Without Benefit
of Clergy

The author in the barnyard of the Ouspensky estate at Franklin Farms, New Jersey, in the summer of 1959.

Without Benefit of Clergy

---

*Some Personal Footnotes to
the Gurdjieff Teaching*

Frank R. Sinclair

To order additional copies of this book, contact:
Xlibris Corporation
1-888-795-4274
www.Xlibris.com
Orders@Xlibris.com
25399

CONTENTS

Acknowledgements

B EGUN AS A simple letter to a relative on a far continent, this attempt to explain something of what drew me to leave my family and my country has taken on a form that I had not foreseen.

I believe I may claim "fair use" of all my source materials, and I have diligently acknowledged them throughout. In particular, I must acknowledge the slightly extended quotations from G.I. Gurdjieff's Third Series, *Life Is Real Only Then, When I Am*, whose copyright is held by Triangle Editions, Inc. I have also referred to some transcripts of Gurdjieff's talks in the 30s and 40s, taken off the Internet, also technically covered by Triangle's copyrights. And I have also ventured to piece together several oral and written recollections of Gurdjieff's Christmas Day 1948 talk at the Hotel Wellington, New York, also technically copyrighted by Triangle. Together, these materials provide the linchpin of my argument that Madame Jeanne de Salzmann brought neither a New Work nor an Old Work, but only Gurdjieff's Work.

I need also to thank a number of people who have helped me take this tiger by the tail. While they are in no way responsible for the basic bias that is so roundly displayed, they have helped in ways that may not always be evident.

The Hon. James Stourton, vice-chairman of Sotheby's-Europe, was generous in sharing correspondence with a contemporary of Benjamin Fairfax Hall, founder of The Stourton Press.

Roger Lipsey generously gave permission to reprint his striking poem about Martin Benson.

Lucy Lady Pentland kindly allowed me to quote from an unpublished paper of Lord Pentland, titled "On Economy of Energy."

Ravi Ravindra pointed me to some delicate esoteric references about the golden embryo, accompanied by suitably appropriate warnings.

Ed Tupta, M.D., permitted me to refer to his recollections of a last meeting with Michel de Salzmann, which helped close the book on some odd consequences of the Ouspensky legacy.

Elizabeth and James Evans, of By the Way Books, Sacramento, California, were generous in making available background material and books they had unearthed about Fairfax Hall.

Stephen Grant cast a custodial eye on an early draft of chapter 12, and concurred that the basic thrust of my observations about the work that Madame de Salzmann brought "is correct."

Martha Heyneman, who was present when I first set foot in the dining room at Franklin Farms these many years ago, quietly urged me to publish while there were still rufflable feathers to be ruffled.

Finally, and not the least, Mary C. Arendt provided invaluable help in preparing the manuscript for publication, policing my grammar, and achieving an uneasy truce between my British "whiches" and American "thats."

Of course, I alone am responsible for the content, the judgments made, and the opinions so freely expressed.

PREFACE

GEORGI IVANOVICH GURDJIEFF has loomed large in my life. But I never met this extraordinary man.

So, I have no doubt that my brief, and largely anecdotal, account of several decades in the surroundings of the Gurdjieff Work in New York will touch some raw nerves and upset a few delicate psyches. Some will call it presumptuous, others will readily call it a betrayal. But I think it can stand being told. It is, as it will become all too clear, no more than a personal footnote to the real history, not that the real history could ever be known.

Measured by the assorted criteria by which so many self-appointed "guardians of the Work" would set themselves apart, I have no particular standing. Madame Jeanne de Salzmann (who never, to my knowledge, claimed the infallibility so readily professed by others) once called me "a child of the Work," but I am not even remotely so, nor have I ever pretended to be. I cannot boast that, as a six- or seven-year-old, I was given bonbons by Gurdjieff, and thus am unable to draw some charming moral for my life-long guidance. I was not around for those extraordinary "toasts to the idiots." I can never claim to have been strong-armed by Gurdjieff to sign a personal check "with many zeroes." I did not stand for a few brief moments in the same room, and then claim forever after that "I knew Gurdjieff." Nor can I indulge in the self-fulfilling uplift and glow—the *darshan*, I suppose—that flowed from having been even remotely in his proximity.

But I take my cue from Gurdjieff himself. There was the marvelous moment in 1948 when he first appeared at Franklin Farms, the Ouspensky estate in Mendham, New Jersey. Those who were there recalled that when Gurdjieff first entered the dining room and looked around at the welcoming gentry decked out in all their finery, he asked, "Who is in the kitchen?" And he saw to it that the poor "working stiffs" in the kitchen were called in to be full participants. Gurdjieff's extraordinary sense of compassion and impartiality is a sobering counter to those who would try to set themselves apart *on any score*. Those who would merely mystify and disorientate may, in all likelihood, have no deep insights or understanding of their own. And not even the ultimate suffering—our own personal tragedies and the loss of loved ones, for example, that place us all firmly within the human race—can be held as the exclusive defining mark of "chosen ones." It is our common lot. Gurdjieff expressed the principle with typical impartiality when he said, "For the man who is working, Nature is a Sister of Charity; she brings him what he has need of for his work . . . . For ordinary man, the man who does not work, there is nothing but chance. But for the man who works, Nature gives him through conscious spirits all that he needs."[1]

As I must emphasize from the outset, I wasn't around in Gurdjieff's day. Instead, I belong to the post-Gurdjieff era, not even remotely a Saul among the Apostles, but a fellow traveler, feeding from those who, like Madame de Salzmann, had been before.

When I first began to set down these recollections of events some 40 or 45 years in the past, my aim was quite simple and modest. It was not my intention to touch on some of the changing perceptions of the teaching, even less to comment on the institutional life that appears to have grown around the Work in that time. My purpose at the outset had been much more personal and much more limited in scope: I wished merely to acknowledge the help, both direct and indirect, that

I received from a few people whose paths had crossed mine. But the landscape has changed.

Inevitably, Gurdjieff has drawn into his massive wake a broad spectrum of pupils, seekers, and searchers, not to speak of adventurers and opportunists (both brazen and subtle) whom it is instructive to discern plying their trade, and all in the name of the Work. Then, too, some extraordinary misinformation, misconceptions, and distortions regarding the work being done in the core Foundations go unchallenged. And if that were not enough to sate the appetite for disenchantment and fantasy, there are all the distortions that have surrounded the extraordinary part played by Madame de Salzmann in the transmission of Gurdjieff's Work.

Chief among these was the charge that she had replaced Gurdjieff's "effort-saturated" teaching with "a mystical illuminism" of unspecified provenance.[1A] As I have tried to describe in the pages that follow, my own experiences from an early age have validated for me precisely that opening to energies from a "supernal source," to use Jame Moore's cogent and "loaded" expression. But it says much for the studied disdain of my elders and peers that Moore's allegations, dating back to 1982, or eight years before her death, about Madame de Salzmann's supposed spiritual malfeasance, were quietly ignored and never mentioned in our institutional circles.

Be that as it may, it is not my role, and no one has asked me, nor do I have the qualifications (whatever they are), to comment on or respond to some of the rather preposterous slanders and rumors, or to point out the more egregious divergences, most of which appear to emanate from the fringe. Nor has anyone asked that I draw attention to the intriguing subversions, not to speak of pathetic pretensions, that have emerged. But there are always these personal agendas. And perhaps Gurdjieff understood completely that these distortions would sound one's alarms and challenge one's vision and call one to ever greater discrimination.

Yet Madame de Salzmann had always urged us to write, and I shall. I was touched that she should say to me after one exchange at the New York Foundation, "I see you are faithful to Mr. Gurdjieff's ideas." And that was after I had publicly demonstrated with incontestable clarity the poverty of my understanding.

To many people professedly "in the Work," reading P.D. Ouspensky's recollections of the Gurdjieff teaching (as recounted in *In Search of the Miraculous* and elaborated in *The Fourth Way*) might imply at times that the teaching is so eminently rational, so logical, and the work for being and consciousness so seemingly calculable, that a simple familiarity with the source literature and the chapter headings would guarantee predictable "results." Perhaps in the shape of an astral body, a real I, real will, real individuality, a soul, and God knows what else. Yet all the while the real significance of our lives remains unknown, inaccessible to the lilliputian egoisms trying to storm the Absolute.

Many of the misconceptions about the Work can be attributed, as Michel de Salzmann felt it necessary to note, to the fact that "Esotericism . . . is not something voluntarily hidden; it is by nature self-protected, since it cannot be grasped without the corresponding inner preparation."[2] It is this necessary inner preparation that is so evidently absent in much of the steady outpourings about Gurdjieff's teaching. Quite a number of new "authorities" have emerged in recent times to expound on the teaching, yet much of their writings, however seemingly plausible, well-documented, and cogently reasoned, all too often display what Dr. de Salzmann characterized as an "unfailing and therefore tragic irrelevance to what is essential."[3] (As my own present musings, too, will surely be characterized both by the sympathetic and the unsympathetic.)

Indeed, if I may risk rousing the scorn of the modern traditionalists—hardly friendly to Gurdjieff, in spite of Guenon's reported but undocumented recantation—it might be said that their criticism of the "mills of academia" as "empty[ing] traditional forms of their qualitative content"[4] surely holds true in the case of the Gurdjieff teaching, too. Yet what could be more traditional a form, and therefore vulnerable a target for some latter-day reconstruction, than Gurdjieff's postulation, "Take the Ray of Creation. At the top is the Absolute, God the Word, divided into three: God the Father, God the Son and God the Holy Ghost"[5]? I do not believe that Gurdjieff's teaching is, as some have said, a new tradition in the making, which is in itself a rather revolutionary thought, but rather that his teaching *is* tradition. At the same time, it is hard to conceive of Gurdjieff as merely a closet traditionalist. For one thing, Gurdjieff certainly appeared to be at odds with the latter-day traditionalists' insistence on "orthodoxy"—and yet to be identified with "esoteric Christianity," as Gurdjieff openly laid claim, is surely the ultimate orthodoxy.

But the apparent changes in form and mode of teaching that intrigue and dismay some present-day observers, and not only those of an academic bent, leading them to the perception that "there is a change in feeling about the nature of the Work,"[6] are understandable distractions, if not real red herrings. Borrowing yet again from Dr. de Salzmann, it seems that the fragmentation that many of these thoughtful observers profess to discern (and, it might be said, often unwittingly foster) occurs only when the teaching "is deprived of the influence from which it originates—which all traditions recognize as being beyond the human level—and which is the only force that can animate it."[7]

I have come to believe that, as a source teaching, Gurdjieff's way points to the same essential truth expressed, for example, by Meister Eckhart, who declared unequivocally that "Every kind of mediation is alien to God."[8] That was no idle Dominican sound bite, as we can gather from the historical record, because Eckhart forcefully reiterated that position: "If we are to know God, it must be without mediation."[9] John

Pentland, one of my own adoptive mentors, appeared to echo this thought (without invoking the well-worn language of formal religion) when he posed the question: "[I]s it possible for me to relate directly to that [higher] energy, as it were on a one to one basis, without intermediary, without fear . . . ?"[10] More or less, one might say, without benefit of clergy—or any formal institutional hierarchy. Pentland's is a question that, for the continued health of the teaching, might even be held in view by a few who profess to be the most devout of his own pupils. We must all come equally under the law.

Even as a particle of the whole (a drop in the vast and endless ocean, to use Gurdjieff's symbolism), one is ultimately on one's own, standing one on one before the higher—or the unknown. And Gurdjieff's Work is, at its heart, a way to approach—and occasionally to penetrate—this mystery.

All the more reason, then, to remember the sage advice of Gurdjieff's first tutor, Dean Borsh. This exceptionally sane man urged that a real education should instill in us "Love of God—but indifference to the saints." *Indifference to the saints*—and perhaps also to the whole pantheon of latter-day expositors (myself included) promoting their proprietary visions of Gurdjieff's intent. I believe the Dean's reminder is especially necessary today, given the proliferation of groups of questionable provenance—and leaders to match. "You are not to follow me," A.R. Orage admonished in his own gloss on Gurdjieff's approach,[11] and as all "followers" (both within and without the formal institutions or foundations) ought equally to be admonished. Perhaps, then, one might need to pen a few extra aphorisms to go alongside those in the old Study House at the Prieuré. Derived from my own modest experience, the first could be quite simply, "Do not be fooled." And certainly not by those thinly disguised personal agendas. As Madame de Salzmann reminded us (and warned us) down the years, all the moments of our inner life, both in the conscious and the unconscious layers, unite to protect the egoism.

Although it was hardly my intention to piggyback on the evident authority with which Dr. de Salzmann spoke about the teaching, I am prompted to repeat yet another of his perceptive comments about the many mutations of "the Work" to be found out there in the marketplace: "It is . . . evident . . . that in the case of 'experiential' disciplines, which are normally included in spiritual teachings at a very high level of sophistication, ideas taken too literally can only lead to sterile theorizing and distortion when their symbolic or practical significance is not understood."[12]

Still, sterile theorizing and distortion are not exclusively attributes of some who are supposedly "beyond the pale." They are equally attributes of those professedly *within* the pale. So, I have titled this present exercise *Without Benefit of Clergy* for some further good reasons. There is a timeless reminder in the liturgy of the Armenian Church (and perhaps in other liturgies) that "The priest is subject to the same weaknesses and sins as everyone else." Group leader or guide or guru or priest—many are equally subject to weaknesses and sins, not to speak of downright ignorance, appalling self-conceit, unexamined arrogance, and presumptuous elitism: how many there are who profess to have been "specially prepared" and singled out (often only by themselves) to carry the torch.

Will these beggarly recollections and comments of mine help the furtherance of Gurdjieff's Work? I doubt it. But they may provide a little encouragement to the simple troops in the trenches, the anonymous practitioners of the Work, the true searchers, quietly (and invisibly) struggling to relate their subjectivity to a more objective life.

Frank R. Sinclair
Grand View on Hudson, New York

NOTES

1. G.I.Gurdjieff, Notes of meetings at 6 rue des Colonels Renard, 1938. Meeting # 20. Probably from Solita Solano's copy in the Library of Congress. Taken off the Internet, 2004.
1A. James Moore, "Moveable Feasts: The Gurdjieff Work," Religion Today, Vol. 9, No. 2, 1982, p. 11.
2. Michel de Salzmann, "Footnote to the Gurdjieff Literature," *Parabola*, Vol. 5, No. 3, 1980, p. 93.
3. Op. cit., p. 92.
4. Alvin Moore, Jr., review titled, "The Only Tradition," *Sophia: A Journal of Traditional Studies*, Vol. 3, No.1, 1997, p. 162.
5. G.I. Gurdjieff, *Views from the Real World*, E.P. Dutton & Co. Inc., New York, 1973, p. 195.
6. Sophia Wellbeloved, "Changes in G.I. Gurdjieff's Teaching 'The Work,'" CESNU-Center for Studies on New Religions, London, 2001.
7. Op. cit., p. 93.
8. Meister Eckhart, "On the Noble Man," *Selected Writings*, ed. Oliver Davies, Penguin Books, New York, 1994, p. 104.
9. Meister Eckhart, "Saul Rose from the Ground," quoted in Reiner Schurmann, *Wandering Joy: Meister Eckhart's Mystical Philosophy*, Lindisfarne Books, Great Barrington, MA, 2001, p. 123.
10. John Pentland, *Exchanges Within*, Continuum, New York, 1997, p. 236.
11. Quote attributed to A.R. Orage by Jean Toomer, in James Webb's *The Harmonious Circle*, p. 551.
12. Michel de Salzmann, op. cit., p.95.

CHAPTER 1

From Where I Was Sitting

NEWCOMERS TO THE mainstream groups of the Gurdjieff Work are, I would assume, generally urged not to speak out of school, and even less to gossip. So, as I launch into these personal recollections of the Work, it is rather instructive to be reminded that Gurdjieff's own chief pupil, Jeanne de Salzmann, herself faithfully complied with this sobering injunction.

Reporting the death of Dr. Michel de Salzmann, about whom it was never any secret that he was Gurdjieff's son, one obituarist stated rather pointedly that, despite his mother's three decades with Gurdjieff, the "final proof" of her "deep understanding of [Gurdjieff's] philosophy was that she never published a memoir."[1] This, the writer added, "was an act of exceptional forbearance considering that anyone who took a glass of Armagnac with Gurdjieff later wrote intimate books on him."

I did not drink Armagnac with Gurdjieff. The few odd tales that I have to tell bear perhaps only remotely on Gurdjieff's teaching, even though I knowingly insert myself into the now densely populated arena of memoirists of the Work. Of course, as a peripheral and rather insignificant participant—a self-assessment not at all invalidated by my having ended up as

Madame Jeanne de Salzmann.
Photo: Institut Gurdjieff, Paris.

"a senior member" of the Gurdjieff Foundation of New York, one of the four founding foundations—I cannot write with anything resembling Madame de Salzmann's forbearance or her strong commitment to the principle that one should speak no more than is necessary, especially about those who are not present or who have gone before. For my part, I have no intimate secrets to impart. What's more, I can comment on outer events only as a mere member of the second generation—or is it the third or perhaps even the fourth?—which consists of those who never knew Gurdjieff but learned from some of those who had.

So, why have I written at all?

It is largely an exercise to recall as simply as I can the search for meaning in my life, beginning with my serendipitous encounter with the Gurdjieff teaching firstly and briefly in South Africa, and subsequently over several decades in New York. I have plunged into this odd endeavor—"memoir" is too grandiose a depiction of the modest effort that follows—for no particular reason other than to register a few little-known, often long-forgotten, and unquestionably "stubborn" facts concerning some inner and outer events surrounding my strange pursuit.

There are of course those who must *still* wonder why I have written, especially since a few egoisms—and not the least my own—may be punctured along the way. But I am telling of *my* experiences, not anyone else's. Like the famous music critic of the *Manchester Guardian* who described a certain piece on a concert program as having been the Ballade in A Flat when in fact a totally different piece had been played, I will only say, "From where I was sitting, it sounded like the Ballade in A Flat."[2]

I am certainly not attempting to "impart" the teaching, an effort with which I, at my rather insignificant level, have been engaged for some time, contributing without a doubt to the inevitable distortion that ensues. (Henri Tracol, late president of the Paris Foundation, once remarked that the teaching was distorted "the moment Gurdjieff opened his mouth."[3]) Rather, this "memoir" is unashamedly personal and totally subjective. I make no excuses for the ready expression of my own particular points of view and my opinions; other people have not spared me theirs, particularly in the name of the Work. Indeed, there were even times that, to my astonishment, I felt I could actually echo Gurdjieff himself in saying that I now had "enemies." Perhaps in reading on, the forbearing reader may sense the drift of my seeming irreverence and occasional iconoclasm.

My anguished sense of alienation during my youth and the ensuing search for meaning eventually propelled me into the circle of those who made up the Gurdjieff Foundation. I would not have known to look for the Foundation as such. Indeed, the Foundation did not then actively proselytize, and does so only rarely now—although one of my old mentors recalled how Gurdjieff himself had told him to go stand on street corners and give away copies of *All and Everything*, then being readied for publication. As it happened, after coming from South Africa I soon found myself admitted to the mother ship of the North American foundations.

If one gives any credence to the ecumenical grumbling of the disaffected and the disenchanted, then the New York Foundation could indeed seem old-line, conservative and reactionary, unfeeling and inconsiderate, as I occasionally characterized it for myself. Yet it is one of the "institutes," or "cells," established under directives stemming from Gurdjieff himself. And these establishments have taken very seriously Gurdjieff's charge that, without the preparation of a certain nucleus, "the action of the ideas will not go beyond a certain threshold." But yet again—and this is another slight justification for this writing—one must be careful not to confuse institutional "office holders" with an "esoteric inner circle." They are not necessarily synonymous. Like the American president who warned against the power of the military/industrial complex in a nation professedly devoted to the democratic ideal, so should one warn the would-be institutional heirs of Gurdjieff to be wary of the forces that they serve.

It took me a long time to appreciate that, in the absence of Mr. Gurdjieff—and later, in the absence first of Madame de Salzmann and then of her son—it is the "institute" that must nurture the light that was brought, and bring the requisite pressures to bear. Or to put it in Dr. de Salzmann's felicitous phrasing, it is the community, or the "church"—that is, all of us, together—that must "save the savior." The messenger has brought the message: it is the role of the "general membership" to keep it alive.

But who or what is the community?

One might argue that institutions, like the warm-blooded entities that make up their membership, endeavor to present some meaningful profile to the world at large. Yet again, the pervasive reality is that *everything* is expressed through the subjectivities of the individual players. *Everything* is colored by the personalities, *everything* reflects their own hereditary and the deep conditioning of their environment. And it is the intense interrelationships between the serious "seekers of truth" on these many levels that give the institution its vibrant and dynamic character. The early leaders of the New York Foundation, for one, would never give up their shared independence of character, even running the occasional ambitious and presumptuous interloper out of town—and squeezing the disaffected into even greater states of disaffection! Yet, under Madame de Salzmann's guidance, they participated wholeheartedly and unstintingly in "the common Work."

There was a time when I was inclined to believe that some of this surrounding ferment was edifying and "evolutionary," so long as I could be one of the seemingly "elect" and could stand above the struggle, as it were. But there is something seriously skewed when some of the self-styled "Defenders of the Faith" should regard an institution as just another setting for endless ego gratifications, the play of great and small ambition, divisive personal agendas, boorishness, inconsiderateness, crass exploitation, and even brazen intimidation. That behavior would be a far cry from the "conscious egoism" that Gurdjieff encouraged as the ground for one's work. Conscious egoism refers to the inner life. Of course, Gurdjieff himself appeared to draw in his wake prize exemplars of all these weaknesses. They were no less likely to be found in the New World than in the Old, even though he expressed his hopeful conviction that the poor and huddled masses who had come to the New World harbored a higher percentage of people in whom the possibility of approaching a true normality "is not entirely lost."

All of this multi-leveled ferment was a virtual galactic journey into an unknown and remote future when, as a young man, I looked for and "found" the Work in Cape Town, South Africa, in 1956—barely seven years after Gurdjieff's death—and began my connection with its activities for the next 40-odd years. Aiming for some eminence within the institutional framework never entered my mind. It is not the point of the endeavor. Yet there was all the evidence around me of all the weaknesses that, down the centuries, contaminate so much of the activities surrounding any spiritual endeavor. Those old Fathers of one of the oldest institutions of them all, the Christian Church, for example, must have been tough eggs.

I have no doubt whatsoever that Gurdjieff clearly understood that the egoistic wish for preeminence and power was pretty much ingrained in humankind—surely one of those "maleficent consequences of the organ Kundabuffer"—and he evidently made full use of it in creating conditions required for the tantalizing work for self-knowledge and the growth of consciousness. Surely, then, the point is not to weaken, while pretenders pretend and sly nepotists ply their trade—all in the name of Mr. Gurdjieff's Work.

In any event, as I began to delve into my memories of events long gone, I chanced upon some recollections written by my wife, Beatrice, about her meetings with Gurdjieff on his last visit to New York in 1948, when she was a young woman newly introduced to the Work. In some notes she made 50 years after the events of those memorable days, and which I have incorporated here,[4] she recalled his saying to her, "Every nationality has dirty side I not like." Now, here was a thought that resounded in me like a loud hosanna!

So, with this implied imprimatur for my lingering and, I trust, objective aversions, and with somewhat of a clear conscience, I will give my own recollections of some events in and around New York without feeling compelled to gloss over the indelicate or the unsavory, since they were real enough, and stubborn facts of the first order. I do so while fully acknowledging that I am equally "under the law"—I too, I should concede, have my "dirty side," which others must find to be far from endearing. As my own old mentor Martin Benson said of his own old master Gurdjieff on more than one occasion, "Gurdjieff must have been a real sonofabitch." That does not mean, of course, that being a sonofabitch is the necessary grounding for consciousness, as some would presume.

I could never succeed, however, in describing with any comprehensiveness the extraordinary influence that Madame de Salzmann had on my life, as she had on so many. Ravi Ravindra, a gifted academic, has made a brave attempt at that through his book *Heart Without Measure* (1999), describing his work in direct contact with Madame de Salzmann since about 1979. Those of us who were privileged to be around her on her months-long visits to New York over several decades had an earlier, more continuous, and longer exposure, but Ravindra describes, at least in outline, the same Work that she had opened to us. A scholar of repute in two disciplines—comparative religion and physics—Ravindra has of course an excellent mind, while mine is like a tattered sieve, so I cannot even essay to emulate his compelling, personal account.

He has been able to convey the special and intense way in which she worked with us. He describes how insistent she was in her demand that we make the special efforts of the Work; how she repeatedly indicated that "ideas are not enough"(that it is not enough merely to have read the central literature and to parrot what Gurdjieff, or she herself, had said); how only one's best efforts were wanted; above all, how she was able to demonstrate by her every word and gesture that there is indeed a science of being.

*   *   *

Meeting Madame de Salzmann barely three months after I had arrived in the United States at the age of 28 was without question the single most significant encounter of my life.

For the next 30 years, whenever she appeared in New York, I almost literally "sat at her feet"—again, as did so many others, most of them perhaps worthier and better prepared than I—to be exposed to the teaching of someone who was unquestionably finer in her being and immeasurably greater in her understanding. I was thrust very early into the so-called Group Two—primarily, let me be the first to admit, because of my having married Beatrice, who had met not only Gurdjieff in New York but also both Ouspenskys and both de Hartmanns. In this scheme of things, I was distinctly "of new formation."

Still, even a tyro like myself could appreciate the rare privilege of being among people 20 or 30 years his senior who had had the good fortune to be around Gurdjieff. But since few of the books of the teaching had yet been published and few records of Gurdjieff's meetings were yet available, most of the people in the group could merely echo half a dozen old sayings of his. So when Madame came to our meetings, I must have been a fresh voice who, if the truth be told, could not care less that Gurdjieff had allegedly said this or that. Acting, as it were, without benefit of clergy and beholden to no one, I wished only to find out—the truth. I ventured to ask my own questions about my own experiences, and Madame responded directly and generously to my guileless wish to know. Once when I noticed that some of the others appeared to resent the attention she gave to my questioning, I decided to keep silent. But soon Madame turned to me and said, "Speak." So there was no point in hiding.

Then, too, there was the extraordinary quality with which she spoke. Some might say that the sound of her voice was mesmeric, hypnotic. I never found it so. Rather, it resonated from a source deep within in a way that evoked a corresponding intensity in oneself. Robert Lawlor, translator of R.A. Schwaller de Lubicz's *The Temple in Man*, notes that ancient peoples did not use words the way we moderns do. For them, he said, words were of a musical nature, so that speaking, as I felt Madame de Salzmann demonstrated, "was a process of generating sonar fields establishing an immediate vibratory identity with the essential principle that underlies any object or form."[5]

This is, as they say, quite a mouthful and perhaps a tall claim. But her voice, when she spoke about essential questions and appeared to probe the depths of her own being to convey her understanding, had a force deriving from some unfathomable reaches within. One was touched, inspired, wishing to be part of the same current of life. As yet another commentator on ancient Egyptian understanding expressed it, "It is the voice which seeks afar the Invisibles summoned and makes the necessary objects into a reality."[6] One felt her deep relationship with the Invisibles, the Unknown, the Immeasurable.

In later years, when it came my turn to speak before the general membership, I recall the occasion when, with Madame de Salzmann sitting a few feet in front of me as part of the "audience," I thought I should express myself with what I considered a measured diffidence. But after a few sentences, she interrupted me. "Speak with more force," she said firmly.

I changed gears, as it were, in midstride, realizing that my attempt at a respectful humility was simply affectation, a hindrance, and a betrayal of what was being mutually explored.

Nevertheless, Madame de Salzmann disclaimed any pretense at being a teacher. For her, Gurdjieff was the teacher, the master, and every action of hers bore witness to her total dedication and devotion to his work. Yet we all accepted unquestioningly that she had a greater understanding than we had. Mrs. Margaret (Peggy) Flinsch confided that after Mr. Gurdjieff's death she had asked Madame de Salzmann to help her "now that Mr. Gurdjieff has gone." Madame responded, "I will help you as far as I am." Mrs. Flinsch repeated that formulation, "As far as I am." To all of us, "as far as I am" was far ahead indeed. For all of us who were able to approach her without any intermediary, Madame de Salzmann was our teacher.

Ravi Ravindra, as I have noted, has given a vivid impression of the intensity with which she called us to work, and the tirelessness with which she expressed the necessity for the appearance in one of a special energy of attention. In her last years, I felt in her a remoteness, a dispassion towards me as a "personage." For a long time I felt very keenly that she had "seen through me," had recognized the shallowness of my understanding, the lameness of my wish, the weakness of my will. It only slowly dawned on me that she no longer had any interest in the formal niceties; she could see through all our unspoken excuses, and it seemed she no longer cared to hold our allegiance through her generosity and kindness, not to speak of her forbearance. Rather, I came to understand her dispassion as an unspoken demand that we work—that we take seriously the need to work for an active presence.

For years she had counseled us that "ideas are not enough," for this was a work for being. Browsing through some of my old, fitful notes, I found two recollections about meetings with her in December 1988, as she approached her

100th birthday. I noted that "she was once again strong and 'dashing.'" And with an evident sense of relief, like a condemned man being pardoned, I had written: "Finally (!), she acknowledged my effort. Almost a kind of drought in the last few years: one could see that she did not remember names and probably even faces." My notes revealed that I felt she had responded to me in this way because I had come "from a more real place in myself, and I had made an effort in the direction she urges." And then, on the next-to-last day of the year: "Another extraordinary meeting with Madame de Salzmann yesterday. [She spoke again of three energies, and] a new understanding for me, as a result, of the 'second conscious shock.'" And I noted, too, that as she had when I first "sat at her feet" in the Foundation, "she once again speaks directly to me." I was not alone in this wish to have the direct "communion." It was a communal need.

Given the profound backdrop of Gurdjieff's Work and its high purpose, what follows may give the impression, then, that I was more often than not just an unruly and crass young rebel, oblivious to some of the basic decencies. But what I intuitively understood was that I, like everyone else, had to search on my own account, "without either hereditary or other right,"[7] for the truth about myself and the world in which we live. And Madame de Salzmann encouraged this search. Once, in my early days, I had brought an observation to a meeting with her, but her puzzling response prompted me to exclaim, "Madame, you are asking me to abandon the ideas." She remained silent. I took this to mean that she did not wish us simply to parrot Gurdjieff, but that there is a search that must reach beyond all forms, beyond words and mental images and symbols. It would be decades before the work in the Silence and the opening to Presence—something akin to the "practice of the Presence of God", as Brother Lawrence had expressed it—became the central reality of my work.

What comes to my mind, then, is the image—itself to be abandoned—of Gurdjieff's powerful movement the "Warrior

Dervish." At the center of a group of dervishes moving to a strong and insistent rhythm is a lone (and certainly senior) dervish. He also moves to the rhythm, turning securely about his own axis, while a single, frenzied dervish dances wildly around him, intermittently bumping into him. The man in the center remains steadfast and unmoved. That to me was the strange situation in which I found myself for many years: while I ricocheted and bounced around with almost reckless disregard, the center was intact in honoring its mission. And at the center were some serious and committed people, struggling with their own frailties and weaknesses—their own questionable "inner beauties," as Gurdjieff expressed it. Which is what these few reminiscences are all about.

Perhaps, then, this little exercise on my part might simply be dismissed as just an idle, foolish, and barely subtle attempt to salve a pathetic egoism. But I have been drawn to it, I suppose, like a Zen monk who, in attentively drawing yet another of his endless circles, essays again and again to try to execute an approximation of the "perfect gesture." And yet, like those "Ladies of the Rope"[8] (and others) attempting Gurdjieff's virtually impossible exercise of trying to tell the story of their lives with absolute sincerity, one discovers that even with the best will in the world certain details are inevitably withheld. They may be far too personal for the encompassing egoism to own to—too revealing, too close to the bone, not fully understood, and even not properly seen.

At the same time (and I shall be repeating this almost as a mantra), in my relation to all these elders and peers, I intuitively but perhaps not always consciously took to heart the principle Gurdjieff derived from his own first tutor, Dean Borsh. From early childhood, the Dean said, there should be instilled in the child "Love of God—but indifference to the saints." Of course, as my mentors must have seen only too well, my early attitude was tainted by a subtle cynicism. This had its roots in a terrible childhood experience that I need not describe. But thanks to my immersion in the Work, to the grace of some remarkable, objective inner events, and not the least to Madame de Salzmann's extraordinary influence, the insights that came with more maturity, if not actual "evolution," have helped me to understand that cynicism, no less than those abundant and dearly cherished personal agendas that flourish in and around the Work, is no ground for growing a soul. Cynicism, no less than those selfish agendas, qualifies, I am sure, as a "sin against the Holy Ghost."[9]

*   *   *

I believe I was rather fortunate, too, in my introduction to the Work in New York. I did not come through the usual group structure, where some people almost inevitably appeared to be beholden—if not seemingly indentured—to their leaders for life. (Michel de Salzmann once expressed the opinion, for example, that so-called group leaders—a term not used by the French, who prefer to refer to "responsibles"—could be considered "black" magicians rather than "white" magicians, to use Gurdjieff's terminology again.) I suppose this possessiveness is a ready temptation for most would-be leaders and masters (not to speak of all those self-proclaimed "Men numbers 5, 6 and 7," and perhaps even higher, to be found on the Internet): having read or heard that Gurdjieff played fast and loose with his adherents, they must see no reason why they should not also play with other people's lives. As Madame de Hartmann observed, "Mr. Gurdjieff could hit you over the head and catch you before you hit the ground. These people only know how to hit you over the head!"[10]

Henri Tracol was equally insistent that "The shocks, suggestions and situations calculated to provoke the disciple's awakening are there *solely to prepare and train him to do without his Master, to go forth under his own steam as soon as he has shown himself capable of doing so*"[11] (emphasis added). In any event, it is often dismaying to see that some "leaders" should delve into people's private lives almost as a feudal right, mold them to their own vision, and practically clone them as faithful images of their own less-than-immaculate understanding. And these faithful, dutiful, and uncomprehending nonentities, in turn, pay the sincerest flattery to their masters (and mistresses) by unconsciously aping their every gesture, their tones of voice, even the way they walk. Not exactly the impression one gains of Gurdjieff's own approach.

As insignificant as I was in the scheme of things, I too was inadvertently tarred with the possessive feather in an account of John Pentland's funeral. As I mention in some later comments on that event, author William Patrick Patterson referred to me as a member of Pentland's groups in his book, *Eating the 'I'*. As closely as I appeared to be associated with some of Pentland's activities, and as closely as I worked for decades with Lady Pentland, I was never in his groups and never pretended to be. And he never proposed or hinted that I cross over. Perhaps he appreciated a certain independence of spirit.

I was fortunate also to learn very early on that it did not matter where one was or what one was asked to undertake, one simply "worked" for its own sake. Within three months of arriving at Madame Ouspensky's estate at Mendham, in New Jersey, this lesson was driven home one memorable evening when it was announced that the "older" people would meet separately with Madame de Salzmann, who was visiting from Paris, while the rest of us would listen to a reading. Since everyone wished to be only where Madame de Salzmann was, the resulting suffering was so palpable one could have sliced it with something as blunt as a telephone directory. I was still a fresh and wide-eyed youngster in the Work, but I think it took me less than a minute to assess the situation. I realized that I was lucky to be there, that I had no conceivable right to be anywhere but with the "younger" members, and that in those conditions I had no choice: I had to work wherever I happened to be.

So these selective recollections concern the personal shape of "my" work, or search, and the inevitable interplay with those who appeared to be a rung or two up the ladder. I have attempted on the one hand to recall briefly my struggles to understand the forces at play in this "too too solid flesh," and on the other hand to understand the lifelong intimations of "another current" of life that have touched my consciousness. Some of those intimations have filtered through with a delicate grace, while others have exploded in and through me with an overwhelming and sometimes shattering force. If it is not too immodest a claim, my experiences illustrate in a microcosmic way the struggle to understand the Gurdjieffian invitation to live, as it were, in two worlds at once. (In actuality, there can be only one world, as the great traditions declare. And yet again, from another perspective, there are *three* worlds: there is a middle ground where the sacred and the profane have their interplay and where the "struggle" for being takes place. That is perhaps what one sense of "being in between" must mean. And that too is partly what I have tried to illustrate in my narrative.)

*   *   *

And so I have attempted this brief accounting as an exercise in recollection, much the way I understand Ouspensky went around in his last years "fixing" impressions of places and people in his memory. I have tried to indicate how the strands of the two currents interweave, so as to illustrate the worldly, or temporal, surroundings of the search. To this end, I have made gratuitous references to certain interesting personalities with their own human limitations and struggles who figured large in my life—people like Martin Benson, B. Fairfax Hall, John Pentland. And at the same time, I have alluded (perhaps not tentatively enough for some) to the inner world, the inner discoveries, in the language that Gurdjieff appeared to use in referring to them, so that a certain acquaintance with his teaching (rather than with the mindless scuttlebutt about his fancied peccadilloes) is more or less a prerequisite.

Gurdjieff clearly understood this necessary interplay between the so-called inner life and the outer. After countless readings of the Third Series, I unexpectedly found that he had described, decades before, what I have painstakingly only just begun to discover for myself:

> My special investigations and experimental elucidations . . . showed me clearly and very definitely that by Great, All-solicitous Mother Nature the possibility is also foreseen for beings to acquire the kernel of their essence, that is to say, their own I, even after entering into responsible age.
>
> The foresight of Equitable Nature consists in the given case in this, that the possibility is given to us after our completed formation into responsible life, by our own intentions *through certain inner experiencings and certain outer conditions* to crystallize in our common presence data for the obtaining of such a kernel—of course with greater difficulty than in preparatory age [emphasis added].[12]

Certainly, I make no claim either to possessing a unique understanding of Gurdjieff's meaning or to having "crystallized" anything towards the formation of this "kernel." But he could not have expressed more clearly for me the process of the Work as "the all-round moral effort" of which Pentland would later write.[13] I suppose it is a moral effort because there is an underlying need for choice (the famous either/or of which Madame de Salzmann constantly reminded us), and also the need for a fundamental transformation of the feeling.

I must also go on record with my omissions: I have made little or no reference to quite a few interesting, often special, and occasionally remarkable people with whom I had so much daily commerce for decades—some of them benefactors in countless ways, such as Dr. Welch, a man of infinite jest and a wealth of worldly understanding. And others, both at home and abroad. Few if any of them have written books or published papers, and so they are more or less "off the map" to archaeologists of these concerns of the spirit. But are they any the less worthy?

There is one omission, however, of which I will not be guilty. Although it is not for me to claim for Gurdjieff a place in the lineage of the Great Knowledge and in the timeless light of tradition, yet that must surely be his rightful due. Inevitably, like the master that he undeniably was, he upended ordinary sensibilities and the cozy assumptions of the uncomprehending. And that process surely includes all the subsequent ferment and confusion in which "Gurdjieffians" of so many diverse persuasions and understandings continue to wrestle not only in the new "institutional" surroundings but also at "non-aligned" public forums, in specialized retreats, in self-adulatory videotapes, in any number of newsletters and books, and on the Internet.

Regardless of the endless and often shallow glosses, Gurdjieff's ideas have an extraordinary power to awaken, because at their heart they defy ordinary understanding. If there are those who now claim to discern a growing and perhaps terminal fragmentation in the teaching, it is not because the teaching *at the invisible core, in the invisible mainstream,* is diminishing in its vigor. Rather, many self-appointed "heirs" of Gurdjieff, who often appear to lack both the vision and an informed surrounding of work, must inevitably fall back on proprietary and limited perspectives.

I am convinced that Gurdjieff, being so prescient and comprehending, must have anticipated the vast misunderstandings, turmoil, contention, and competition that would inevitably surround his teaching. What better ground for the appearance, in the committed ones, of the energies demanded in the movement of return? What more fertile surrounding for the emergence of conscience? At every turn, the "crunch" of the old and the conditioned—and the need to break through to a real inner freedom. There is, for instance, a profound echo of this understanding in Lizelle Reymond's sensitive account of her time spent with Sri Anirvan in India. Anirvan notes how the continuous pressure exerted by the rigid Hindu society on "a delicate being" will "cause beings ready to throw off the yoke to 'explode.'" This effort, he says, "is a movement of the essence, still incoherent but already prepared to pay the price of independence."[14]

It was perhaps some recognition of this sort that motivated Gurdjieff to create surroundings for himself that challenged all complacency, all egoistic gratification, and enabled him (he said) to experience the assorted human manifestations that, had Beelzebub himself known of them, would have grown horns "even on his hooves."[15]

The movement of return (to "the Most Holy Source of everything existing"[16]) is clearly a merciless process in which the wheat is separated from the chaff, the fine from the coarse. So those who would wish to be in the invisible mainstream must continue to refine and purify their work, like that master dervish at the center, aware of—but impervious to—the turmoil. And this invisible mainstream must identify with no set form; it may go underground in its proper time; and it must have as its deepest aim the striving to be whole.

If some of this understanding has appeared among mere members of the second (or perhaps the third or fourth) generation, then Madame de Salzmann—a woman of extraordinary insight, fortitude, and creativity—did indeed help to ensure that a healthy nucleus had taken root around her and, as Henri Tracol would say, bears witness to the Work.

*   *   *

NOTES

1. Writing in *The Independent*, London, September 21, 2001.
2. Neville Cardus, *Autobiography*, William Collins and Co., London, 1947, p. 224.
3. This remark does not mean to impute Gurdjieff's profound understanding or his integrity in matters both lay and spiritual, but rather to emphasize the difficulty of speaking about the great mysteries
4. See chapter 7.
5. Robert Lawlor, Introduction to *The Temple in Man*, page 11.
6. Gaspar Maspero, quoted by Lawlor, Introduction to *The Temple in Man*, page 11.
7. G.I.Gurdjieff, *All and Everything: Beelzebub's Tales to His Grandson*, Viking Arkana, New York and London, 1992, p. 353.
8. William Patrick Patterson, *Ladies of the Rope*, Arete Communications, Fairfax, California, 1999.
9. I have always felt, for example, that a "death wish" is paradoxically made with the energy of life: another "sin against the Holy Ghost." See Matthew 12: 31, 32, and P.D. Ouspensky, *A New Model of the Universe*, Alfred A. Knopf, New York, 1931, p. 203.
10. Olga de Hartmann, quoted by Dushka Howarth, *The Gurdjieff Heritage Society*, The International Humanities Conference: All & Everything 2003, Bognor Regis, UK.
11. Henri Tracol, quoted in the annual report for 2001-2002 of the Gurdjieff Society, London, p. 29.
12. G.I. Gurdjieff, *Life is Real, Only Then, When "I Am,"* p. 107.
13. John Pentland, Foreword to Jean Vaysse, *Towards Awakening*, Harper & Row, San Francisco, 1979, p. x.
14. Lizelle Reymond, *To Live Within*, Doubleday & Company, New York, 1971, pp. 186-7
15. G.I. Gurdjieff, *Life is Real, Only Then, When I Am*, p. 46.
16. G.I.Gurdjieff, *All and Everything: Beelzebub's Tales to His Grandson*, Viking Arkana, New York, 1992, p.1029.

Jacob's Ladder: The author on the crux pitch of the
Jacob's Ladder climb, Table Mountain, South
Africa, about 1956.

CHAPTER 2

At the Cape of Good Hope

INTERTWINED WITH MY youthful dreams of ascending Mount Everest (not to speak of climbing the north face of the Eiger, sailing alone around the world, and playing cricket like the incomparable Don Bradman), experiences that I can only describe as mystic or spiritual or sacred have been persistent phenomena throughout my life.

I dare say that the use of any such terms is immediately repugnant to many, especially since Gurdjieff sought to use a language largely unglued from religious terminology, as noted, for example, by Jerzy Grotowski.[1] Acknowledging that "There is something religious there" in Gurdjieff, Grotowski notes also that it is "not for display." Yet Gurdjieff was, to put it mildly, as God-intoxicated as Spinoza, and *All and Everything* itself sprang from "a revelation [to Gurdjieff] of the book from beginning to end," according to A.R. Orage. So I will try to navigate these tricky waters, well realizing that some things are inevitably on display, disguise them how we will.

To some, the mystic and the spiritual must suggest that one is otherworldly, perhaps effete, barely able to suffer the daily grind. To me, however, these experiences reflect the curious interplay of two great currents in our lives—the sacred and the profane. One current gives intimations of a "separate reality," the noumenal world underlying the world of action and phenomena, while the other seemingly more obvious current represents the play of forces—including that of one's "functional" nature—by which one is interminably driven and commanded. So it is that the search for meaning is played out on many scales, in many realms, and through many facets of the human structure—not just in the exploration of great ideas in hallowed halls, or in meditation and retreats, but out there in the marketplace, on manure piles, and in the daily rounds of family affairs, business, and politics.

I have rarely spoken about my experiences, particularly the more intense ones, because one's very motives for speaking tend to arouse suspicion. These experiences and insights are easily misunderstood and misinterpreted. Fortunately, the extraordinary comprehensiveness of Gurdjieff's teaching helps one find one's bearings. As it becomes so clear from a study of his teaching, a mere study of his psychological ideas is meaningless without the perspective that is brought by his cosmological ideas—and, in fact, by the metaphysics underlying the great traditional teachings. Evelyn Underhill, a venerable avatar of the mystic vision, underscores the value of the mystic experience when she states that, far from being "a byway of religion," it represents "in its intensive form the essential religious experience of man."[2] She elaborates at great length on this thesis: "Speaking always from experience—the most complete experience achieved by man—[mystics] assure us of an Absolute which overpasses and includes the Absolute of philosophy, [and] far transcends that Cosmic life it fills and sustains."[3] Even Alfred North Whitehead, a philosopher committed, in his philosophy of process, to the "love of concrete immediacy," points to the fact that "It is only by drawing the long bow of mysticism that evidences for [God's] existence can be collected from our temporal World."[4]

My own need for concrete immediacy evoked in me the ancient questioning, but yet not so clearly articulated, Who am I? Why am I alive? And mystified? I had many early recollections—as doubtless many others have—of feeling that I had been simply "dropped on the planet," out of nowhere. As a boy, I would be walking home from school, immersed in the bewildering wonderment of being alive, like an alien being on an alien planet. I also wondered who these people were who were my parents. How had this all come about? If, as Plato appears to suggest, one actually chooses one's life and therefore one's parents, why them? Perhaps because they were simple and honest. And they left me unhindered, while I sulked and brooded like Achilles alone in his tent, trying to fathom these mysteries.

*   *   *

In retrospect, my "beginning" was somewhat serendipitous if not entirely auspicious: I was born on St. Andrew's Day—November 30—in 1929 in a suburb of Cape Town, South Africa. Neither my parents nor I gave any thought to patron saints—we had too many other pressing preoccupations—and I did not do so until late in my life. Coming from a totally different tradition and culture, Gurdjieff set great store by his own, St. George. Coincidentally, St. Andrew is the patron saint of Scotland, which introduces another slight thread of interest (or more properly, diversion) to what follows. It is a strand that began to weave its way only after I had been for some time in the Work.

South Africa was at that time a member of the British Commonwealth of Nations. It was only in my late teens that apartheid—the oppressive segregation of the races—became institutionalized, but the overriding fact of life down at the tip of Africa was a keen sense of race and racial difference. My mother, Nellie (Liebenberg), was a country girl, an Afrikaner. Her father had passed away by the time I was born, but I knew her mother briefly towards the end of her life. My grandmother died in our house in a suburb of Cape Town. I am not given to seeing ghosts, but to this day I have a clear recollection of having seen something wraithlike flit through the hallway soon after she died.

My father was a Sinclair—William John Sinclair—the youngest of seven children. His father, Francis William Thomas Sinclair, owned a coach-building business. I remember my grandfather as smart and formal, quite Old World, in his dress. He remained active until shortly before he died in 1948 at the age of 85.

What I am about to add here about the family origins is hardly germane to the main thrust of this account, but I will indulge for just a few paragraphs, since this began, after all, as a letter to a relative in a far-off land. I owe most of this information to my father's sister, Frances Sinclair Gorrie, a source whom I tapped much too late. She must have been over 90 when she wrote down some of this history for me in her beautifully clear script. Her grandfather—my great-grandfather—David Gunn Sinclair, she wrote, "was born in Aberdeen, Scotland, in 1838. He at the age of about 19, being in an adventurous mood, set sail with 6 or 7 young men round about his age, on a voyage to Africa along the west coast and headed southwards. During a storm, the small sailing boat was driven ashore and wrecked on a rocky coast. All of them fortunately reached the shore safely. It appears that [David Gunn Sinclair] chose to make his way southward, and arriving at a small settlement then called Loerisfontein decided to stay there. Incidentally, a lighthouse was erected and named the Columbine Lighthouse—Columbine being the name of the boat, so it is reputed. It was there at the small village where [he] met and married Magdalene Homewood." They had one daughter and four sons, the eldest being Francis, my grandfather.

A further digression. Magdalene Homewood was the daughter of Captain William Homewood, a master mariner, who as a 27-year-old had arrived in Cape Town and set up business as a trader and shipowner, organizing trading expeditions into South West Africa (then known as Great Namaqualand, and now as Namibia). The South African author Lawrence Green describes some of Captain Homewood's activities in his book *On Wings of Fire*, adding that he was "one of those pioneers whose diary (if he had kept one) would have made a great story of adventure."

David Gunn Sinclair and Magdalene were later buried on a farm called "Heuningklip" (rough translation: "honey stone"), about a mile from Vredenburg.

Re-reading my aunt's material, I was struck by the odd forces that must have been at play, since as a young man I had gravitated towards that area of the Cape Province without knowing exactly why. I would go to the Cedarberg mountains on week-long hikes, and once visited an eccentric yachtsman, Frank Wightman, who was living alone on his home-built yacht, the *Wylo*, in Langebaan Lagoon. (Obviously, too, I appeared to have some farming instincts, which found expression once I got to Franklin Farms.)

Being the youngest of their respective families, my parents had a special relationship to their older brothers and sisters. My mother, especially, was always considerate to older people, regardless of race. She would not hesitate to quietly flout convention by having a Cape Coloured lady (that is, a person "of mixed blood," in the language of the Cape) stop off for tea. In the South Africa of the time—even before the formal policies of apartheid institutionalized this squalid discrimination—my mother's natural decency towards people of other races was quite the exception. This sense of decency appears to have been "in the genes," because years later (in the 1990s), my first cousin—her brother's son, Chris Liebenberg—although not a politician, was brought by Nelson Mandela into his new cabinet as the transitional minister of finance, and Mandela publicly commended him as "a man of social conscience."

My parents married during the Depression years, when life was especially hard. It was a time when people were migrating from the countryside to the cities. Neither of them was especially well-prepared for urban life, and they had a long, painful, and difficult struggle to make their way. It must have been especially difficult after I left South Africa for the United States. I left just when I had begun to be relatively secure in my job, and they told me later of their many trying experiences because of the economic hardships ensuing from apartheid.

For years, the thought that I had abandoned them was a private and personal burden. I felt uncomfortable and remorseful to be living at a great distance from them, in the United States, and devoting myself to my "hobby"—to find the sense and meaning of my life through the Gurdjieff Work. I had my own great difficulties in making my way in New York, yet as remote and distant as I was, I tried to make good the errors of my younger days (and these are poor words) with generosity, openness, and acceptance, behavior that was in sharp contrast to what I had shown as a selfish and inconsiderate young man. Gradually I came to understand Gurdjieff's great insight, that the "search" for the truth about myself could only be grounded in real sincerity towards myself. Only in this manner, it seemed, was I able to reach to and support them in ways both visible and invisible. Being caught up in all the activities of the work, it was perhaps 20 years before I saw them again after having left South Africa. It was a profound shock on meeting them again to realize that all those years had vanished, and in the quiet of my room that night I wept.

*   *   *

This "search" for meaning and purpose was second nature to me from the earliest. Perhaps it was my real nature. Metaphysically speaking, I would say that the search and the need to know were there before I was.

Whatever the unbelievers might say, the mystical—or, if you wish, spiritual—experiences were not flights of imagination or idle daydreams or attempts to escape the "harsh reality" of life; they were real, objective inner events. I only gradually began to understand these events as pointers to the presence of another reality, a "real world," from which one is veiled by one's ignorance, one's sleep, and one's total infatuation with the shadow world to which Plato and other traditional figures so clearly refer.

In later years, I found an extraordinary corroboration of these traditionalist ideas in physicist Shimon Malin's insightful study of the relationship between quantum physics and the Western philosophical tradition. "Great discoveries in science and great works of art," Malin observes, "are grounded in transcendent experiences."[5] The accounts of such experiences, he notes, "indicate that moments of such creations and discoveries are moments of contact with the noumenal realm." Furthermore—and this is one of the main thrusts of Malin's studies—"An experience of insight can lead to a direct knowledge of reality as it is in itself, a knowledge that comes with the feeling of utter certainty."[6]

I should add one caveat, which Malin, a careful and sensitive mind, expresses with true scientific dispassion—that "the certainty of the experience of insight does not lead to certainty in the conceptual formulations that result from it."[7] The actual experience connects one with what Werner Heisenberg, in speaking about a seminal experience of his own, called "the central order," while the attempt to communicate and explicate the experience, as Malin notes, depends on the current paradigm and the personal limitations of the one who has had the experience. Malin notes, too, that there are different levels and different kinds of experiences of the noumenal.

Without laying claim to any special expertise, least of all in Malin's own field of physics, I can only state that in some indefinable way my experiencings left their indelible imprint. The first of these mystical experiences that I can still recollect occurred when I was about eight years old, or perhaps younger. I had been to our church Sunday school earlier in the day. Lying in bed that night, I began to think about what one of the teachers had said. I suppose that he or she had responded to questions about the "first cause" by declaring that God had created the universe. Pondering these questions, I remember asking myself, "But then who created God?" For years after, I could recall that, at that questioning, "I disappeared in a blaze of light."

One might say alternatively, that a blaze of light enveloped me, or overwhelmed me. Or even that I *was* the light. Many years later, when I began to discover that others shared such experiences, I found references in the work of Mircea Eliade, for example, to the "blaze of light" as an archetypal mystical experience. And even more recently, I have discovered (if that is indeed the proper terminology) that the Church of Gurdjieff's youth, the Eastern Orthodox, is replete with accounts of such experiences. As Vladimir Llosky notes, light "is both that which one perceives, and that by which one perceives in mystical experience."[8]

One of the things that caused me to turn away from Sunday school and the rather shallow Christianity as practiced in the church to which I belonged was a typically insensitive remark, probably made with the sincerest of good intentions. Our pastor, a well-meaning gentleman, had brought in a singing coach. It turned out our coach was a rather crotchety local pharmacist. His small claim to fame, it seemed, was that he was the brother of Sir Norman Birkett, later the lead British prosecutor at the Nazi war crimes tribunal at Nuremberg following World War II. He had us sing a hymn. We launched into singing in our usual unruly way. After one verse, he stopped us. "There is something I want you to understand," he said in a firm, prosecutorial manner, no doubt modeled after his brother's. "I want you to know that little birds who won't sing will be *made* to sing!" That effectively ended my interest in formal or—to use Gurdjieff's terminology—exoteric Christianity.

Since it had become all too clear that I could not derive any help from this source, I continued to read . . . and read . . .

and read, voluminously, trying to find some clues about the real meaning of life. I became more and more solitary and more and more unhappy. Still, the sacred experiences persisted. Once, in my late teens (probably around the time I had begun to attend the University of Cape Town), I had cycled from our home in the suburbs through the Tygerberg hills to Blaauwberg Strand. Blaauwberg was a beautiful beach on Table Bay across from Cape Town, with Robben Island—the island where Nelson Mandela was imprisoned in later years—a few miles offshore. I was tired from the long ride and decided to lie down and rest for a while behind one of the dunes. Hardly had I lain down than there was again an experience of passing out in an overwhelming blaze of light. In later years I would often remember the smell of seaweed and the salt air associated with that occasion.

I have to say that I had been rather proud of being appointed head prefect, that is, head of the student body, of my high school—a largely empty role, but unusual in that I was an English-speaking boy in a dual-language but predominantly Afrikaans school. After matriculating, I went on to the University of Cape Town. I chose courses for my undergraduate degree that more or less approximated to my "search," still with no clear idea of how I would earn a living. I kept hoping that I would find "answers" in some of the material I chose to study. My parents were having a difficult time—for many years painful for me to recall—but they made the further sacrifice for me. I had one pair of trousers and two shirts to my name when I enrolled.

The campus of the University of Cape Town lies on the eastern slopes in back of Table Mountain, and from it one may look to the range of mountains known as Hottentots Holland, on the far horizon. The university is beautifully located, and not only by virtue of being at "the fairest cape in all the circumference of the world," to quote the circumnavigator, Sir Francis Drake. Years later, I discovered that I was not the only one on campus—or elsewhere, for that

The campus of the University of Cape Town, on the eastern slopes of Table Mountain.

matter—who had special or mystic moments. In his book *The Mystic Light*, published about 10 years after I had left the university, Professor J.H.M. Whiteman, professor of mathematics at the university, described an experience of the "Archetypical Light" [his words] that he had had at the age of 28.

This experience was cited, and given great credence, by Mircea Eliade because "its author is at the same time a careful observer and an informed scholar."[9] I always thought it an interesting, if not extraordinary, coincidence that the two of us probably passed each other a few times on that hallowed ground, I as a raw and rather footloose undergraduate and he as a ranking academic. As a trained observer, a man "familiar with the metaphysics and mystical theology of both East and West," as Eliade describes him, Whiteman's report on his mystic experiences helped to authenticate my own experiences for me. Academically, however, I was not in Whiteman's league. I was not a good student, because I was plagued by my "burning questions." But I won the medal for ethics one year, and earned distinction in political philosophy.

*　　*　　*

One of the most profound of my early spiritual realizations occurred in my mid-20s when I had taken to rock climbing, primarily on Table Mountain, which had some classic climbs. I was trekking alone through the Cedarberg mountains, about 120 miles north of Cape Town. I believe this occasion was my second visit to the Cedarberg. At the time, because I was so self-absorbed—still marred by the devastatingly traumatic experience, to which I have referred, when I was probably no more than 10 or 12 years old—I was entangled in a strangely warped relationship with my parents. I was practically a character out of Dostoyevsky. Today I think of it, still with great dismay, as a groping, ill-informed, ignorant, and convoluted attempt to understand the profound alienation from life that had crept over me.

I believe I had just recently met the ideas of Gurdjieff, whose teaching about our mechanicality and sleep spoke directly to my concerns, because my unease about the way I conducted myself towards my parents was gnawing at me. In any event, on this occasion I had hiked for several hours until I came to a plateau between two long, high ridges. It was cold and gray. A strong wind blew. I was miserable and lonely. It was finally dawning on me that I was not the immaculate and self-sufficient loner that I liked to imagine I was. To one side, a strange 60-foot-tall natural rock formation known as the Maltese Cross loomed above an intervening low ridge like one of H.G. Wells's Martian creatures, a kind of mute witness to my unhappy progress. Finally, I stopped. I realized that it was pointless going on in that way. My heart wasn't in it. I was pursuing a hollow and empty dream.

What did it matter that, on one hand, I enjoyed cheap triumphs, like working out for hours in the gym and getting stronger and healthier, or that I had achieved a petty security in my newspaper work, where I was making a small name for myself, while on the other hand I led a fraudulent, hypocritical, and hollow life in relation to my parents and others. All of these thoughts and feelings bore in on me with overwhelming force. I turned around and trekked back to a stone hut on the plateau, where I spent a miserable night, wracked with remorse. The next day, I hiked back to the ranger's station, and from there drove straight home, determined to change my ways without knowing exactly what it was that I needed to do.

The profound hypocrisy of "seeking the higher" while acting heartlessly and selfishly towards my parents caused me such anguish that I could not rest until I could begin to exorcise that awful trait and—as I later learned Gurdjieff would say—to "repair the past." I realized then that I had been made to feel, through the force of conscience, the truth of the commandment, "Honor thy father and thy mother." However, it was only *after the event*, as it were, that the actual words of the commandment had come to mind. *Feeling* the truth about this necessity had preceded the verbal articulation. For me, this experience was an early corroboration of Gurdjieff's teaching not only about the existence of a "higher feeling center" and the powerful impact of the experience of remorse of conscience, but also about the different speeds at which thought and feeling function.

It was only when I faced and struggled with this terrible contradiction in myself (my heartless behavior on the one hand and my wish for "spiritual" growth on the other) that I could honestly begin to undertake the search for the "elevated" knowledge that I have come to know to be at the heart of the so-called perennial teachings.

*　　*　　*

There were also two "brushes with destiny" in those early years that always haunted me in later life. Once, as a boy of 8 or 10, I had run out of our home early in the evening to go to a store nearby. Without looking, I darted across the road right in front of a car that sped on, missing me perhaps by a fraction of an inch and a fraction of a second. That timeless moment is still etched in my memory. Later it would occur to me from time to time that perhaps I was not "destined to die" just then.

The other occasion arose purely out of my own stupid egoism. Although I had only the most minimal experience and no real training in rock climbing—apart from some hair-brained solo efforts—I was determined to tackle the "big stuff." The orthodox approach would have been to join up with experienced climbers, but as a loner I had no real wish to go that way. I had set my sights on a spectacular climb, Jacob's Ladder, close to the western edge or summit of Table Mountain. Finally I ran across someone who said he would join me. We did reasonably well until we came to the main section of the climb. While he belayed me, I led the way up the exposed face. I was at the end of the 120-foot rope, out of his sight, when I got to the crux pitch. From the description given me by someone who had climbed it, I knew there was to be a delicate maneuver. I simply could not figure it out, and I clung to the face in the same spot for several minutes, trying various moves. Suddenly, my strength gave out. I blacked out and fell off the face.

I woke up to find myself gently dangling out in space.

I swung back on to the face, and climbed quickly to the crux spot again. I realized that I was at the limit of my strength, and that I had to get through or bust. There was no time to try to figure out the required moves. To my astonishment, my body made the moves, and I breezed through to the stance above. Again, it was only later that I understood something of what had transpired: that the body has its own intelligence, and in relinquishing the "control" of the (usual) mind I had allowed it to act without any encumbrance of some low-order and tired old discursive thought trying to figure things out. There was no fear. Instead, I experienced a totally focused attention on what was in front of me, as if all my parts—the head, the body, the feeling—had been galvanized into totally unified action. This was a taste for me of what Alfred North Whitehead may have meant in saying towards the end of his life that "the creative principle is everywhere." It manifests itself with this purity especially in such moments of danger, when there is a demand that exceeds one's ordinary limits.

There have been over the years innumerable corroborations of this fact, but few as dangerous or potentially catastrophic. I would wake at night in years after, realizing that I had not been well prepared for these adventures. And I realized how reckless and uncomprehending I had been in the way I had laid my life on the line.

*   *   *

After leaving the university, I was fortunate to land a job on the editorial staff of the *Cape Times*, the English-language morning newspaper in Cape Town. The *Cape Times* was a rather exciting place for a young journalist. My unofficial mentor was Dudley R. D'Ewes, the assistant editor. He had evidently been passed over for the top job because of alcoholism, but that slight, it was said, had sobered him up for good.

I spent eight years at the *Cape Times*, but even in that brief time I was able to appreciate, as so many others had, the great sobering influence that D'Ewes exerted over the conduct of the newspaper during the critical years when the apartheid policies of the Afrikaner government were being instituted. He was known, an informal history of the *Cape Times* observed, as "A writer of singular grace and polish."[10] He was, the history also noted rather tersely, a "Rhodes scholar, steeped in the classics and theology, a BA of Keble College, Oxford, and an MA of the University of Cape Town. Lean, ascetic and incisive in thought and speech, D'Ewes was destined for the Anglican ministry but found that he 'could no longer accept the objective existence of the Holy Spirit as a person.'"[11] His apparent rejection of Anglican orthodoxy and the doctrine of the Trinity as a metaphysical first principle were unknown to me at the time, and would not have meant anything had I known. But learning of this several decades later when I had begun to delve into such questions for myself, I received some hint of the conflicts that must have wracked this intelligent man and driven him to drink. After all, "this obviously unanswerable question"[12] about the relation of Jesus Christ to God the Father has been perhaps the most contentious issue in the history of Christendom, as John Julius Norwich so succinctly characterized it. Down the centuries, esoteric issues like that have pushed many an otherwise sane and sober man over the edge.

In any event, even though everyone spoke knowingly about his past, D'Ewes was totally sober when I met him. He was recognized, too, as a pioneer conservationist and environmentalist and had served for 18 years as president of the Botanical Society of South Africa. The *Cape Times* historian noted that he kept to "a punishing schedule of afternoon and night work," to which all of us could attest. Many a night, as

I walked to the railway station from the office after putting the last edition to bed, Dudley D'Ewes would go jogging quietly past me to catch the last train to his home. He was truly an honorable man. He had none of the obnoxious pretensions and other airs so assiduously cultivated by the British of the time and their colonial imitators; their pomposity and arrogance and condescension could make one puke. There is a distinct difference between that conditioned behavior and the contained intelligence that Gurdjieff found so admirable in some of the truly cultured people of Asia. In hindsight, I had felt that quality of contained intelligence in Dudley D'Ewes, and I was ever grateful that our paths had crossed.

NOTES

1. Jerzy Growtowski, "A Kind of Volcano," in *Gurdjieff: Essays and Reflections on the Man and his Teaching*, ed. Jacob Needleman and George Baker, Continuum, New York, 1996, p. 98-99.
2. Evelyn Underhill, *Mysticism*, New American Library, preface to the 12th edition, 1974, p. vii.
3. Ibid, p. 42.
4. Alfred North Whitehead, *Adventure of Ideas*, Macmillan Publishing Co. (Free Press edition), New York, 1967, p. 169.
5. Shimon Malin, *Nature Loves to Hide: Quantum Physics and the Nature of Reality*, Oxford University Press, New York, 2001, p. 156.
6. Ibid, p. 158.
7. Ibid, p. 158.
8. Vladimir Llosky, *The Mystical Theology of the Eastern Church*, St. Vladimir's Seminary Press, Crestwood, NY, 2002, p. 218.
9. Mircea Eliade, *The Two and the One*, Harper & Row, New York, 1969, p. 72-75.
10. Gerald Shaw, *The Cape Times: An Informal History*, David Philip Publishers, Cape Town, 1999, p. 137.
11. Ibid, p. 139.
12. John Julius Norwich, *A Short History of Byzantium*, Alfred A. Knopf, New York, 1997, p. 45.

CHAPTER 3

The Outsider

IT IS DIFFICULT, if not impossible, to recapture or even
understand the old anguish and heartaches and
sufferings viewed from 40 or 50 years on. So I was truly
surprised to find among my papers an old, yellowed
manuscript of a book review dating back to my first real
discovery of Gurdjieff's ideas. The review, which I wrote in
my middle 20s, reflected the craving for sense and meaning
that dominated my every waking moment, colored all my
thoughts, and made me feel myself a kind of "pathetic
wandering phantom" in an alien universe, to adapt South
African philosopher Jan Smuts's felicitous phrasing.[1] I read
the florid idioms of the review, with its tone of ornate
imprecision, with some embarrassment now, but there it was,
the mirror of my state at the time.

I say "first real discovery" of the Gurdjieff ideas, because
I had come across a reference to Gurdjieff almost 10 years
earlier, when I was about 19, but I had not grasped the
significance of it. This was in an article in the September
1949 issue of the English publication World Review, which I
had acquired because it carried an article on T.E. Lawrence
by Andre Malraux titled "The Demon of the Absolute." Just
coincidentally, there was also an article by J.G. Bennett titled

"Living in Five Dimensions." In that article, Bennett made specific reference to Gurdjieff. From the copy still in my possession, I find that I had marked several passages that clearly corresponded with my interest. Bennett put it very succinctly: "We pass a great part of our lives conscious of very little. Our functions work mechanically under the combined influence of our established automatisms and the stimulus of the external world. We are, in fact, very much less conscious than we think we are." I had been living with this awesome realization for most of my waking life until then, and I was destined to suffer this for five or six more years without sensing any hope. I think I had made only half-hearted attempts to track down Gurdjieff and Ouspensky. There was actually a copy of C. Daly King's *The Oragean Version* in its original format in the Cape Town Public Library—pretty much my spiritual home in those years—but it had no appeal for me. And Bennett's own references seemed too intellectual or abstract to have any practical significance for me at the time.

I suppose it was by the sheerest chance that David Castle, the book review editor at the *Cape Times*, asked me to review a book by an unknown 24-year-old British writer, Colin Wilson. Actually, he did not ask me: he simply handed me the book with the unspoken understanding that I would produce some sort of review. He did not suggest any specific length, and I imagined he had no particular interest in receiving any but the most cursory review.

The book, which I still have on my shelves, was *The Outsider: An Inquiry into the Nature of the Sickness of Mankind in the Mid-twentieth Century*.

Reading the book, I was astonished to discover how many other historical figures had had the same interest that I had in trying to fathom the meaning of their lives. I was obviously not alone! Among the figures he cited were T.E. Lawrence, Friedrich Nietzsche, and Dostoyevsky. I had read them all, been infatuated by them, felt they had suffered like me.

Wilson threw a totally new light on this particular animal, the Outsider, and on my own desperate gropings. Only later, after I had delved into Gurdjieff's teaching and taken up with the Work, did I realize the extent of Wilson's unspoken and unacknowledged indebtedness to Gurdjieff. He did not in any way appear to own to the fact that he had derived his main categories of analysis from Gurdjieff. I suppose this is not important. So many of Gurdjieff's insights have passed into common currency, known perhaps only at second hand, distorted and misunderstood, that it is almost pointless to lay claim to proprietary rights on his behalf.

I suppose that what prompted the publication of my piece was my reference to the "house poet" of the *Cape Times*, a curious fellow named John Howland Beaumont. I had never met him, but I would clip the occasional poems of his that the newspaper ran in its editorial column. It turned out that he was actually a proofreader at the newspaper, slaving away in some dingy warren in back of the press room. He produced a steady stream of poems that probably few people understood clearly. In any event, my little analysis that follows appeared to provide a satisfactory take on his public cries of anguish. Today I have a different understanding of some of the terms I used in the review—terms like the Socratic "know thyself," for example—and I would certainly try to use expressions like that with a new precision. But I will give my piece in its entirety, even forgoing the temptation to expunge one or two even-at-this-stage embarrassing adjectives. I cringe today at my liberal use of words like "seminal," "quest," and "bogged." Naturally there was at least one reader of the newspaper who wrote in to take me to task for claiming that Beaumont's poems were seminal. And he was absolutely right in his criticism. My biggest presumption was, of course, to equate this rather minor poet with those larger-than-life sufferers like Nietszche, Lawrence of Arabia, Nijinsky, et al. But there I was, at the tip of Africa, off the beaten track, "contemplating day and night" and the eternal verities in total isolation, like the lone Bushman in a well-known Afrikaans poem picking away at his one-stringed instrument under the southern stars:

> *Op my ou ramkietjie,*
> *met nog net een snaar,*
> *speel ek in die maanskyn,*
> *deurmekaar.*

Roughly translated, this reads:

> On my little old guitar
> With just one string
> I strum in the moonlight,
> All over the lot

*   *   *

The Outsider: A Study of the Unquiet Mind.

Thou wouldst be happy, wouldst thou?—Then be a fool, George Borrow advises in *Lavengro*. And those who would be happy would be wise not to read Mr. Colin Wilson's remarkable study of the unquiet mind—the pervasive malaise of our time.

It is not for the squeamish or the staid or the sleek-headed men who sleep o'nights. It is not for those who contemplate life on a complacent belly. It is, as Mr. Wilson says, only for those who "are interested in man in extreme states."

This book is doubly remarkable. Firstly, it contains some of the most seminal criticism of the archetypes of the unquiet mind, such as T.E. Lawrence and Dostoyevsky particularly, that is to be found in print, and secondly, it professes to be a Guide for the Perplexed, pointing to some of the "traditional" ways out of the murk.

It is the most penetrating analysis that I know of the Demons of the Absolute, those luckless men who, like Lawrence and poor proud satanic Raskolnikov in *Crime and Punishment*, deal only in the elemental disjunctions, the primal either-or of behaviour. It is, to bring their study to readier subjects, the key to understanding "the heart's defiant thunder" that the South African John Howland Beaumont sounds in poetry that marks him as one of the major poets of our time.[2] And it helps to explain the nameless quest of Frank Wightman, the Hermit of Constable Hill, the yachtsman-author of *The Wind Is Free*. It is a book about the anguish of men who, in Wightman's words, refuse to be "incarnated cliches," who revolt at being jostled in the "March of the Slaves."

There are fundamentally two ways of looking at the universe, perhaps never so well expressed as by General [J.C.] Smuts in his celebrated address to the centenary meeting of the British Association, when he said that "the human spirit is not a pathetic wandering phantom of the universe, but is at home, and meets with spiritual hospitality and response everywhere." Mr. Wilson's study is about the wandering phantom, or, as he calls this luckless spirit, the Outsider. The Outsider feels with excruciating clarity (and I use my own metaphors, not Mr. Wilson's) that it is easy to profess sanity and sobriety if one has God on one's side: if one is blessed by God (or Nature) with a plenitude of ability *and* the quiet mind. He feels, like Lawrence, that "books and bikes and music" are barren things, and like Hamlet he looks at life and cries: "What to me is this quintessence of dust? Man delights not me—nor woman neither, though by your smiling you seem to say so."

Suffering and involved, all things conspire to his solitariness. So he shrivels up like a beetle, a tsotsi [3] of the spirit who stalks the barren byways of the soul—like Lawrence in the RAF [Royal Air Force], a leaf in the wind (his posthumous journal, "The Mint," shows a wandering phantom made articulate); or like H.G. Wells finally, his mind at the end of its tether; or like Nijinsky, Van Gogh, Blake and George Fox; or the veritable host of figures in life and literature that Mr. Wilson's wide reading has discerned.

The Outsider becomes "a hole-in-the-corner man" (Mr. Wilson's phrase). He is reduced to solitude by his unquiet mind. He has—and I borrow perhaps the most apt description of the malaise from the work of John Howland Beaumont—"a bleak heartbreak in his blood," which bogs the will and all endeavour, and stifles all enthusiasm. Like Macbeth he has a "rooted sorrow" in the mind; like [Walt] Whitman, he has a "hungry gnaw"—call it what you will. In his solitariness the Outsider learns the excruciating truth that though the old Socratic injunction to "know thyself" may be the first step to wisdom (and to sanity and sobriety), it is also a first step to a resounding and seeming neuroticism of the order of Raskolnikov or T. E. Lawrence. He is a votary of the barren view. He is enthralled by his twilight self, and breathes blasphemies to the night. He turns the old sods over and over in the mind, till there is not a worm to feed on anymore. He knows only solitariness and the anguish of blunted sensibilities, or responses not evoked. He goes stalking through a little life (rounded each day by a fitful sleep) like a demonic being.

The Outsider is the man at the barrier. So his quest is to try to resolve the unquiet mind. He seeks to resolve the bleak heartbreak of the blood. *He seeks his other self.* He seeks a nameless fulfillment of all his nameless longings—but he seeks it with the urgency of a man who feels deep in the marrow that there can be no deferring of the fulfillment of a doubtful hereafter: he wants to escape the frustrating prevision of hell.

Though the "afflictions" of the Outsider may be construed to support a Freudian appraisal—Beaumont deaf, Wightman a small man, Lawrence bogged by his family "secret," Dostoyevsky an epileptic, Nietzsche tormented by his disease—the Outsider must go beyond psychology and philosophy. No Freudian analysis ever explains exactly how and when an "affliction" becomes a bleak heartbreak that stifles all enthusiasm. What seems incontestable is that an "affliction" and a seeming neurosis heighten the awareness of otherness, of being not as other men; and the bleak heartbreak, in turn, intensifies the neurosis. "We are all victims," Beaumont has said.

So the quest for sanity and sobriety—for the other self, for full self-expression, for the condition in which he may savour "all things lovely"—is a religious quest. "The individual begins that long effort as an Outsider; he may finish it as a saint," Mr. Wilson says.

He *may* finish. For though Mr. Wilson outlines some of the successful quests, he also emphasizes the great failures, the archetypes of men who have succumbed at the barrier— the men who have been fated to go plunging into nothingness till madness or "mind-suicide" (Lawrence's term) overwhelmed them. The analysis is not for the squeamish.

"The primary aim is to live more abundantly at any cost," Mr. Wilson says. "Blake . . . agrees with Nietzsche, Dostoyevsky, Hesse; the way forward leads to more life, more consciousness.

"Suicide is no answer, nor mind-suicide, nor the idea of 'an allegorical abode where existence hath never come.' Heaven-after-death is irrelevant. The way lies forward, into more life. Van Gogh shot himself and Nietzsche went insane, but Raskolnikov and Mitya Karamazov went through with the terrifying crucifixion of the answer to the Outsider's problems: to accept the ordeal; not death, but 'ever further into guilt, ever deeper into human life,' into the ten years' exile, the purgation. Life itself is an exile. The way home is not the way back."

The first necessity (and he says there is no division of opinion about it) is to "go to extremes." In this religious quest the Outsider must go the whole hog; the mystic alone is rewarded. The Demon of the Absolute must change his very marrow. He must burn, to be consumed in the flame of his own metamorphosis.

*   *   *

But some of the luckless ones never burn entirely in the flame. As in Beaumont—and we have the evidence of each new poem—there is always a residue of the questing self that in due time becomes the fuel for stoking yet another blaze, from which the essential core of his being emerges each time with a still keener temper for clanking down the dark byways again, reaping newer experience for the burning.

Beaumont's poetry is a distinct contribution to the study of the unquiet mind not simply because those great slobbering characters in the vast Russian novels may seem a little remote but mainly because his work is a consistent elaboration of "the heart's defiant thunder" of a questing spirit who cannot fathom "this monstrous wrong of life." It is perhaps the prime platitude of philosophy that language is inadequate to express the deepest intuitions, yet a poet of rare perception such as Beaumont brings to the common currency of language the inarticulate connotations that delve deep into the Darkness. [Footnote in the original: Dr. I.D. du Plessis (a well-known South African literary figure of the time) rightly described him in an article in the *Cape Times* on February 14, 1950, as a major poet of our time—*but for the wrong reasons.*] To Keats the poet is a chameleon. He has no identity. He is "continually in, for and filling some other body." And pervading Beaumont's poetry is this sense of the poet's peculiar communion with what the philosophers would call the secret character of the nature of things, those pulse-felt articulatenesses that are

> All gathered with the secret silent art
> Of vanished summers in the sun.

He has himself drawn the portrait of a chameleon—the poet's self—that takes its impress from its environment. This chameleon-poet, Beaumont, is a "beast of ancient sorrows," coloured (or marred) by some aboriginal calamity or a monstrous wrong,

> . . . An eternal shame of man
> Or some bleak heartbreak in his blood.

This poet's vocation then is to shed the "foolish tears of some old pain," to pour out some of the "sullen thunders of the soul." That is the only story worth the telling—the sullen thunders that shake the spirit, the nails of doubt that eternally crucify; the harrowing heartaches that sap the will; the heroic gestures that come from deep in the guts. Thus if we believe with Walt Whitman that "the poems of life are great, but there must be poems of the purport of life, not only in itself, but beyond itself," then we may truly regard Beaumont's sullen thunders as newer insights into some of the mysteries of the workings of the world.

> Mine was the task of the word
> And the bitter design of the word.

The word—and one remembers that the Christian mystique has found a ready accord with others of his kind who have been racked by their nameless longings—is also "the Word that was in the beginning": there is a *bitter design* to the universe. It is a time-clock universe which clocks him

> . . . out of time and life
> And count my destiny by each day's strife.

For Beaumont is the Poet of the Barrier. Like Ulysses, cast ashore "from wanderings," he remembers (as Lawrence remembered most "the agony, the terrors and the mistakes") the "cold and weary care" of his quest as he gazes

> . . . across the foam to Ithaca,
> Dove-haunted, honey-golden land
> Of all our dreams . . .

Racked by the excruciating reality of the chaos of his emotions—"your foolish flesh, your feet of lust"—he has dipped into the Darkness and professes to see an order in the universe, "a song of an infinite harmony" that "sings in star and sun and stone and tree": *but it is an alien order.* It is a time-clock universe

> That counts nor efforts of the mind nor grace
> Of thought, but with unstinted justice pays
> For my immeasurable gift of days
> The measured coppers of my toils—
> Sweat-stained, clock-docketed and time-watched
>   spoils
> Of hungry man's immortal heritage—
> The thirty silver pieces of the age.

Suffused with his nameless longings, the formless yearning of the unquiet mind, he sees wide forecourts (or the ocean foam) separating him not only from the true character of a universe that presents to him a "metalled and fast-figured face," but often also from *his own true character.* He feels himself "part of nothing but the darknesses of fate": he has not resolved the dichotomy between his questing self and an alien universe. [Footnote in the original: In spite of what Dr. Du Plessis has implied.] He has not yet made his "peace with the fool or the bitter earth." He is at the abyss, the great gulf. He is a singer of ancient sorrows, bogged in "the everlasting now" because (I borrow words quoted by Mr. Wilson) he has exhausted the future: "*I had foreseen* the bitter dew," Beaumont says in his "Portents from Macbeth." He is bogged by the bleak heartbreak in his blood:

. . . No labour's balm or death
Of slow day's life brought me the breath
Of murdered sleep or curse of time.
The hurt mind of embattled rhyme
Had drawn the last of grace long ere
The restless ecstacies of care
Revealed the fearful truth of youth
And the afflicted dream of youth.

The dreams of shaken nights are deep
In hidden sanctities of sleep,
While yet I hear a voice cry: Sleep
No more.

—But here I balk at going farther. The Demon of the Absolute must work out his own salvation, and the mind boggles at the thought of the paths Beaumont's questing spirit shall explore.

Perhaps he may win through to that condition of which he has had his glimpses, as of that "one small bright bird" which

. . . Sang the pride of earth and for

The joy of life as if but in a dream.
I did but sleep—ah me, I dream, I dream!

Beaumont's quest is to make the portent of that dream the pervasive reality of his life. Those who admire his achievement must be thankful that

As yet the citadel still stands
With flaming battlements within the fire—

and hope that he shall not succumb, like the luckless ones whom Mr. Wilson lists. One hopes that he shall not fall at the barrier, where

. . . in the Darkness then the night
Obliterates all but a name.

I commend both Mr. Wilson's seminal book and
Beaumont's poetry (the Collected Poems are overdue) to all
who are interested in the archetypes of the unquiet mind—
but with the warning of Boehme's which Mr. Wilson endorses:
"If you are not a spiritual self-surmounter, let my book alone."

*　　*　　*

So much for that youthful and purple prose. I owe it to
Wilson that I returned to the shelves of the Cape Town Public
Library to look again at Gurdjieff and Ouspensky. When I
had first glanced at *Fragments* and seen the abstruse "table
of hydrogens," the stark "ray of creation," and the forbidding
"food diagram," I had simply put the book aside. I had wanted
help of an unknown order, not diagrams. Now I went back to
find out what these men were really saying. I knew now they
were speaking to me.

What astonishes me these four decades later is how the
basic or classic terminology of the human search—the Great
Knowledge with which Gurdjieff aligns himself—can be
saddled with such diverse and shallow meanings. The
Socratic injunction to "know thyself" has nothing to do with
either introspection as such or with neuroticism: if it is
assumed to have such a consequence, it is because the process
known in the perennial philosophies as self-inquiry is not
only tainted and distorted but also not understood.

Having been led to Gurdjieff's ideas and immersing myself
in the processes of the teaching, these old dark-of-the-night
yearnings quietly receded and soon evaporated. They had
served their purpose. They had brought me to the threshold
of the Work. I realized I needed help. Not the ordinary sort,
nothing to do with "making it through the night," but the
help of a completely new order of knowledge.

So it was that I gobbled up Ouspensky's books. I recall to this day my walking down Government Avenue, the pedestrian walk from the old Dutch East India Company's gardens that ran alongside the Houses of Parliament, while reading Gurdjieff's tale of the Armenian wolf and Ouspensky on recurrence. I was totally absorbed and fascinated. Here was a new world of ideas and meaning to be explored. I remember it vividly. Ouspensky "spoke my language." So that was what Nietszche was really about. And now the idea of self-remembering. I recalled all the moments I had "woken up," to wonder what I was doing there, as if I had been dropped on to the planet from outer space. As Bennett had expressed it in his article, I had come to realize that "inner freedom must be bought and paid for," and that there undoubtedly were people who could point the way.

At this point, I was determined to "find the teaching."

NOTES

1. J.C. Smuts, "The Presidential Address to the Centenary Meeting of the British Association for the Advancement of Science," *The Speeches of General J.C. Smuts, P.C., C.H., K.C., D.T.D.*, Truth Legion, Johannesburg, 1940, p. 178.
2. "[O]ne of the major poets of our time . . . ." An embarrassing claim, still!
3. Tsotsi: a South African gangster type.

CHAPTER 4

Benjamin Fairfax Hall
and The Stourton Press

E ACH OF US receives the call in his or her own unique
way.

My search for a real teaching was "all my own work,"
undertaken in solitariness and quite distinctly without benefit
of clergy. It was something I was compelled to pursue. But I
owed my actual entry into the Gurdjieff Work to the brief but
fortuitous appearance of a gentlemanly and unassuming English
expatriate who lived, as I did, at the tip of southern Africa.

Our brief acquaintance, which lasted little more than two
years, opened the way to my coming to the United States. In
retrospect, it seems a strange confluence of events that would
take him to South Africa, where I would meet him, the sole
"representative" of an unknown and mysterious teaching.
Soon after he had steered me to the States, he himself pulled
up his stakes and returned to his homeland. From my
personal, subjective point of view, it was almost as if he had
done a duty in being on hand for me. I never saw him after
that.

It was sometime in 1956 or thereabouts, at which time I
was 26 years of age, that I realized it was Gurdjieff's ideas

that offered me the help I sought. I set out to find someone who could introduce me to them. It is a reflection of my ignorance of the world that I did not think to write to the publishers. Instead, I did what appeared to be the most logical thing: I placed an anonymous advertisement in the personal columns of the afternoon newspaper, the *Cape Argus*. (I did not do so in the *Cape Times*, its morning counterpart, because I worked for the *Times* and I did not want to reveal my interest in any way.)

A few days after placing the advertisement, I checked in at the *Cape Argus*, which was actually just around the corner from the *Cape Times*, to find that there were four replies—and a package. The package contained a copy of Gurdjieff's *All and Everything*, with a penned inscription in the front that read: "From one human being to another, that both may have more of themselves to give." With it was a note saying that I was not to reveal to anyone how I had received the book. After all these years, I believe I may report that I still have the book, and to this day I have no idea who left it for me. The handwriting had the feel of an older person. I know that some of J.G. Bennett's people made their way to South Africa during and after World War II, so it's possible that one of them left it for me. But there is no way of knowing if this was indeed the case, since there were a few others who appear to have "discovered" Gurdjieff for themselves.

I followed up three of the leads that were closer to home, but I knew immediately upon meeting these people that they were not ones who could offer me anything to resolve my thirst for meaning. Reluctantly, I contacted the fourth, who had written a note that, along with the address, convinced me that he was a "typical expatriate Englishman," for whose type I had a distinct aversion at that time. I recollect his name as Rodney Stone. He lived on a small farm north of Cape Town and was married to an English-speaking woman who had grown up in Argentina. They were friends, they said, of B. Fairfax Hall, who had been P.D. Ouspensky's printer. I learned that Fairfax Hall had had a group, which was inactive at the time. He confided to me that Hall had actually told him his "chief feature," and I must admit that to this day he is perhaps the only person who has made such a statement. (I suppose "group leaders" make these declarations all the time, just as they freely give Gurdjieff's "stop exercise," although publicly they never admit it.)

I had a very jolly, alcoholic dinner with this couple, and found myself making many visits to their toilet, which, being on a farm, was a septic unit—a hole in the ground. The copious quantities of wine and my frequent retreats to the hole helped establish a certain informality to the mutual "interrogation." I was on the editorial staff of the *Cape Times*, and this had a certain cachet. The Cape of Good Hope was—and probably still is—a cosmopolitan outpost at the tip of Africa, and in a city of perhaps no more than 500,000 people (at that time) I had a small reputation as a journalist: my byline appeared quite regularly. So, in a small way, I suppose I was also someone to cultivate.

Following that "interview," they recommended that I telephone Fairfax Hall, and so I arranged to meet him. I did not yet have a car, so we arranged that I would take the (electric) train to Rondebosch, and he would meet me at the station. On the appointed day, I took the train there. As I sat in the waiting room after arriving, I watched through a window as he drove up in a massive fin-winged Chrysler—a rather ostentatious display of wealth down at the Cape in those austere post-World War II days. I faced a terrifying moment of truth. I was in a funk, tempted just to stay in hiding. It was such an automatic and unthinking response, which now after many decades in the Work I am able to recognize as the basic stuff of self-observation but which at that time presented a difficult struggle. I realized that for most of my life I had had a failure of nerve at such critical moments, but this time the inner need overrode the weakness. Sober reason prevailed: I was desperate to meet someone who could shed light on my questioning. So, summoning my courage, I went out to meet him. And in a way, the rest is history!

As James Stourton, a friend of his in later years, perceptively described him in the British publication *Matrix* in 1992, Fairfax Hall had "the quiet manner of a retired Treasury official." Fairfax Hall professed to know something about me already. He had asked members of his group to read one or two things I had written—probably some book reviews and my precious little essays on cricket—and he criticized one anonymous editorial that I was a little vain about. I am happy to say that after all these years—more than 40 years later, in fact—I am probably a lot less sensitive to that sort of comment.

Fairfax Hall struck me as very honest. He conveyed only what he felt he understood about the Work ideas. He had no pretensions about his role. I learned that he had come to the Cape in 1949 (after World War II) to get away from the rigors of post-war England—and, I suppose, to hold on to his money. It was rumored among the group members that his family had been in the printing business for generations, but I subsequently learned that these reports were not accurate. [1] Late in his life, he wrote an account of his career in printing for *The Private Library* in which he said, "Printing as a pastime was not a thing which had any family or youthful associations for me. It was more or less by chance that I heard The Nonesuch Press mentioned when I was an undergraduate, and began to look with admiration at books which had been printed with them." He had launched The Stourton Press in 1930, and now at the Cape he had continued to ply his craft. I did not learn until 40 years later that he was already renowned in printing circles for *A Catalogue of Chinese Pottery & Porcelain in the Collection of Sir Percival David, Bt., F. S.A.*, by R.L. Hobson, C.B., which dated back to 1934. It has been described by James Stourton as "the masterpiece of the Press and indeed one of the most impressive private press books of all time."[2]

I was able to piece in a few early biographical scraps when James Stourton very kindly shared with me some correspondence he had had with Charles Middleton, of Henley-on-Thames, Oxfordshire, at the time of Fairfax Hall's death, in February 1982.

Charles Middleton had been an "exact contemporary" of Fairfax Hall at Trinity College, Cambridge, from 1923 to 1926, after Fairfax Hall had come up from Harrow. He remembered Fairfax Hall as "generous and good-natured with lots of money and an inquiring mind. His apparent worldliness (creature comforts, cars & cigars etc.) was superficial & never led him into dissipation or excess. Temperamentally he was patient and painstaking . . . ."

After leaving Cambridge, he entered his father's firm of B.J. Hall, and according to Charles Middleton, "His chief preoccupation had become study of Indian philosophy & the occult . . . . He had already traveled a little in India in the interval between Harrow & Cambridge, & the subject always interested him."

With typical reserve, Fairfax Hall never spoke to me of the circumstances in which he had met Ouspensky, and I never asked.

Only at the turn of the last century and long after his death did I learn that he had served a remarkable self-apprenticeship in printing. Towards the end of his life, Fairfax Hall recalled that he soon became his own pressman, photographer, lithographer, plate-maker, type caster, and compositor. He had acquired a thorough knowledge of his craft. And from James Stourton's account in *Matrix*, I learned for the first time the origins of the name Fairfax Hall had adopted for his press. He had begun his printing while working in Stourton House, Westminster. James Stourton wrote: "This was on the site of a house which my family owned in the 18th Century and Fairfax adopted this name—having sought with characteristic courtesy permission from my great grandfather—for no stronger reason."

After 1934, Fairfax Hall printed no more books until 1947, by which time, James Stourton wrote, "he had acquired an improbable fascination in Russian Mysticism, and in particular the writings of P.D. Ouspensky." This, James Stourton observed, became the main theme of the press for the next 18 years.

When I came on the scene (about late 1956), Fairfax Hall's press was housed in what I recall as a virtually spotless whitewashed cinderblock building in his yard at "Boschheuwel" in the Bishopscourt area—perhaps the most select community at the Cape in those days. Following my arrival, Fairfax Hall reactivated the group and reinstated the practical work. The group had previously begun to set galleys for a work titled *Self-will*, which (if my memory serves) we proceeded to print. Strangely, this book was not listed in Fairfax Hall's own checklist of his publications in *The Private Library*. Earlier productions of his included Gurdjieff's *The Struggle of the Magicians* (1957) in an edition of 10 copies; a book on *Surface Personality* (published in 1954); *Memory* (1953); *Negative Emotions* (1953); *Notes on Work* (1952); and *A Record of Meetings* (of Ouspensky, 1951).

James Stourton, for whom it may have been difficult to understand Fairfax Hall's devotion to Ouspensky, not to speak of his "improbable fascination in Russian Mysticism," more or less dismissed their significance as examples of the printing craft: "Fascinating as these books are for the light they shed on the personality of Fairfax, they are of no interest from a typographical point of view except that they are mostly set in Aries 14 pt," he wrote.

Still, they constitute a special testament to Fairfax Hall's commitment to the Work ideas as received through Ouspensky. *A Record of Meetings* was initially published in a limited edition of 20 copies, but it later made its way into paperback when Madame Ouspensky's granddaughter, Tatiana Nagro, reissued most of the Ouspensky titles. All of the Ouspensky books printed by The Stourton Press were excerpted by Fairfax Hall from Ouspensky's lectures or responses. I recall seeing the many volumes of the original meeting transcripts in his library at Boschheuwel. But the first South African-produced volume was evidently Rodney Collin-Smith's *The Theory of Eternal Life*, published anonymously in 1950. This was published more formally three years later by Vincent Stuart, London, under Collin-Smith's pseudonym, Rodney Collin.

As a newspaperman, I was in my element at the press. At the *Cape Times*, it was often part of my job to go down at 1 a.m. to oversee the "lock-up" of the last galleys on the late pages before the presses ran. The old linotype machines at the *Times* made a distinctive clatter and there was always the smell of ink. Fairfax Hall had two nice antique Albion presses; each impression required a lever to be pulled horizontally in order that the paper be pressed down onto the type (again, if my memory serves). It was a very traditional process, which involved considerable "make ready."

Again, it was only through James Stourton's recollections of Fairfax Hall in his old age that I understood how absolutely painstaking and extraordinarily meticulous he was in his approach to printing. Stourton observed that "The guiding deity of the whole operation was a micrometer installed in a red leather box. Evidence of its workings were . . . everywhere in the form of carefully cut scraps of paper containing precision measurements down to several hundredths of a millimeter for all stages from casting type[,] for which it was very necessary[,] to make ready." Stourton felt that this "was the basis of his superb ability as a colour printer." I should note that my experience of the operations of the press did not run to color, since we printed only black and white while I was there.

Fairfax Hall used a typeface known as Aries that had been designed especially for him by Eric Gill and was the exclusive property of the Press. The only sizes made were 10, 14, and 18 point, while his display was set in Perpetua titling. Aries, to the cognoscenti, is essentially a Perpetua type. We actually cast the type ourselves. He set me one day to do the casting: this required my turning a crank handle that made me bend so low on the downstroke that my face was only inches above the little cauldron holding the molten lead. On one occasion, just as my face got the closest it could to the pot, he called the "stop." The stop exercise (described in Ouspensky's *In Search of the Miraculous*, chapter 17) requires one to freeze where one is at the command and not to move a muscle. As I looked into the pot of gurgling lead I was terrified that it would splash into my eyes, and I flinched. After a minute or two, he told us to resume our activities, and I told him of my fear. He assured me there was no danger. But he did not call the "stop" in that circumstance again.

It was somewhat reassuring to learn, four decades later, that I had not been alone in my awe of this procedure. James Stourton described a demonstration of "this brontosaurus of printing technology" by Fairfax Hall when, in 1981, he passed the equipment over to Stourton shortly before his death. "This was a terrifying operation for which Fairfax put on a butler's apron," Stourton wrote. "First the compound of type metal was heated until it bubbled and gurgled like a volcano on the verge of eruption. When the matrix was in place, for whichever character was to be cast, Fairfax worked the lever that precipitated a tremendous crashing of parts. A lone piece of type spilled out with a small nick which had to be filed off by hand. Fairfax was very frail at the time and one half expected he would be blown away by the impact."

It was at the press that I discovered for the very first time what it means to be "asleep" in Gurdjieff's sense. I was given a very long paragraph to set. When the proofreaders later pulled a proof of the galley, they were puzzled to find several lines that they could not account for, since they were not in the original text. They asked who had set that particular passage. I was so embarrassed that I professed not to know. What I had set was pure fiction, sheer imagination: I had been dreaming, yet I had dutifully and meticulously set the passage letter for letter and "justified" the type (i.e., equalized the spacing for each line of type and fitted it into the galley). It was a real shock to me. Which is the real point of the practical work in the Gurdjieff way: it is only in these conditions that one begins to see the truth about oneself—to see one's lack of attention and lack of presence.

Fairfax Hall was very careful in his responses to our questions about the Work. He required us to bring written questions, to which he would not respond right away. Rather, he would go to the transcripts of Ouspensky's meetings, excerpt Ouspensky's responses to similar questions, and then read them to us the following week. As honest as he was, this method lacked spontaneity and immediacy. But we were drawn to him for his modesty and sincerity. And in what appeared to be the typical Ouspensky method, our questions about the cosmological ideas or the food diagram would see large diagrams brought out and placed on easels, while one of our number, Hein Kropholler, who later became a full-fledged chemistry professor, I believe, would run us through the explanations. It was all very formal.

While he was always quite dispassionate in his responses, I recall one time when he was ever so slightly pleased with himself. It was at our very first meeting. He told me of the response he had made to one of Ouspensky's chief aides, Dr. Francis Roles, who had written to him urging him to join with Idries Shah, the Sufi. A number of people had been touting Idries Shah as the supposed successor or heir to Gurdjieff. Fairfax Hall told us he had written to Roles to say that if one wished to cross a raging river one could not do it "by straddling two horses."

When in 1957 the Soviet Union launched the first space satellite, *Sputnik*, which could be seen in orbit over Cape Town, he asked us to write about our understanding of its significance. I do not recall that anyone of us quite anticipated his observation that the launching was part of the process of "feeding the moon." I have never been totally comfortable with that thought, but I dare say he was broadly correct in his interpretation.

After our group had been meeting for a year or so, he announced that he had arranged that those who wished could go in turn to the United States and spend two months at Madame Ouspensky's estate at Franklin Farms, in Mendham, New Jersey. As I noted earlier, I flew there by way of London and Prestwick, Scotland, in August 1958, and did not return to South Africa for perhaps 20 years. I never saw Fairfax Hall again. I had never had a "personal" relationship with him, certainly not anything like that which I had with Martin Benson or any others down the years. I did come within a hair, as it were, of seeing him when I was traveling through London after visiting France in 1979—some 20-odd years after last seeing him in Cape Town. He had left South Africa in the meantime to live again in London (at 36 Trevor Square). I had obtained his telephone number, and when I got to the Underground station at Piccadilly Circus, I went to the telephone intending to call him to arrange a meeting. With the crowds milling by me, I wrestled for 10 or 15 minutes with the notion. But in the end I convinced myself that I had nothing at all to speak to him about. He had never met Madame de Salzmann, whom I had come to regard as my teacher and mentor, and I could only imagine a very formal and awkward encounter. So I gave up the thought.

It was perhaps around this time that Pentland looked in on me while I was working with a young group in the Gallery (on 62nd Street in New York), which was used more or less as an anteroom for groups not yet admitted to the Foundation. He asked, in a somewhat conspiratorial way, that we go outside, and out there on the sidewalk he mentioned that he had had a meeting with Fairfax Hall in London about some publishing matters. He said that he had wondered how to approach Fairfax Hall, with whom he also had not had any dealings for many years. Then the idea came to him, he said, to thank Fairfax Hall for "sending Sinclair to us." I found it momentarily flattering, but I was also grateful that at least he must have told my early mentor that I appeared to have found my home in the New York Work.

Fairfax Hall had been one of the people who had compiled the Ouspensky book titled *The Fourth Way*, excerpted from the transcripts of Ouspensky's lectures. I had also been told at Mendham that The Stourton Press had also privately published Collin-Smith's book *The Theory of Celestial Influence*, which some people had thought to be written by Ouspensky, but this book is not shown in Fairfax Hall's own checklist. It was subsequently brought out by Vincent Stuart Publishers in 1954 under Collin-Smith's pseudonym, Rodney Collin. Evidently there had been rumors that *The Theory of Celestial Influence* had been written by Ouspensky, so the formal publication was undertaken to make it clear it was not an Ouspensky work, although it was inspired by Ouspensky's conversations with Collin-Smith. That, at least, was the story told at Mendham.

I should note too that Fairfax Hall was one of the circle of diehards who had chosen not to visit Gurdjieff in Paris after Ouspensky's death. He held to the old Ouspensky line that Gurdjieff had taken a wrong turn and that he was not to be trusted. When I had asked him to clarify this in our very first meeting, he mentioned how insane it was to have sent Madame de Hartmann back to Essentuki during the Russian Revolution. "I would not have sent a dog back there," Fairfax Hall said to me. There is also a hint of Ouspensky 's "hard line" on Gurdjieff in the note Fairfax Hall appended to the five little volumes he excerpted from Ouspensky's transcripts. When they were subsequently reprinted in 1979 in one volume under the title *Conscience* (edited by Merrily E. Taylor), the book carried this one-sentence disclaimer: "The compiler of these essays wishes to state that, though formulated with more precision by Ouspensky, some of these ideas were first introduced into Europe by G.I. Gurdjieff." This is followed by the initials B. F. H. He was loyal to the end.

In any event, carrying on the Work in South Africa was already becoming very difficult during those early years under apartheid, when the government was ever ready to cast its jaundiced gaze on everything non-Afrikaner as alien and suspect. The group appeared to have disbanded soon after I left, and Fairfax Hall returned to England in 1961. Before leaving, he reportedly donated his Albions to the Michaelis School of Fine Art(s) in Cape Town, retaining, however, the typecasting equipment.

My one last indirect contact with him took place several years after he had left South Africa. I am a little unsure about the exact order of events, but this is roughly what I remember. I had done some elementary block printing on a small platen press obtained from a well-known type founder, The Kelsey Company, in Meriden Connecticut, now unfortunately gone out of existence through the advent of computerized printing. At Christmas 1970, I sent him a rather nice block print of my own design, and he responded by sending me a copy of one of the last books he had published at The Stourton Press in its new London quarters—a book of linoleum cuts by Rupert Shephard, titled *Passing Scene*. But I waited 10 more years before I felt ready to undertake a real printing project, because he had set such a high standard. And it was his book that prompted me to include linoleum cuts in the printing projects that we did for a few years at Armonk.

More than 25 years later I discovered among my papers a generous letter he had sent me outlining his very practical approach to the craft. Dated January 14, 1976, his letter said:

> If the questions of outlay and space are important to you, then a flatbed press would be better because you could use it also as an imposing stone.
>
> In the Cape, you will remember, we had two Albions: a demi and a double-demy. They are a great pleasure to use but you need a lot of time and

patience. I think a flatbed *cylinder* press is much better. Vandercook of Chicago make several models. The electrically driven ones are very heavy and very expensive but they make a smaller model which is operated by turning a handle. The cylinder packing is simple and almost no make-ready is required. The forme is rolled automatically as the handle is turned. You knife on a little ink on to the idler roller after about every ten impressions. With this kind of press you can get precise register and can print letterpress or half-tone blocks, linocuts, copper & wood engravings.

There is no doubt that Vandercook make the best universal proofing presses in the world, and that is all you need for small editions. But platen presses such as the Cropper treadle are cheaper and turn out the work more quickly, but the quality is not so good.

When I returned from South Africa (& prices had not rocketed) I bought an electrically driven Vandercook and it was on that that I printed *Passing Scene* of which I sent you a copy in April 1970. This was done from Rupert Shephard's South African linocuts in three colours. I have no personal experience of a hand operated Vandercook but I have seen one at work in a commercial printing plant. It was making four-colour proofs from copper plates and seemed to me much the same as my machine except for the physical labour involved.

He ended his letter with kind references to friends in the Work in London and New York, and a generous comment on the role that I appeared to be playing. I was glad to hear that he was not totally out of touch with events that seemed to have passed him by. And he signed it "Fairfax," an intimacy I had not been accorded when I first appeared on the scene 20 years before.

I was fortunate indeed to have met this good, honest, courteous, unassuming, and supremely efficient man. On the practical and worldly side, he instilled in me a love of printing and the printed page, and on the spiritual side he made it possible for me to go and live on Madame Ouspensky's estate. I find it hard to believe that our meeting could have been mere chance.

NOTES

1. I was put on the trail of Fairfax Hall's printing roots through the good offices of Elizabeth and James Evans, of By The Way Books, Sacramento, California.
2. The Honorable James Stourton, vice-chairman, Europe, for Sotheby's, to whom Fairfax Hall later sold the equipment, type, and name of The Stourton Press.

A former governor's mansion, the main house at Franklin Farms seemed little changed in 2003 after being vacated by the Work 40 years before.

CHAPTER 5

"Where Is He That Is Born?"

I BELIEVE THAT Fairfax Hall had few illusions about his ability to communicate the Work and that this surely prompted him to offer members of the Cape Town group the opportunity to visit Franklin Farms.

Several of us took it in turns to make a visit of two months' duration. As my two months drew to a close, I extended my own stay for two more months in order to be there when Madame de Salzmann came. Once having met Madame de Salzmann, I gave up my job at the *Cape Times*, and eventually my original two-month visit to Franklin Farms lengthened to a stay of about a year and a half, until shortly before Madame Ouspensky's death.

Among the small group of people in residence at Franklin Farms was Beatrice Rego, who had been living there for almost 12 years. I recall very distinctly that I had had a premonition as I said goodbye to my parents at the railway station in Cape Town (for the journey to Johannesburg and the subsequent overseas flight to New York by way of Gatwick, Scotland) that I would meet my wife in the United States. It just came to me out of the blue. I gave it no further thought. But there she was, and a year after I arrived, we were married.

The wedding took place on October 23, 1959, a date more or less dictated by Miss Dorothy Darlington, the head of Madame Ouspensky's devoted caregivers, so as not to conflict with the celebration a week later of the anniversary of Gurdjieff's death. On the day of the wedding, which took take place in the Presbyterian church on the hilltop in Mendham (preacher: the Rev. Robert Burns, fortuitous bearer of a classic Scots name), there was of course no letup in the usual activities around the farm. Martin Benson just led me off, almost unceremoniously, to do the usual chores after breakfast—feeding the chickens and pigs and working around the estate. Then around lunchtime, he looked at his watch and announced that I had better get ready for the church ceremony. Back at the main house, I pulled out my only suit, which I had not worn for a year, only to discover that there were moth holes around the fly. I took the trousers off, and Miss (Margaret) Capper sewed them right then and there as I stood by. That done, I made my way downstairs, where my best man was waiting. (Ken Ward, an aeronautical engineer who had been spending time at Franklin Farms, had been commandeered for this role.)

Suddenly, as I followed him through the door into the so-called boot (or ante) room, I "left my body." This is the first and perhaps only time I shall have reason to use such an expression, replete as it is with so many New Age connotations.

I found myself—a "disembodied" self—observing (or more properly, witness to) an extraordinary segment of a shallow arc stretching horizontally before me. Neither "end" of the arc was visible. Later I could only describe it as a "segment of eternity." I was in another dimension altogether. All of this took place in the space of one stride. I must have stood there, transfixed, immobile, because Ward turned around and said rather sharply, "This is no time for dreaming. Let's go."

In later years, when I came to read about the life of Ramakrishna, I felt the similarity to what he evidently experienced on a rather frequent basis, not to speak of his evident reluctance at having to "return to earth." There is also a reference by the Frenchman Romain Rolland to an experience that he too described as "a sensation of the eternal." Plotinus speaks in the Enneads of being "lifted out of the body into myself." If this was, as I felt it to be, the experience of the noumenal world, it is indeed experienced, as Shimon Malin expresses it, "as more real than the sensible world; ordinary experiences pale in comparison, to the point of becoming devoid of meaning."[1] And there are evidently many, many, other similar accounts in mystic literature.

This experience and others like it were simply lodged, or "incorporated," into me: I did not go about imagining special powers and qualities, nor did I seek them. I certainly did not go around speaking about them. For me, they were indeed intimations and—more than that—direct evidence of another, unfathomable and unutterable reality, the realm of the sacred. Karlfried Graf Dürckheim, for example, writes of those moments "when the Absolute erupts commandingly into consciousness."[2] Of course, Gurdjieff himself might have questioned von Dürckheim's reference to the Absolute as being "too high." Be that as it may, by now I had come to accept these extraordinary inner events as both normal and natural, perhaps even the "birthright" of a human being. But I was too involved in the profane, or everyday, problems of living. My mentors, like Martin Benson, were all too cognizant of human frailty (including their own). That particular understanding appears to be at the heart of Gurdjieff's teaching. And I was always very practical, hardly your dreamy type. The urgent admonition of Nietzsche's Zarathustra, "Stay loyal to the earth, my brothers," was more my style. In fact, Dr. Welch once said, in an expansive moment, "You're a Renaissance man!" Hardly, Doctor, hardly. But I was no mean hand at shoveling manure, and like so many others, I learned through the intense practicality of the Work to do many things, certainly not professionally, but well enough to pass muster.

The commercial world, meanwhile, with its obsessive pursuit first of the pound and later of the almighty dollar, was always a difficult one for me to fit in comfortably. What was I really fit for, I wondered. I had been fortunate to gravitate almost intuitively to journalism, finding an interesting job at the *Cape Times* right out of university. But here now, in the United States, I did not relish the idea of pounding away at a typewriter for hours on end. So one year I decided to get some professional career guidance. The search firm put me through a battery of psychological tests conducted by a psychology professor from Columbia University. When the day came for him to announce his assessment of my abilities, he sat down opposite me, pulled out a small stack of file cards, and, pausing for effect, read off the first card: "You are a mystic," he pronounced.

Secretly I was taken aback, since I had been trying to slant my responses to his tests to suggest that I was really hard-nosed and obsessively dollar-driven, someone who (as the saying goes) would sell his grandmother down the river to make a dollar. I wondered what precisely had given me away, but I could never be sure. However, my dissembling must have been convincing too, because he added, "And you are also a sonofabitch."

Obviously I had learned nothing new from this costly little venture. But I was also gratified to receive this small corroboration that I did in fact possess some desirably profane qualities that might serve me well in the marketplace. As I had come to say, using a "Bushman saying" of my own invention, "If you want to feed with the lions, you must learn to love raw meat."

My extraordinary experience in the boot room at Franklin Farms had come almost exactly a year after my first encounter with Madame de Salzmann. Having originally come to Mendham for two months only, I had taken a leave of absence from the *Cape Times* for this purpose. However, as these two months were drawing to a close I learned that

Madame de Salzmann would be coming. My old journal notes reveal that the people of the farm were encouraging me to stay, since I was proving to be useful around the estate, so I arranged to stay another two months.

I had no idea who Madame de Salzmann was. Fairfax Hall had never even hinted of her presence. In fact, I had had no idea that she existed. When I asked about her, the women looking after Madame Ouspensky said with their typical British understatement that she was "an interesting person." I think Martin Benson, too, must have encouraged me to stay on because he was clearly devoted to her, considered her the real leader of Gurdjieff's work, and wished for me the opportunity to meet her. Benson was a "Gurdjieff" man through and through. I, on the other hand, without having known about such critical distinctions, had come to the Work and to Mendham through "the Ouspensky side," as it were. I should note again that Fairfax Hall, unlike a number of his contemporaries in the Ouspensky sphere, had chosen not to visit Gurdjieff in Paris after Ouspensky died. I had understood that Fairfax Hall not only considered Gurdjieff to be of unsound mind—off his rocker, as it were—but he was also perhaps even afraid of Gurdjieff. He had a more than comfortable life, he was content with Ouspensky's exposition of the "system," and he evidently felt no need to expose himself to Gurdjieff's seeming irrationality, unpredictability, and well-known disregard for the niceties of "proper" society. And those were the days when everyone was addressed rather formally as Mr. or Mrs. or Miss, a custom that lingered on even until the last days of Franklin Farms.

The occasion of my first encounter with Madame de Salzmann—a momentous event for me—was the commemoration, on October 29, 1958, of Gurdjieff's death. Each year, October 29 is specially marked by the people in the Work. Back then, with Madame de Salzmann in attendance, the more senior members in New York would join those in residence at Madame Ouspensky's estate. There were perhaps 12 in all who were in residence, including Madame Ouspensky's grandson Lonya Savitsky, Tom Forman, Martin Benson, Miss Dorothy Darlington, Miss Daphne Ripman (later Mrs. Carlos Macielajcwic), Miss Margaret Capper, Bill Forman, Miss Nancy Pearson, Miss Rowina Dickson (a Scotswoman), Miss Elizabeth Harper and Beatrice (both Americans). Also living on the estate, but in their own cottage, were two out-and-out Ouspensky "loyalists," Dr. and Mrs. Ralph Phillips, while Pierce and Barbara Wheeler were living in the Turkey Cottage opposite the barn. As the lowliest and newest and most temporary of the residents, I was evidently considered a virtual nonentity, although I was not yet fully aware of my preeminence in this regard.

In the days leading up to the dinner, Madame Olga de Hartmann and others arrived to help plan the dinner. I saw very little of them except at mealtimes, since my days were taken up with the endless chores around the estate: keeping the small coal-fired furnace for hot water stoked, shoveling manure at the barn, grinding wheat for the coarse farm bread we ate, and working with Martin Benson at all other times. Late one afternoon I went into the kitchen to pick up a bucket of scraps for the pigs. I heard the planners speaking in the next room, known as the back kitchen. As I bent down to pick up the bucket, I heard Madame de Hartmann say with a voice of pitiless contempt, "Oh, Sinclair? He's just a piece of the furniture." At that moment, the world came to a full stop. I virtually "died" where I stood. I was devastated. Here was another crushing blow to my fragile and pitiful egoism. With my hand on the handle of the bucket, I froze where I was for what seemed like ages. Numbed by this shock, I slowly came erect with the handle of the bucket still in my grasp. I stole out quietly, and made my rounds like a zombie. My suffering was awesome, mind-boggling, and overwhelming, and I was crushed.

It took a day or two to get over the shock. Gradually I came to accept that I was simply a guest in Madame

Ouspensky's house, more or less a "temporary sojourner," as Africans were contemptuously categorized in my own homeland at that time. I calmly reasoned to myself that I was fortunate just to be there in that special surrounding. I had no place else to go. If it was decided that I could not be part of the event, I could find lots of things with which to be occupied on the 300 acres of the estate.

Then, to my surprise, I learned on the day of the event that I had been included after all, in the team of waiters. Wesley Addy, a well-known screen actor and companion of Celeste Holm, an icon of the New York theater, headed the group. It turned out that I was truly the last and least of the team, like the runt in a litter. My task was to carry dishes from the kitchen to the threshold of the dining room, where I handed them to the waiters. I had only a vague impression of Madame de Salzmann and the others. When we had finished serving, we were "allowed in," as it were, to sit at the tail end of the tables, just inside the passageway from which we had brought the food. By this time, everyone else had finished dinner and was having coffee and dessert. But then, while we were eating, Madame de Salzmann came over to our table, and standing there, spoke to us about our experiences as members of the team of waiters. Since none of my newfound colleagues had much to say, I found myself responding to her and, to my own intense astonishment, asking many questions, questions that I had no idea I had.

Since it appeared that Madame was spending more time than expected in talking with me, someone brought a chair over to her. She sat down, and continued the exchange. I found myself articulating questions and thoughts that I had never expressed before. Here, for the first time in my life, was someone who spoke to my deepest concerns, who undeniably had an inner presence (a thought that I had no way of articulating at that time) and at the same time actually "included" me in that presence, who listened in some unfathomable way, and who actually "saw" me before her and spoke to me as a real human being.

I might now, four decades later, risk saying that she resided in the essential, and respected the iota of the essential in me. Even that is a pitifully inadequate formulation. Perhaps I was experiencing for the very first time in my life a sense of trust, a trust in the absolute integrity of her work. At one point, I found myself saying to her: "Madame, it is easy for you who are Madame de Salzmann, and for Mr. Gurdjieff who was Mr. Gurdjieff, to talk about remembering yourselves. But what about me?" She responded by saying that when she was a young woman she had said exactly the same thing to Mr. Gurdjieff. She recalled that he had told her, "If you come by my room at two o'clock in the morning, you will hear me gnashing my teeth and weeping bitter tears on my pillow."

The point of that exchange was, as I need hardly say, that real self-consciousness has to be earned. Moreover, it has to be earned (to use Gurdjieff's comprehensive expression) through "conscious labors and intentional sufferings." There was a great deal more, none of which I could remember. But I noticed as we spoke that people began to bring up chairs to listen in on our exchange. She was no doubt speaking for everyone's benefit as much as for mine. Finally, Madame de Salzmann looked around at her audience, chuckled in the way we came to know so well over the years, and said that she had to stop.

It goes without saying that I was irrevocably "hooked." This was where I wished to be. At the same time, being a virtual beginner and a mere visitor, I had no means of access to Madame. Yet I wished to hear her speak to my concerns. It was probably soon after, on a Saturday afternoon, that she called a meeting of the permanent residents. With them out of the way, the estate was practically deserted, so I went up to my room on the third floor. As I sat there looking at the walls, I heard a measured voice speaking in the room below. Listening intently, I realized it was Madame speaking with the forceful authority that was her special quality.

I could not make out the words, but I wished to hear her speak. I put my ear to the heating vent. That didn't help. I rolled up the rug and lay with my ear to the floor. That didn't help either. I went downstairs to the basement, putting my ear to the ductwork, but I still could not get closer to the source. I even went up a more or less secret back stairway that I had discovered and that, I seem to recall, led to Ouspensky's library, but I was still unable to get near enough. Reluctantly, I had to admit defeat.

And then there arose in me the resolve to find a way to have Madame speak directly to me. How was I to accomplish that? I still was not familiar enough with the language or the practices of the Work to speak up at the large Saturday and Sunday meetings. It was only several months later, when conscience struck and the enormity of my inner slavery was unequivocally revealed to me (an event I will try to describe), that I found the freedom to speak with a new sincerity and not out of a subtle fog of egoism and pretension.

Being in those conditions was like coming home. I was indeed a prodigal son. I had never encountered anyone like Madame de Salzmann in my life, and there was no one like her back in South Africa. Nor was there anything comparable to the conditions offered at Mendham. In addition, I had just been introduced to the Movements, which had revealed to me my total lack of attention and my appalling lack of connection to my body, even though I had prided myself on having played soccer for my university and cricket for my town, and had become a fairly good mountaineer. I could not go back to a barren life. So I decided to give up my job, "abandon" my family, and turn my back on my mother country. Without much of a struggle, I resigned my job at the *Cape Times*, extended my visa several more times, and a few months later took out permanent residence in the United States. (Ultimately, after almost 40 years, I took out U.S. citizenship, since traveling on a South African passport was often difficult. Ironically, I took my oath of allegiance to the United States on the very day it was announced that Nelson Mandela had been awarded the Nobel

Peace Prize, and indirectly I had regained some legitimacy as a South African.)

Over the years Madame de Salzmann was the person to whom I gave my total allegiance in the Work. And like so many others, I suppose, I always felt that I had a special relationship with her: it was a dispassionate relationship, without any sentimentality or imagination on my part or mystification or manipulation on her part. One learned to have none of the ordinary fears in front of her—only, it seemed, the fear of not measuring up to the demand which she so clearly emanated. Not the least of the things that I felt I learned from her example over the decades was the wish to serve. Ultimately, to serve God—the All-Embracing Creator Endlessness, as Gurdjieff phrased it.

In time, she opened up many opportunities for me, despite my relative youth and inexperience. In fact, when Henri Tracol (her chief aide and president of the Foundation in Paris) met with me one day to discuss a new challenge Madame had given me, I was so moved that I blurted out, "You know, Mr. Tracol, in my next lifetime I would wish to be born Madame's son!" This was not a plea on my part for privilege or power or recognition, or a statement about something as exotic and perhaps as questionable as the idea of recurrence. I was simply expressing my astonishment at the extraordinary warmth and openness that she displayed towards me. Tracol received my rather strange declaration in his usual unruffled and gentle way, and quietly replied, "Ah, you have to earn that right." Which was a whole lesson in itself. In those days, I did not even know that Madame did indeed have a son. And after coming to know him, I could see how presumptuous my innocent wish was.

*   *   *

Having expressed these high ideals here, I must balance the record of my stay at Mendham by admitting that I was soon given a rude reminder of my real inner situation. And arising from that, yet another remarkable mystical experience—or better yet, *a profound and miraculous objective inner event.*

Before launching into a description of this extraordinary event, I should properly assume the attitude of the hapless Karapet, whistle blower of Tiflis,[3] turning to all points of the compass and roundly cursing all within range to counter the insalubrious vibrations that will be directed my way. Because there are those "establishmentarians" who will automatically denounce one's speaking about deep experience. And my speaking will no doubt be considered a betrayal of some cherished principle of the Work. Of course, there are many who are able only to indulge in the "tidy and endless 'psychological knitting'" to which Dr. de Salzmann has eloquently and pointedly referred.[4] That, unfortunately, is as much as they are able to encompass of "the Work." There are others who, understandably, balk at any reference to "a higher" that we can know, any suggestion of "the miraculous," any hint of "another current," any opening to the mystery of Presence, call it what you will. And well they might balk, given our common propensity to dream about far possibilities. At the same time, one respects their serious concern that the inner processes of the Work should unfold in orderly stages—nothing before its time.

Still, I expect to be consigned to that questionably exclusive netherworld of those who might appear to have laid public claim to the experience of a second body. To my knowledge, the leading *declared* occupant of this special domain is Bennett. "One of the key moments in my life," he writes, "was when I was with Gurdjieff in Vichy, France, in 1949. I knew by certain signs that my body kesdjan was formed. Gurdjieff said to me, 'Now you can have paradise, but not be satisfied. Necessary to go to *soleil absolu.*'"[5] It is, of course, a matter of record that Gurdjieff himself openly asserted that Bennett "already has his kesdjan body."[6] But I am not making that claim for myself. I am simply reporting on a strange, miraculous, objective inner event. And I am saying that this extraordinary event points to an occurrence that is clearly integral to Gurdjieff's teaching.

It is perhaps not inappropriate to say a word or two about Bennett, whom I met only once, and then only in a most cursory fashion, as I describe in a later chapter. Bennett appears to have a decidedly (and probably justifiably) "mixed" reputation around the Work. As Dr. de Salzmann has charged, Bennett was a follower of many teachers in succession and made "a mixture of teachings that is difficult to sort out." Furthermore, he indulged in "highly speculative interpretations of Gurdjieff's works and life—which, needless to say, have been thoroughly exploited by commentators of all breeds."[7]

Some of the basic distrust of Bennett that I have sensed around the Foundations was conveyed by Stanley Nott in *Further Teachings of Gurdjieff* (1969), where he concluded that Bennett had not spent as much time with Gurdjieff as he would have people believe. I myself had tried to estimate how long Bennett had been around Gurdjieff, so it was interesting to read Nott's estimate: "His personal association with Gurdjieff was for a year and a half, with intervals, till Gurdjieff died. Twenty-five years before he had been at the Prieuré for about two weeks," Nott reported.

Still, in reading John and Elizabeth Bennett's fascinating account of their weeks in Paris in Gurdjieff's last days, I was struck by their recollection of Gurdjieff's having said that "real, imperishable 'I'" could not be achieved through the "bodily suffering" that Bennett was inflicting on himself at that time. Nor could real knowledge be achieved, Gurdjieff insisted, through the kind of intellectual onslaught that Bennett was making. "Mathematik is useless. You cannot learn laws of world creation and world existence by mathematik," the Bennetts report Gurdjieff to have said.[8] (One wonders whether Gurdjieff acted then in terms of what some now allege to be the "Old Work" or the "New Work." To my mind, as I shall argue in a later chapter, there was—and is— only one Work, which was totally encompassed in Gurdjieff.) Bennett's vast ambition was well known around the Work, and as James Moore reports, his "rich spirituality . . . moved almost too excitedly through a terrain of fasts, vigils, ordeals, temptations, signs, portents, special graces, and mystical climaxes."[9]

In any event, I have tried to respect the implicit prohibition on speaking too casually about the "miraculous." I think this injunction makes great sense, given the common, egoistic predisposition to lie, to pretend, to fabricate, to claim special powers, to profess to have an edge on the common run of humanity. On entering a group, one is urged to be careful not to dream of remote eventualities when the primary demand is, instead, to bring one's "functional" aspects into a true receptivity—that is, to begin the long work of providing a proper support for a new circulation of energy. Or as Dr. de Salzmann put it, "One of the particularities of Gurdjieff's teaching is the noteworthy emphasis on the importance of the first phase of harmonizing the functions and acquiring the center of gravity of the individual presence . . . ."[10]

At the risk of giving a totally erroneous impression, I have studiously avoided writing about that fundamental aspect of the Work in these pages. It is enough to say that there are no shortcuts, no overnight sensations in the work for being. As Pentland put it, it is necessary to come together and to stay together "until real results are achieved." This is well understood where the real nature of esotericism is respected, as among the Sufi esoterics. Ibn al-'Arabi, one of the greatest of them, "cautions the Sufi esoterics against becoming deluded by the revelations or 'unveilings' which come to them from God such that they depart from . . . obligatory works," such as prayer, fasting, pilgrimage, and so on.[11] A sobering admonition, indeed.

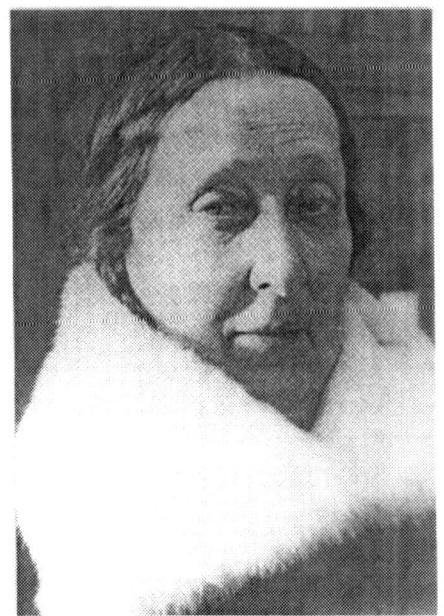

The Madame Ouspensky that I never met. A formidable presence, she wielded great influence from the remoteness of her bedroom off the second floor red corridor, even though she was bedridden for years.

Madame Ouspensky's grandson, Lonya Savitsky, sketched by Beatrice Sinclair at Mendham, about 1959.

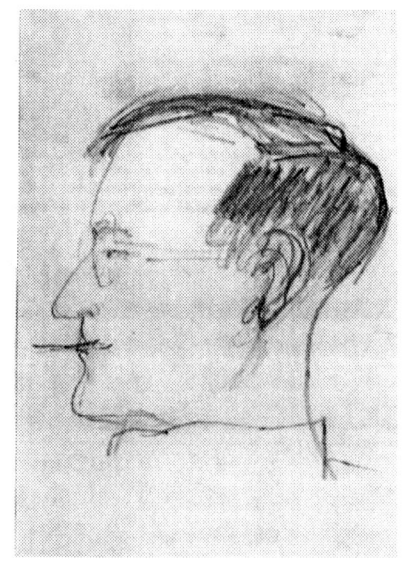

Madame Olga de Hartmann on the grounds at
Armonk in 1965, about four years after the
Mendham era ended.

The entrance to the "boot room" at Franklin Farms. Daphne Ripman is at center, and Joseph Senfeld, Foundation attorney, at right. About 1959.

Margaret Capper, one of Madame Ouspensky's
faithful attendants. About 1959.

Rowena Dickson
and NancyPearson
at Franklin Farms.

Dorothy Darlington in a pensive mood
on her weekly outing.

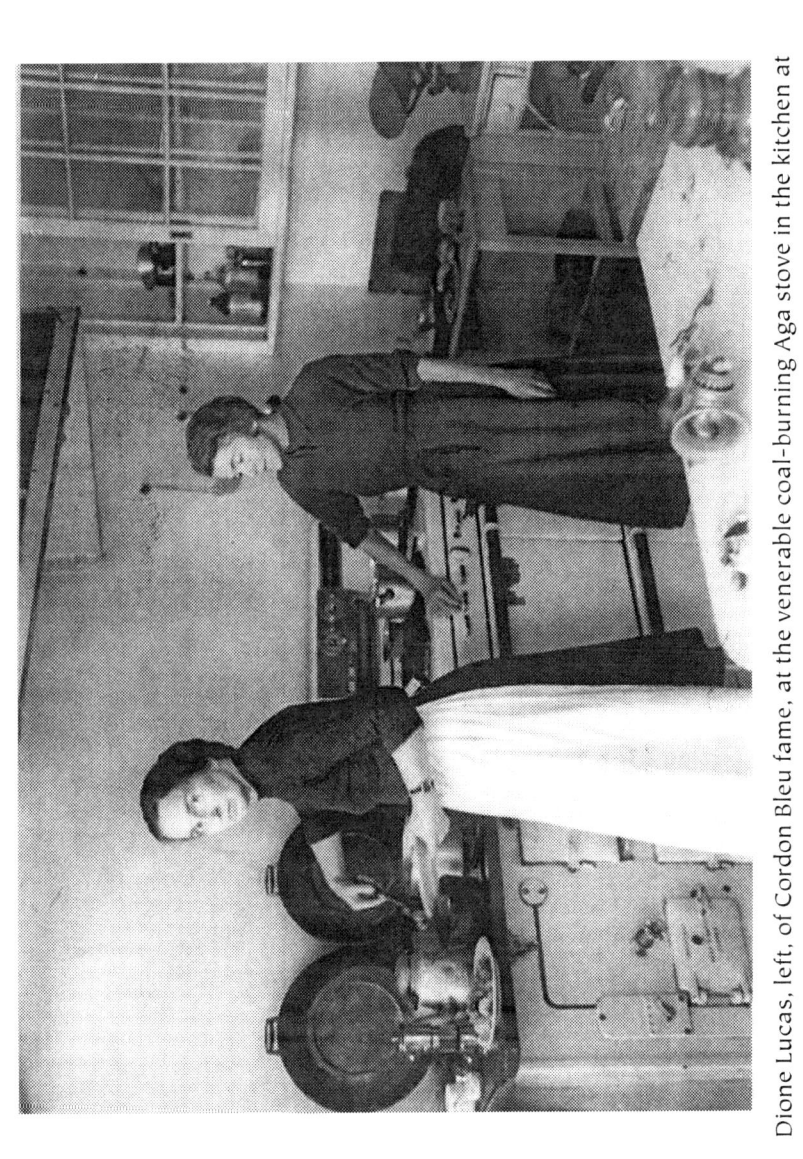

Dione Lucas, left, of Cordon Bleu fame, at the venerable coal-burning Aga stove in the kitchen at Franklin Farms, about 1959. Nancy Pearson, the regular cook and a peerless translator, looks on.

Photo: Library archive, Gurdjieff Foundation, New York.

Jessmin Howarth, center, venerable and dedicated movements instructor to several generations, center, on the south porch outside the dining room at Franklin Farms.

Photo: Library archive, Gurdjieff Foundation, New York.

The dining room at Franklin Farms in an early configuration. At left is the passage through the kitchen pantry to the kitchen. The three French windows face south. This set-up was replaced by having a heavier main table placed to the left in front of the fireplace (not visible here). Date: perhaps sometime in the mid 1950s. *Photo: Library archive, Gurdjieff Foundation, New York.*

Life could occasionally be elegant at Franklin Farms. This was probably a Thanksgiving dinner in the main dining room, about 1959.

Women picking peas at the top of the
kitchen garden, Franklin Farms, 1959.
Beatrice Sinclair faces the camera.

*   *   *

Be that as it may, we had been working all day baling hay out on one of the sections of the estate known as "67 acres" that bordered on Jockey Hollow Road. When I got back to dinner, I was more or less "wiped out." I was not only physically exhausted but there was also all the new uncertainty of launching out into life in a new country and the need to go prospecting for employment in New York City. (Beatrice had left the farm a few days before to take a teaching job, while I remained on for a few days. I don't recall all the circumstances, but I believe everyone had felt I should stay on for a week or two and continue to help around the estate while I explored the job market and Beatrice settled in at her own new job.)

When I got to the dining room, Madame Ouspensky's grandson Lonya Savitsky, sitting in his customary place at the head of the large dining-room table, immediately made some insulting and uncalled-for remarks about Beatrice and me. I don't recall what the substance of his remarks was, but I was astonished that he would turn on me like that. Someone later said he ridiculed me for "loafing" around Mendham while my wife was out in the world earning a living.

I answered him back, and he got more insulting. I found myself matching insult for insult with increasing anger. Getting into the spirit of things, I began to describe rather graphically and with rather perverse pleasure what I would do to him. (Although Benson was reputed to have said of me that I was "as strong as an ox" in those days, no one could know that my threats were purely verbal. But in the face of his distasteful taunts, it seemed I had to make my points with emphasis.) In no time, some of the shocked household passed the word upstairs, and Miss Darlington and others began to hover around. By then, the damage had been done.

I was so dismayed by this turn of events that I did not go to the kitchen and do the washup, but instead went down the road to Benson's cottage. Benson had not been at dinner. I am sure that had he been, Savitsky would not have gotten very far with his cynical taunts. As the shock of the encounter sank ever deeper in me, I was absolutely mortified at what had happened. The charming and gentlemanly image I had of myself had been blown to smithereens. I felt totally annihilated. I told Benson what had happened. And then I lay on his living room floor and wept.

I don't know how long this lasted. But as I lay there, wracked with remorse, utterly devastated, my face buried in Benson's carpet, an extraordinary thing occurred.

There appeared in me a brilliant, shining, golden embryo. (My original preference was to recall this as a golden fetus, and although I have adopted "embryo" as the term most conforming to the subsequent references that I have unearthed in traditional texts, I still think that "fetus" is the better term, since its human characteristics were quite "advanced.") I won't go into further detail. But lying there prone on the floor, I suffered terrible remorse and shame at having behaved as I had done, *and at the same time* I was witness to the miraculous appearance in me of this brilliant, glowing, golden being. It glowed in a surrounding vivid blaze of light. (Again, this encompassing brilliant light.) I experienced intense suffering and intense joy simultaneously—as if they were one and indivisible.

I shall say little, if anything, more about this actual event. There is, as I have said, an unwritten and unspoken understanding that one does not speak too freely about such things. In time, I came to think of this event in terms of Gurdjieff's teaching about the different bodies. *I have absolutely no doubt as to what I had witnessed.* I can speak of it with "the feeling of utter certainty" that Shimon Malin declares to be the hallmark of these "experiences of insight."[12]

At the risk of being thought presumptuous, I felt this experience meshed with Gurdjieff's statement that "the human organism, that is, the physical body, has such a complex organization that, under certain conditions, a new independent organism can grow in it." This new body, he added, is known in Christian terminology as the natural body, and in theosophical terminology as the astral body.[13] But I never spoke about this experience to anybody, not even to Benson, although he had stood over me—a veritable spiritual midwife—all the while this invisible process took place. I did not even speak about it to Madame de Salzmann, to whom I was as yet a virtual stranger. It was not something to speak about, it had been so profound and overwhelming.

Meanwhile, everyone around me at Mendham could only know the external events: my standing up to Madame Ouspensky's grandson, whom I felt to be a cynical and supercilious idler, a common or garden bully—and my crude and exaggerated threat to put him in his place.

Over the ensuing years, I turned again and again in my reading to see if any of the literature of the great traditions threw light on the phenomenon of the golden embryo. Occasionally I regret that I did not speak to Madame de Salzmann about it. I did not ask her because I was sure she would simply counsel me not to imagine things about it, but to work more seriously. It was also understood that one did not speak about such experiences; if they were real, one let them be. I felt she knew with absolute certainty how shallow my efforts were and how appallingly infantile my being was. I imagined her saying to me that to concern myself with this particular inner event would be a major distraction.

But I began to gather evidence that indicated such a phenomenon was not entirely unknown or unrecorded. I could not claim to have brought it about, as it were, since it appeared in me as if by grace, the intervention or emergence of another order or level of being. It certainly did not result from any arduous, single-minded, concentrated esoteric exercises such as those described, for example, in some of the ancient Chinese literature. Perhaps only an idea as esoteric (and ultimately as questionable) as recurrence might contribute to an understanding of this. Was this, in fact, as the "early" Krishnamurti expressed it (rather naively, as he himself appeared to recognize), the culmination of lifetimes of struggle and suffering? Looking back to my youth, before this "breakthrough," it seemed as if those presumed and unseen lifetimes had found a culmination in a few concentrated decades of suffering and alienation. Who could know?

Some light is shed on this experience by Thomas Cleary, of Harvard, who in a scholarly note to his translation of *The Secret of the Golden Flower*, a classic Chinese guide to the alchemy of inner growth, states: "The term embryo of sagehood or the embryonic enlightenment is very common in classical Buddhist texts of the Tang and Sung dynasties. It seems to have passed into Complete Reality Taoism from Chan, but a parallel idea occurs in certain pre-Chan Taoist scriptures. The formation of the embryo represents the initial awakening of the mind. Nurturing the embryo, a term frequently found in Chan, refers to the process of development and maturation after awakening."[14] In a further note, he refers to "the creation of the transcendent being by concentration of spirit: 'In the midst of ecstatic trance there is a point of living potential, coming into being from nonbeing, whereby the spiritual embryo can be formed and the spiritual body be produced.'" To underscore his point: the spiritual body is born within the corporeal. At the same time, and this probably reflects his academic orientation, he does not appear to be saying that this is an "object," such as I experienced.

There appear to be similar hints in Richard Wilhelm's rather questionable translation of *The Secret of the Golden Flower*, but if Thomas Cleary is to be trusted, and I believe there is every reason that he should be, Wilhelm's text "was in fact a garbled translation of a truncated version of a corrupted recension of the original work."

I also came across a tantalizing reference in the Rig Veda: "Hiranyagarbha, *the golden embryo*, arose in the beginning: . . ."[15] Who knows what the ancients meant by this? Then there are explicit references to the golden embryo in the Chinese text *The Secrets of Cultivating Essential Nature and Eternal Life*, by Hsin Ming Fa Chueh Ming Chih, translated as *Taoist Yoga: Alchemy and Immortality*. [16]

And hovering over all of these sources is Meister Eckhart, with his profound mystic understanding. Eckhart actually poses the essential question about the "new birth": "Where is he that is born?" Eckhart appears to refer to this birth not as producing an object—an embryo, for example. Rather, he speaks in terms of an awakening to another level of consciousness. Obviously, too, I believe I am speaking about two seemingly intertwined phenomena. One has to do with the dawning, if only momentarily, of a "new consciousness" (perhaps self-consciousness, in Gurdjieff's terminology), and the other has to do with the emergence or materialization of the necessary "support," that is, the "subtle body" required for the passage of these energies. But I already hear murmurs offstage, and I will not try to dissect these experiences much further.

Rather, I sense the extraordinary implications of my experiences. All the efforts to work in the way to which we were called (and still are being called) by Madame de Salzmann, following Gurdjieff, leads in some unfathomable ways to the growing presence of "a body of attention," or, as David Appelbaum expresses it, "the secret birth of awakened consciousness." [17]

Eckhart, for example, speaks of a "birth" that takes place "in the inmost part of the soul." I sense many echoes in his sermons of an event, or events, or types of experience, that appear to have a great similarity to what I witnessed. (At the same time, there are, of course, other possible interpretations of Eckhart's meaning.) Somewhat tangentially to my thesis, Eckhart writes, for example: "It is a property of this Birth that it always comes with fresh light. It always brings a great light to the soul, for it is the nature of good to diffuse itself wherever it is. In this Birth God streams into the soul in such abundance of light, so flooding the essence and ground of the soul that it runs over and floods into the powers and into the outer man. The superfluity of light in the ground of the soul wells over into the body which is filled with radiance."[18]

Certainly, Madame de Salzmann appeared to point me to this kind of Eckhartian awakening when I later recounted an experience I had had on the streets of Midtown Manhattan. In anticipation of a meeting with her later in the day, I had slipped out of my office and gone into a church nearby. I worked very intensely for half an hour, and then went back out on the street. The intensity, I should note, was not in some mighty striving to achieve a new state, but rather in the purity of the wish simply "to be." I was in an unfamiliar and unaccustomed state as I walked through the milling people. I was totally contained, totally free of fear, free of considering, free entirely of any egoism. I began to describe this experience in the meeting. She stopped me with a slight gesture of her hand. I thought to myself, "What have I missed?" Then she said, "That is real 'I.'"

In hindsight, I could easily say, "Of course! How could I not have known?" Yet this is precisely the nature of the oral teaching, that the required guidance is received in a direct encounter. So this experience was not of the "real I" of my imagination, an "object," some stiff embodiment of a superior being (the Übermensch, or whatever), but an ineffable encompassing sense of Presence and freedom, and what seemed to be the taste of pure being. It was necessary to hear this from her, who was many steps—light-years, it seemed—ahead.

*   *   *

To continue this awkward exploration of the subtle interplay of the sacred and the profane—of the "double movement of life in ourselves," as Pauline de Dampierre expresses it[19]—the external events surrounding the appearance in me of the golden embryo are a story in themselves, but they are of little importance now.

When I had regained my composure, Martin Benson advised me to go back to the main house. I would face the music. In the kitchen, I apologized to one or two of the older women who were there. Dione Lucas, the famous founder of Cordon Bleu, who worked tirelessly and devotedly in the kitchen on many a weekend, looked askance at me. She said she pitied me. I heard her without any self-pity. I was beyond that.

Savitsky soon wandered into the kitchen and gloated over my "downfall." He declared, "You are finished." The "management" called a meeting that very evening, and Miss Darlington then told me they had decided I was to leave in three days. I said I would leave that evening instead, and telephoned Beatrice to come and get me. If Beatrice was shocked by my "disgrace," she did not show it. I supposed she had "seen it all" in her time at the farm.

But I was back the next weekend. The Work held primacy, and no one but Savitsky declared me an outcast. However, the word soon reached me that he now carried a loaded pistol when I was on the estate. I saw him ostentatiously fondle it in his jacket pocket whenever I was around. I learned that he showed the pistol to people in the kitchen, and made no pretense of hiding his hatred of me. Here was irony indeed: I had come to Franklin Farms "to grow a soul," and Madame Ouspensky's grandson planned to blast me to kingdom come. It was not quite the route that I had planned on taking. Later, the Foundation attorney at that time, Joe Senfeld, who was not impressed by Savitsky's antics, told me that Savitsky had asked him how he could shoot me and still make it appear that my death was "accidental." Naturally, Senfeld counseled him not to attempt anything of the sort. I, on my part, wondered how I could pass him on the narrow stairs leading up to the bedrooms and not be shot. I racked my brains over that problem. I think of that as the most concentrated thinking

I had ever had to do until then. This was no joke: it was a matter of life and death. Eventually the solution came to me: when I walked up the stairs or in the hallway, I would bury my hands in my trouser pockets and keep them there, come what may, so that if I were shot it would be obvious that I had made no threatening move.

It was only many years later that I learned that some of the key people at the Foundation in New York were angry that I had been made to leave. Still, it was only right and just that I had been thrown out, since (as Forman admitted to me 20 years later) the old Ouspenskians were afraid that Savitsky would indeed shoot me. I was not at all proud of having acted as I did, but at least I had stood up to a bully. In the process, I had unwittingly challenged their whole order, and I know that I was never forgiven. In time, the Ouspenskian core dissolved, with Miss Darlington going off to Australia, the Phillipses moving away, and most of the old stalwarts fading from view.

Savitsky himself came to an unfortunate end several months later (sometime in the fall of 1960, about a year before his grandmother's death). It was all hushed up. He had evidently turned the pistol on himself. I surmised that he could not face the prospect of an uncertain and perhaps very lonely future as the Foundation made moves to withdraw its support from Franklin Farms, which it did not own. The estate passed to his half sister, Tatiana (Tania).

Savitsky must indeed have been a troubled soul, even though many people, including my wife, appeared to find him quite endearing. In the months after his death, several people spoke of having encountered his ghost in the red corridor, that is, on the second floor where he had lived. One woman, as sane and sensible as they come, even said that his ghost had appealed to her, "Please help me." I have never doubted the authenticity of these reports. They are as credible to me as Gurdjieff's accounts in *Meetings With Remarkable Men* of his own youthful experiences of the supernatural.

*   *   *

In any event, because of my experience, I came to understand that a man too can be "with child." Benson, at least, had understood something of the remorse that I suffered during that process. Pacing the room as I lay on the floor, he had said, among other things that I hardly registered at the time, "You are one of my people."

The inner event, however, was to me a matter of grace, some unfathomable action of "the Higher." As I do not tire now of noting, Gurdjieff himself states, when writing of the "inner world of man," that there is a saying, "common to all the old religious teachings, that 'man receives all his possibilities from On High.'"[20] In some incomprehensible way, then, through the force of conscience, the "inner conditions" were exactly appropriate for this extraordinary event to occur.

The experience faded that very evening. I learned in reading Ouspensky that this too is lawful. He reports Gurdjieff to have said, "A shock can for a short time open up higher centers and connect one with them for a moment. It can concentrate for a certain time all the energy in our body that is dispersed everywhere, and draw it together . . . but as a rule you fall more deeply asleep later. You can even lose consciousness."[21]

I simply let the mysterious event be. I had to get on with facing the "present reality" of my life, and the overriding need to integrate the "outer" and the "inner" worlds. I did not have a clear grasp then of the idea of two currents, but I sensed intuitively this need to integrate the inner and the outer. "Where is he that is born?"—It was as if this new presence had "gone to ground," receded from my ordinary consciousness, and now resided invisibly—where? Frequent intimations of this presence re-emerged in later years, but not with the clarity, precision, and comprehensive impact of its first emergence. In many ways, it would appear that the work to establish a "body of attention" (felt as a subtle presence) is the precursor to—what? The soul? Henri Tracol appeared to intend something of this when he wrote of "an inner process of becoming."[22] The point, he emphasized, was not that the "imprisoned soul" seeks to be liberated from the "accursed body," but that "man's true destiny on earth is linked to his effort to bring about the laborious fusion of the opposing tendencies in himself." It is not enough, he added, "to awaken to the evidence of a more inner, more subtle presence. It is necessary to have an exchange in which he takes part as a whole being." And so it was the intuitive recognition of this need for "the laborious fusion" that helped to keep me grounded.

$*$ $*$ $*$

There were other experiences, some difficult to explain without recourse to the insights (such as those I have cited) of "those who have gone before." One that stands out occurred when I was to speak at one of the Foundation's large Tuesday-evening exchanges on the ideas.

I had prepared my brief presentation quite thoroughly—or at least, as best I was able. I planned, as I usually did on such occasions, to have in the back of my mind the skeletal outline—say, six propositions—that I would flesh out as I spoke. I announced the theme, as was customary, and paused. Suddenly my mind was still. Absolutely still. Absolutely quiet. It dawned on me, without words, that this state was what I had "worked for" all my life. I would have been content to stay that way for time without end. Then, in taking in the scene around me, I realized that the members of the audience—there were about 120 or more people—were quietly and expectantly waiting for me to begin. They were there, not to look at me, but to hear something said. But no thoughts came. My mind was brilliantly lucid, undisturbed, peaceful, and totally empty. There wasn't a murmur or a tremor of anything resembling my usual kind of thought. No "ripple on the still waters." There was "nowhere to go" and no need to go anywhere at all.

I could see all the faces clearly, all looking at me. I tried to disturb this extraordinary stillness by trying to visualize the propositions I had written down earlier, but try as I might, I could not visualize anything. I said out loud, "Bear with me for a moment." (The transcript of the meeting actually reports my having said that.) I dare say that no more than a minute had elapsed, yet it felt like a lifetime. Finally, I unearthed from some remote part of my mind—from out of the "dim recesses of [my] ape-like consciousness," as Whitehead would say—one proposition, not exactly in the order I had intended, and began with that. I was compelled, as it were, to "muddy the waters," and soon I found myself back once again in my customary state. Obviously, it was not intended (by the powers that be?) that I should go farther in the Silence.

Again, I have been struck by some clear similarities to this experience in reading about the lives of Ramakrishna, Krishnamurti, and of course Meister Eckhart. Eckhart speaks of the absolute silence in the "inmost part" of the soul, which is "an impartible stillness, motionless in itself, and by this immobility all things are moved."[23]

What I experienced, therefore, appears to echo the quintessential and timeless (and I shall say it again) mystic experience: that an undeniably direct communication with "the Higher" is possible. As Eckhart puts it (somewhat heretically, for a Catholic), "Every kind of mediation is alien to God."[24]

It is not totally inappropriate, then, to cite Meister Eckhart once more, as he gives glimpses of the return to the Source, as if this were the real goal of life, the true aim of the Work, the purpose for which one is born. Of course, I do not claim to have anything but a partial grasp of his probable meaning: "When I was in the Principle and Ground of Godhead, no one asked me where I was going or what I was doing; there was no one to ask. On my return to the Principle and Ground of Godhead, where I am formless, my breaking through will be far nobler than my going forth; no one will ask me whence I came or whither I went, no one missed me. There, God-as-Other passes away."[25] One thinks here of the extraordinary correspondence in the experiences of people as disparate as Gurdjieff and, say, the physicist Erwin Schrodinger. On the one hand, there are Gurdjieff's own great insights in the Gobi, for example, and on the other there is Schrodinger's declaration in *What is Life?* (1943): "The mystics of many centuries, independently, yet in perfect harmony with each other (somewhat like the particles in an ideal gas) have described, each of them, the unique experience of his or her life in terms of what can be condensed in the phrase: *Deus factus sum* (I have become God.)"

Indeed, I have inferred yet another possible meaning to my own experience. In some ways, it seems, the taste of the annihilation of the egoism (of course, now reinstated once again in its full splendor, as this memoir illustrates) may be a fulfillment of Gurdjieff's promise to "destroy, mercilessly . . . in the mentation and feelings . . . the beliefs and views, by centuries rooted" in oneself. I think this is the "destruction" that some perceive to be his aim in writing *All and Everything*. My reading of this inner event is perhaps no more fanciful than other interpretations of Gurdjieff's ideas and teaching.

But I must not overreach. The point to this recitation of references is really, as Basarab Nicolescu writes in his study of Jacob Boehme's cosmology, that a man's life "comprises two births: biological birth and a self-birth or self-engendering. The new birth implies death to oneself, a singular, mysterious process which takes place in the secrecy of the interior life."[26] And the point that Madame de Salzmann labored to communicate to us uncomprehending souls was not that I, through my aspiration, can reach to "God," but, as Nicolescu asserts so convincingly, "This new birth is a birth from above."

I sense that I am treading some delicate ground, with the danger of mixing terminologies, misunderstanding different insights, confusing disparate experiences—and appearing to profess an understanding of the incomprehensible that is not my intention. But my reading in some of the classic traditionalist and perennialist literature—the documentation, as it were, by Plato, St. Augustine, Eckhart, and a host of other timeless sources of the Great Knowledge of which Gurdjieff speaks—would indicate that I am not necessarily a prospect for a straitjacket and heavy sedation. As their latter-day counterparts unabashedly aver, "Traditionalists recognize in mysticism and metaphysics the true center and depth of every religious tradition, the depth at which we can say that every religion, from its necessarily unique perspective, is talking about the same Divine Reality."[27]

Still, there was another extraordinary corroboration of this awakening to the real when I had two unexpected heart attacks in my late 60s. As I lay on the operating table in the emergency ward, and the cardiac team hovered over me to thin my blood and lower the heart rate—and remove the massive elephant that was standing on my chest—I experienced an extraordinary egolessness, a freedom from the customary sense of "I and mine," and an unaccustomed impartiality. I was able to be a silent witness to, and a participant in, the medical team's efforts to stabilize my condition.

For several weeks I could savor this lifting of the burden of the egoism. It soon crept back in as I "returned to normal" and gingerly ventured out "into the marketplace" once more. But with these experiences now indelibly part of me, I could understand Nietzsche's description of Zarathustra on his descent from the mountaintop: "There was no loathing about his mouth." Life, I realized more fully than ever before, was an extraordinary gift. Indeed, and this discovery came long after the event, I could see why Gurdjieff might conceivably have said, "Once being alive there is no choice, we must live forever."[28]

I realize that I may have belabored the point that objective inner events such as I have described are no figments of the imagination. I should not, then, go on with this recitation of the evidence of the miraculous. Enough to say that, many years later, I learned from Dr. de Salzmann that Gurdjieff actually had special exercises for nurturing this inner life. One of them was titled, "Food for the second body." It was no surprise to me.

NOTES

1. Shimon Malin, *Nature Loves to Hide*, p. 195. I take issue with J.G. Bennett, who dismissed "out-of-body" experiences as "superficial manifestations of the world of spirits." See *Deeper Man*, Bennett Books, Santa Fe, New Mexico, 1994, p. 175. Be that as it may, I experienced myself in a totally different realm, and the body had vanished.

2. Karlfried Graf Dürckheim, *The Call for the Master*, E.P. Dutton, New York, 1989, p. 75.

3. G.I. Gurdjieff, *All and Everything*, Viking Arkana, 1992, p. 41.

4. Michel de Salzmann, "Footnote to the Gurdjieff Literature," *Parabola*, 1980, p. 94.

5. J.G. Bennett, *Deeper Man*, Bennett Books, Sante Fe, New Mexico, 1994, p. 189.

6. J.G. and Elizabeth Bennett, *Idiots in Paris*, Coombe Springs Press, 1980, p. 50.

7. M. de Salzmann, op. cit., p. 92. It should be noted that the fallout from Bennett's inventiveness regarding the sources of Gurdjieff's teaching, for example, continues unabated. Even though James Moore and others have effectively demolished both Idries Shah's claim to be an authentic Sufi master as well as Bennett's case for the Naqshbandi Order of Sufism as a key source of Gurdjieff's ideas and practices, Anna T. Challenger's recent book, *Philosophy and Art in Gurdjieff's Beelzebub: A Modern Sufi Odyssey*, perpetuates these assertions. See L.P. Elwell-Sutton, "Sufism and Pseudo-Sufism," *Encounter*, Vol. 44, No. 5, pp. 9-17, and James Moore,

"Neo-Sufism: The Case of Idries Shah," *Religion Today*, Vol. 3, No. 3, pp. 4-8. For a more generous appraisal of Idries Shah and his influence, see Müge Galin, *Between East and West: Sufism in the Novels of Doris Lessing*, State University of New York Press, Albany, NY, 1997.

8. Bennett, *Idiots in Paris*, p. 27. There is an interesting echo of this understanding in an article titled "Neurons and Mind," by Wolfgang Smith, himself a mathematician, in *Sophia*, Vol. 10. No. 3 (winter, 2004), p. 29. He cites the experience of Roger Penrose, the Oxford mathematician, whose "inquiries have disproved the notion that we can somehow calculate our way to knowledge and understanding."

9. James Moore, *Gurdjieff: The Anatomy of a Myth*, Element, Rockport, Massachusetts, 1991, p. 294.

10. M. de Salzmann, op. cit., p. 95

11. Charles Upton, *The System of Antichrist: Truth & Falsehood in Postmodernism and the New Age*, Sophia Perennis, Ghent, NY, 2001, p.91.

12. Malin, op. cit., p. 158.

13. P.D. Ouspensky, *In Search of the Miraculous*, pp. 40-41.

14. Thomas Cleary, *The Secret of the Golden Flower*, HarperSanFrancisco, 1991, p. 84.

15. *Rig Veda*, X, 121.1 and 2, quoted by Ravi Ravindra, *Whispers from the Other Shore*, Quest Books, Wheaton, Illinois, 1984, p. 34.

16. I am indebted to Ravi Ravindra for this source.

17. David Appelbaum, Introduction to Reiner Schurmann, *Wandering Joy: Meister Eckhart's Mystical Philosophy*, Lindisfarne Books, Great Barrington, Mass., 2001, p. ix.

18. Meister Eckhart, *German Sermons and Treatises*, translated by M. Walshe. Quoted by Robert K.C. Forman, *Meister Eckhart, Mystic as Theologian*, Element Inc., Rockport, Maine, 1991, p. 176.

19. Pauline de Dampierre interview, "The Present Life," *Material for Thought*, vol. 12, 1990, Far West Publications, San Francisco, p. 49.

20. G.I. Gurdjieff, *Life is Real, Only Then, When "I Am,"* p. 173.

21. P.D. Ouspensky, *The Fourth Way*, p. 317.

22. Henri Tracol, "The Mystery of Rebirth," *Parabola* magazine, Vol. X, No. 3, 1985.

23. Meister Eckhart, *German Sermons and Treatises*, Vol. 2, p. 101, translated by M. Walshe, quoted by Robert K.C. Forman, op. cit., p. 172.

24. Eckhart, On the Noble Man, *Selected Writings*, Penguin Books, New York, 1994, p. 104.

25. Eckhart, quoted by Alvin Moore, Jr., "Nature, Man and God," *Sacred Web*, vol. 2, p. 51.

26. Basarab Nicolescu, *Science, Meaning and Evolution*, Parabola Books, New York, 1991, p. 88.

27. Charles Upton, op. cit., p. 61.

28. G.I. Gurdjieff, a talk ostensibly given in Essentuki, 1918. Found among Madame Olga de Hartmann's papers.

Madame Ouspensky's funeral, January 3, 1961: Wesley Addy, a film and television star, far left, and Alfred Etievant, far right, at the hilltop graveyard in Mendham.

Photo: Library archive, Gurdjieff Foundation, New York.

CHAPTER 6

"Every Nationality Has Something I Not Like"

The following recollections of Gurdjieff's last visit to New York in 1948 were written 52 years after by Beatrice Sinclair as the "first impressions of a young and naive novice."[1] They were originally written for inclusion in the New York Foundation's privately compiled History of the Work in New York. I include this further edited version because it conveys some of the extraordinary quality of, and the mystery surrounding, Gurdjieff's presence. While Beatrice was always proud of the fact that Gurdjieff had said to her, "I like your type," I must point out again that I myself never met Gurdjieff.

ALTHOUGH GURDJIEFF'S VISIT lasted only a few months, it seemed a lifetime, so great were the impressions of the time spent with Gurdjieff at the Wellington Hotel, New York City. We heard astounding insults, roars of laughter, and many stories poking fun at the peculiarities of the English, Scots, Irish, and so on. Some of these stories were captured on tape at those dinners, and one can still get some taste of the uproarious proceedings presided over by Gurdjieff. [2]

Beatrice Sinclair, at Mendham, about 1960.

Gurdjieff endlessly repeated his story about the cow returning to the barn whose door had been painted a new color during its absence in the field: "Cow look at barn door, used to be green." It stood there puzzled; it recognized its old quarters, but then again it could not be sure.

There were, of course, also very serious hours. The manuscript of Gurdjieff"s master work, *All and Everything: Beelzebub's Tales to his Grandson*, was being prepared for publication. He was delighted. "Take out into the street and give to the people," he said. But we who were in the Work, on the other hand, were asked to pay a hundred dollars for an autographed copy. [3]

Gurdjieff showed us large, glossy photos of a chateau that, he said, he wished to purchase in France. Thus he was engaged in his famous practice of "shearing sheep" and asking for checks with many zeroes. Dorothy Wolfe took me up to Gurdjieff, who was sitting on his couch, one leg tucked under him. No, he said, he would not accept my one hundred dollars. He said to Dorothy, "She very naive about money."

Gurdjieff had by now stopped teaching the way he did during the period recorded by Ouspensky. Instead, he met with people individually or taught through his famous lunches and dinners. Because I had a job teaching in Riverdale, I could only attend the evening gatherings. This began with movements in the late afternoon at Carnegie Hall. The dust rose from the floor with all those rhythms and many rows of people. Gurdjieff had two assistants: Alfred Etievant[4] and Aubrey Wolton. Once while we were working on movements that Gurdjieff had begun, a sudden sense of quiet attentiveness spread throughout the class. Gurdjieff had entered through a side door. We could not see him, but we felt his presence.

With many "alley-oops," Gurdjieff had this class of very many rows go down, head on the floor, and with many "alley-oops" we came up in stages.

He started "American Number 7" with us, which we did night after night. He instructed us to feel our right side as we lifted our right arm, and then sense the left side. And as we did the rhythm, with the head turned, one had a strong sense of presence. Of course, it was all derived from him, or imparted by him.

For the movement "American Number 10," Gurdjieff balanced one arm on a chair and then lifted his leg, bent at the knee, sideways. It was an event never to be forgotten. Having seen how Gurdjieff made this movement, there can be little wonder that I still say, "We never truly sense ourselves."

The multiplication "American Number 11" seemed a special, interesting movement for Gurdjieff. At one point, he asked us to sit in front while two rows multiplied. Madame de Salzmann played the piano. Gurdjieff loudly tapped out the rhythm on the piano. Many times, Gurdjieff seemed to be creating a movement as we went along.

I had been introduced to movements by Mrs. Jessmin Howarth only a week before Gurdjieff's classes. So it was all new to me. One evening, as I struggled to keep up in the rear, I was shocked to hear him call out my childhood name: "Ah, pequina. No imitate."

I had no preconceptions about the movements; there was not yet any literature on the subject. And apart from *All and Everything* there was nothing on the teaching itself. During the "American Number 11," with all its criss-crossing files, it suddenly became an astounding movement of such great force, of such magnitude, and at such a great speed, that I knew I did not count in it at all. It is said that the movements have a message, but never have I experienced the like of that moment again. For years I kept quiet about it all. Then one day I spoke of it to an older person. Those forces, she said, were "absolutely ruthless."

One evening at the end of movements, Gurdjieff pulled out a large handful of lichee nuts. Throwing them in the air toward the class, he said, "Here—catch!" There was a great rush of all the people in the class. "STOP!" he called. I can still feel myself in a half-turned posture and my somewhat stupefied astonishment. This impression of myself remains vivid to this day. An older person said he felt himself as an animal.

At another time, at the end of movements, Gurdjieff said to the class, "At this time [around Christmas], many people pray. Their prayers go only so far up in the atmosphere. You can suck these into yourself; this force."[5]

At the Wellington

Once as we walked from the movements hall to the hotel, someone asked, "What do we do with all this energy we have collected in movements?"

As we entered Gurdjieff's apartment at the hotel, some people sat on the most comfortable easy chairs. Gurdjieff admonished them: "You not see older person there? No seat!" We all felt the lack of outer considering towards Gurdjieff. Someone plunked herself down cross-legged on the floor, and he called her a camel. To another woman, he said, "Your hair like shit." He referred to one or another of us, "She young, she old," regardless of chronological age. He had an acute perception of every person.

It was here that Crocodile (Kathryn Hulme) told her famous story and shed many tears as she told of Sissy, "this little girl, so brave," whom she pitied for having had to travel all alone across the Atlantic. Gurdjieff asked Hulme, "Your name is crocodile?" And amidst great hilarity he told the children, "Now children, what she told, never take extérieurement such." But for their inner worlds, they should ask their mother, father, "somebody you know, serious person only, what means 'tear of crocodile?'" Gurdjieff had also just given the children presents, asking them, equally famously, if they would have paper money or coins.

We then entered the larger room where Gurdjieff sat on his couch. A younger person entered and said, "Good evening, Mr. Gurdjieff." He mimicked her in an exaggerated, very amusing way. I will never forget this impression of Gurdjieff's wit.

The most amazing thing about Gurdjieff was that at one moment he was most amusing, but then, as you looked again, he appeared to be in touch with something greater—God?—and with apparently no obvious transition from his role playing. You saw all this in his eyes, turned slightly upward. Everyone felt this other level—of love, divine love. Perhaps this is why we were able to take so many of his shocks and insults. (Later, so many group leaders tried giving similar shocks, but people reacted. That great sense of love that you experienced in Gurdjieff was not there.)

As we became seated for the reading, Gurdjieff turned to Frank Lloyd Wright, who had just opened the window a bit. Gurdjieff said, "Close, so vibrations stay in." He turned toward a woman and gave her a verbal thrashing for the horrid manifestation of her ethnicity. Gurdjieff saw my distress. "Not to worry," he said. "She like duck; shed water from feathers." Later Gurdjieff, who found out everyone's nationality, explained to me, "Every nationality has dirty side I not like."

The Chapter on America, Again?

Mrs. Rita Benson, a well-known Broadway actress, enunciated every word most articulately as she read the chapter on America. Gurdjieff watched us all to see our reactions. One young man laughed at the description of Professor Kishmenhof's chicken darting through the kitchen "at full speed." Mr. Gurdjieff said, "Good, eh?"

Next, it was into the dining room. The chain of loaded serving dishes came from the bathroom (which served as the kitchen, with the cooking done over the bathtub). Tonight—the delicious, and frightening, sheep's head. "Eyes most good," he said with delight.

One evening, at the beginning of dinner, Gurdjieff asked to have me sit by him. I had been standing in the large doorway, being most critical of his stories. I said to myself, "To think I have come here to learn something important!" A stool was placed in between the crowded chairs by his side. "Drink up!" he said to everyone at the table. "Drink up!" There is no question in my mind that Gurdjieff had special powers. He was able to enter the body of someone and communicate that way. For instance, sitting close to him, he first touched the cord (the jugular vein) at the left side of my neck—perhaps to see if I was relaxed. And indeed I did feel him as "my dear grandfather," although I had not yet read *Beelzebub*. At least I had the presence of mind to be very attentive to Gurdjieff and not wander off into my own inner talking. Unbelievably, he was able to have a long, continuous conversation with me while still engaged in conversation with the older people sitting at the table.

The most important time at dinner was devoted to the "toast to the idiots." We tried to decide what they might mean and which idiot we would choose. Sometimes Gurdjieff decided someone was a certain type of idiot and said, "Used to be [such and such] idiot and is now advanced to [such and such] idiot."

During dinner there were more shocks. The older people seemed ready to withstand their reactions or not react at all. One woman showed no emotion when Gurdjieff maligned her daughter. Once, a priest, not in the Work, was asked to dinner. Gurdjieff cut him down to nothing. It went on a long time. We never saw the priest again.

But Gurdjieff was also capable of great kindness. One night, I sat at a small table by Gurdjieff's side. He spoke to the "important" older people about my "heredity," and went on at great length about my possibilities. He said he liked my type; I was like his childhood friend. I was amazed that they— so advanced—should be obliged to listen to this. But how well these people treated me later.

Gurdjieff's Music

Gurdjieff sat down close to us with his harmonium. With no real knowledge of the Work, I simply gave myself up to these divine feelings. At one time, I felt I had actually left the planet. Another evening, I found myself crying on the way home in the subway—not in sorrow, but more with joy. The crust of myself seemed to have melted away.

Gurdjieff had asked that I make an appointment through Madame de Salzmann to see him. I had not been able to arrange this, and he must have sensed my distress, because he "visited" me in the night while I was sound asleep and asked me many questions.

Gurdjieff's Departure

After Gurdjieff's name day, on which we had a great celebration, Gurdjieff had to leave us to return to Paris. We stood in line and he kissed us, each and every one, on both cheeks. We thought we would surely see him in a few months.

After Gurdjieff's death, Madame de Salzmann and her entourage came to Mendham. Madame de Salzmann, sitting at the huge oval dining-room table, said to Madame de Hartmann, "Life will never be the same." In spite of Gurdjieff's passing, we all felt we had been left with tremendous energy; anything in this life seemed possible.

NOTES

1. Originally written in or about October 2000.
2. Gert-Jan Blom: *Gurdjieff: Harmonic Development: The Complete Harmonium Recordings, 1948-49*, Basta Music, 2005.
3. Both Martin Benson and Beatrice Sinclair spoke of Gurdjieff's having said that *All and Everything* should be taken and handed out to people on the street. According to the editors at the Traditional Studies Press, in Toronto, "galley proofs were shown to Gurdjieff on his deathbed in 1949," so what people saw on Gurdjieff's last visit were probably bound copies of the typescript, which had been read to his pupils through the 1940s. The actual book was only published in 1950. Beatrice's own first edition copy (number 69) carries Gurdjieff's (evidently) printed signature.

4. According to the unpublished history, *The Gurdjieff Work in North America: The First 75 Years*, assembled by Group Two, Alfred Etievan added a final "t" to his surname when he applied for United States citizenship. His widow, Lise Etievant, reverted to the original spelling when she returned to France.

5. See chapter 12 for more on the centrality of the work to "suck" in the energies of common prayers. Here this work was communicated quite openly to an audience of both new and older people.

Martin Benson on his 60th birthday,
Franklin Farms, 1959.

CHAPTER 7

Martin W. Benson:
A Guardian at the Gate

T O THE WORLD "out there," the Gurdjieff teaching has a certain taint of intellectualism, of being "biased towards the head." I suppose that Ouspensky, a brilliant mind and a mathematician to boot, unwittingly helped to give it that bias. Then there were all the other gifted early adherents, like Dr. Kenneth Walker, a Harley Street physician; Dr. Maurice Nicoll; A.R. Orage, and later Lord Pentland and Dr. William J. Welch—to name only some of the English-speaking intellectuals who were drawn to the Work. There were also many "lesser" lights in the "mainstream" of the Work who, perhaps unconsciously, conveyed this bias.

I had this same initial misunderstanding. Having majored in philosophy during my undergraduate years, mainly to try to find if any other members of the human race had had the same burning questions that I had, I thought to pursue this lofty calling until the pressing necessity of earning a living— reinforced down the years by the realization that my mind was like soft cheese, and moreover, with holes in it—brought me down to earth. So it was quite a shock to be thrown in with Martin Benson when I got to Mendham.

Groves of Academe: Martin Benson, right, expounds on some essential facts of life to Jack Moscrop, center, while Tom Forman, left, takes the lie of the land. Photographed in the kitchen garden, Franklin Farms, 1959.

Now a word from our sponsor: Martin Benson with his favorite Schmidt's of Philadelphia beer. Thomas Forman approaches at right rear. Franklin Farms, 1959.

Now, after almost five decades of being "in the Work" and trying to fathom the truth of what my life is about, I can declare with uncompromising certainty that the Work is not the exclusive preserve of intellectuals; it is also equally there for those who have no conception of (say) the square of the hypotenuse—or of astrological correspondences, for that matter. In fact, as Ravi Ravindra, an academician of note, points out, hardly any of the great spiritual teachers have been scholars or learned men. [1] Madame de Salzmann herself expressed her understanding of the role of the (ordinary) mind very directly in a sitting in New York: "The mind must admit it does not know."[2] It is clear now that the prerequisite for the appearance in one of a "higher energy" is a new balance, a new alignment between the basic intelligences of the human "structure"—the "mind" of the body, the "mind" of the feelings, and the "mind" of the mind. Without that support, these higher energies are denied us, however much one may pretend, or wish, or hope, or attempt to command that they appear.

I am not, however, about to argue that Martin Benson was even remotely a "spiritual teacher." He was by any measure a "simple country boy" with, of course, a distinct difference: he had a passionate and serious wish to understand the meaning of life. Despite his patent limitations and weaknesses, he played a large part in my life and the lives of some others around the Work.

He probably had not made it past the sixth grade in school. His obituary in *The New York Times* called him an agriculturist. I dare say that a few strings were pulled to get those few lines in the *Times*, because, apart from being the husband of one of George M. Cohan's leading ladies on Broadway, he had absolutely no position of note in "ordinary" life.

The word around Franklin Farms was that Gurdjieff had said of Benson that he was "more in essence than in personality." I learned this after only a week or two at the estate when I told Miss Darlington, Madame Ouspensky's dutiful aide, that I couldn't make head or tail of what Benson said. At times he could not articulate more than a sentence or two about his understanding of the Work without spluttering and waving his arms. "You've got to smash your way into the fourth dimension," was a typical Bensonian declaration as he punched a hole in an invisible wall in front of him.

Having started my "apprenticeship" under Fairfax Hall, who was as careful, formal, and precise as any true-blue British follower of Ouspensky might be, Benson's strange ramblings were decidedly disconcerting to a greenhorn like me. Miss Darlington's quiet assurances put me at ease, and I set myself to listen and to forbear. Benson himself professed that he had been sent to Franklin Farms by Madame de Salzmann "to bring some life to the place." By the time I arrived on the scene, all the great names had gone—Ouspensky himself, Thomas de Hartmann, and assorted members of the British gentry whose names and reputations were merely a blur to me. Benson was the only one among the residents there who had not known the Ouspenskys. Another less flattering reason for his being there may have been that his own farming ventures had failed and his marriage was said to be on the rocks. He and his wife, the former Rita Romilly, were so diametrically opposite in their characters—she the Broadway prima donna, he the "agriculturist"—it was hard to imagine a more incongruous couple. She it was who had warned at least one young man, "Mr. So-and-so, I have a volatile nature. I have had to live with it, and so will you." Benson made a serious, and I would say a conscious, effort to show a "united front." It was often an effort of Socratic scope.

It was only over time that I began to piece these puzzling impressions together. When I first arrived, it was like coming home: the people at Franklin Farms were "my kin." They took me in. I was not used to the consideration and the basic kindness that these strangers showed towards me. And I soon had the run of the place, but always under the tutelage and general supervision of Benson. Where he went, I went. From the crack of dawn until late at night. For almost 18 months, I spent most of my day in his company. We ate together, worked together, drank together.

Mendham (or more properly, Franklin Farms) was a world apart. The main house itself was the domain of the women, with Madame Ouspensky's grandson, Lonya Savitsky, under their protective custody. I doubt that Savitsky could have earned much of a living out in the world. He was probably about 47 years old when I arrived. He would stay in his room on the second floor (the red corridor) watching television for most of his day, showing up only for lunch and dinner. When he did venture out, it was to drive off in his Chevrolet convertible and play tennis somewhere. Or he would practice his golf shots, driving the balls into and over the woods while those of us working in the so-called kitchen gardens ducked instinctively when we heard them ricocheting towards us through the trees. A few of the young men who came there on weekends felt he was callous and uncomprehending in his total disregard for the harm he might cause.

Savitsky was unsparing in his often penetrating judgments of, and comments, on others. But this was, I learned only much later, all too familiar to the faithful at Mendham. James Webb, writing in *The Harmonious Circle* (1980), noted that Savitsky had been the cause of "some internal dissension and faction fighting" dating back 20 years to the days at Lyne, the Ouspenskys' workplace in England. Savitsky, he wrote, "made incessant demands on the patience of the Ouspenskys' pupils, and many thought Mme. Ouspensky blind to his faults. However, to some of 'Madam's people,' [Savitsky's] behavior seemed to be yet another deliberate provocation in the sense of the Work. Ouspensky himself admitted that his step-grandchild was a thorough nuisance, but in this—as in other matters—allowed himself to be swayed by his wife."

More or less "in charge" of this strange ark-like enclave was Dorothy Darlington, a small Australian who had been

Ouspensky's secretary and now devoted herself to caring for Madame Ouspensky, bedridden with Parkinson's disease. I myself never saw Madame Ouspensky alive. For about a year or more, I was responsible for bringing firewood to the box outside her door on the second floor, but I never ventured farther, nor would I have been invited to do so. Only at her death did my wife lead me into Madame's room to spend a few minutes by her body as she lay where she must have lain for several years until then. Even then, one of the older women indicated by her uneasiness that I did not really have the right to be in the room. To her, I was just a presumptuous interloper, as well I must have been.

At the risk of being considered a total ingrate, I must admit to having many mixed feelings about Madame Ouspensky as a model of the Gurdjieffian way. I have never felt at ease about all the stories of her dictatorial manner. I have felt that kind of behavior might be appropriate in dealing with feudal serfs, or all those indigent relatives to be found on the old Russian estates, or (and here I betray the basic anti-colonialism of my time) the British gentry, who clearly needed to be prodded and shocked out of their condescending superiority and overweening sense of caste. In any event, the notorious "enameled self-assurance" and "air of ineffable superiority" so supremely displayed by people like Lord Curzon, Her Majesty's Viceroy of India, and others of that ilk are things now long past.

James Webb, for example, writing well after the events he described, put it very bluntly: "Sophia Grigorievna Ouspensky was to all outward appearances a termagant." A termagant, to the uninitiated, is an overbearing shrew. Some of the tender psyches so abundant around the Work today might not have the stomach for close encounters with her kind. Be that as it may, I have never been able to square Madame Ouspensky's well-documented authoritarianism with the search for truth. But tell that to a Zen master.

Of course, Madame de Salzmann could not have been

more explicit about her own high regard for Madame
Ouspensky when she wrote her famous letter to the residents
at Mendham and the older ones in New York at the time of
Madame Ouspensky's death. "We have lost our dearest one
in the Work," she wrote. I have no right to repeat the full
contents of that extraordinary letter, although I have no doubt
it must have found its way onto the Internet by now. Yet I
can't forget the impact it made on me and perhaps a dozen
others when we heard it read in the dining room at Mendham
a day or two after Madame Ouspensky died.

"In the name of my relation to Madame Ouspensky who
was the nearest soul in my work, I wish to tell you this," she
wrote. "Once more I recognize the truth I experienced in front
of Mr. Gurdjieff's body, and which has become a certitude:
There is no death. Life cannot die." She added a few more
sparse lines that went to the core of Gurdjieff's teaching, could
we indeed understand their significance: "If we wish to know
life, we need to die, to die to the known and enter the
unknown."

It must have been a life of great privation—indeed, of quiet
desperation—for those devoted women. Lacking funds for any
but the most basic necessities, they lived a kind of hand-to-
mouth existence. All, of course, except Savitsky. While the
rest of the household picked at their leftovers, he would dig
into a steak—and if he was not satisfied with the way it had
been broiled, he simply tossed it to his dog Tsung, while many
lustful eyes followed its trajectory. After a few weeks, I
realized how unappetizing the food was, and how skimpy.
And there they were, living frugal, Spartan, and rather joyless
lives in a former state governor's mansion set on 300 beautiful
acres of farmland and woods. Some said the estate had also
been the property of George Washington Hill, inventor of the
instant-coffee process, and must have known more sumptuous
times.

From what I could make out, Benson certainly helped to
bring a little joy. I think he was only reluctantly accepted by

some of the old Ouspenskians. He must have been a somewhat rude intruder where once Ouspensky himself and others of the old intelligentsia had held sway. He told the same simple stories over and over again at lunch and dinner—stories about the humdrum events on the estate, stories about his youth, recollections of his time with Gurdjieff. We would all listen attentively to his brazenly ethnic story about the Russian intellectual reduced to being a sightseeing guide on a Moscow tour bus after the revolution, or the story of the two French-Canadian lumberjacks manipulating a log flow down a raging river. The lumberjack story, being more politically correct, can be repeated. The lumberjacks battled with their logs from early in the morning until late in the afternoon, until one of them suddenly looked around and called out, "Jacques! Jacques!" "What is it?" his companion asked. "Jacques! Jacques!" he said, "We are not here—we are 20 miles from here!" To Benson, that story was all about our work for Presence.

I think he felt he had lived before as a combatant in the American Civil War. He loved the war songs from that time, and he would listen to them in the evenings. (Those were the days of record turntables. I think hi-fi and 33 1/3 rpm records had just taken hold.) From little scraps of information I gleaned over the years, I gathered that he was the son of a sea captain who owned three vessels. He was gassed during World War I, and evidently spent some time after the war in the Ramapo hills in New York State, where the mountain air helped to clear his lungs. He told of some adventures in looking for stolen railroad property in what were then somewhat untamed surroundings. He recalled that many Hessian soldiers had either deserted there during, or settled there after, the War of Independence, and he seemed to suggest that some of the folks he had met there were just a little on the far side of normal. In any event, he had a sister who lived on Staten Island, which helped explain his acquaintance with a group of Sicilian immigrants who had adopted a curious ritual out there. As Benson told it, they found being cooped up in Manhattan so alien to their way of life that they would take the ferry to Staten Island on weekends, where they would squat together in the woods and take "a communal crap." That was vintage Benson, and these stories made him fun to be around. We were quite happy that the women were out of the way, occupied with their own activities in the main house.

He was a good if somewhat crude craftsman. I called his specialty "elemental engineering." He would fret for a week over the building of a simple wooden ladder down into the pig pen. My job was to stand by him as he worked, handing him the hammer or the saw as needed. A grim discipline for me, as I tried to keep my attention from wandering, or to not go to sleep just standing there. Tools and equipment were always in short supply. But like a true outdoorsman, keenly aware of his surroundings, he would tell me (say) to go down to the barnyard and look behind a certain pillar in the tractor shed, where I would find a big bent nail, which we would duly straighten and use. We also did some general plumbing repairs around the property, and he liked to point out that plumbing terminology, with its nipples and male and female connections, was replete with references to sex. Once, with a young visitor from the far north of Canada, we spent a whole week in the basement of the main house carefully dismantling and repairing a big rusty storage tank, which we dared not damage any further, else there would have been no hot water. Benson, the visitor, and I went down to work on the boiler after breakfast all week and only came out around 5 p.m. to feed the animals. For a year or two afterwards Benson and I received regular letters from this young man recalling what an unforgettable time he had had.

Benson had a wonderful rapport with animals. One of his favorites was a lame white hen whose legs had been damaged by some wild animal. He would greet her warmly each morning and talk to her like a friend, and she would crawl awkwardly towards him with evident joy at seeing him. There was also a large white sow, which he treated with great respect and friendliness. Then one fine day it was decided she had to be slaughtered, and it fell to him to do the deed. It was a difficult thing for him to have to do. He spoke with feeling about having to put his emotions aside.

One evening I told him I could not understand the Law of Three. With scarcely any hesitation, he told me to get into his car and we drove to a field of crab apples. He pointed to the stumps, to which he had grafted stock for edible apples. To him this represented the way in which the life force could be tapped into and redirected by our intervention. To this day I am not sure of the exact relevance or the connection, but it made me think.

We would spend the whole day together, working around the estate. Then, after I had washed the supper dishes, he expected me to go down to his cottage at the main entrance. There I would sit upright on the couch while he sat opposite, and he would ramble on about the Work, often until past two in the morning. This was some of the greatest physical discomfort I have known. If I nodded off, as I would after a hard day's work, he would poke me in the chest and say, "You don't do that." I learned to ask him the appropriate questions. But I never dared to point out the contradictions, of which there were many, or say, "But yesterday you said such and such." Only later did I understand that he was, as it were, trying to formulate ideas, that he was actually learning to express his thoughts. As Roger Lipsey so eloquently put it:

> He spoke in waves—
> You couldn't parse his sentences
> Any more than you can parse waves[.]

Then one day, while I was raking some leaves near his cottage, perhaps a year or two after I had arrived, he said to me, out of the blue, "Sinclair, I don't know why you came, but I'm glad you came." That was the only acknowledgement of the sort that I can remember. Indeed, it was rare for him to even call us by our given names: usually it was simply, "Hey, Oscar." And we felt we were part of a privileged set. (Years later, I thought to address the young son of a woman in my group as Oscar, and she roundly dressed me down.)

But it wasn't at all easy, when one considered that Rita Benson was inseparably part of his world—she was testy, unpredictable, and, it seemed (although one could never be sure), often near-hysterical. I soon made it clear that I wasn't to be bullied: indeed, she retreated tearfully from the first of our many confrontations, and I thought that that had soured my relations with Benson, but he didn't utter a word of reproach. As I would later say of John Pentland, Benson only gave me his work. (Rita Benson it was who declared to all within earshot one midnight in the Foundation when we were preparing for the January 13 celebration that I was a black sheep, not worthy of her trust, not fit to be among her dutiful aides, and many more choice sentiments to that effect. I had merely stated the obvious: while she could rise at noon, I could not stay up so late, travel a long distance to my home out of town, then return to the city in the morning and continue to hold down my job. But there were those among her people who actually envied me my escape.)

Martin and Rita Benson were total opposites. In my estimation, she was always "on stage." Everything seemed to be an act: her enthusiasms, her rages, her professions of sincerity. One never knew what to believe. I suppose that like the intense actress she was, she must have fed off the extraordinary example of Gurdjieff—the most consummate actor of all—to the point where it was hardly possible for the casual observer to distinguish in her the player from the role.

She must have spent an intense and enviable apprenticeship under Gurdjieff, having hovered in his orbit for many years. Decades after her death, I learned that on Gurdjieff's visit to New York in 1929, "Rita Romilly circulated the story that Gurdjieff had asked her to marry him."[3] She had also been charged with some of the hectic fund raising that Gurdjieff demanded in the closing days of the Prieure. And she could indeed be quite brazen. Finding a few bundles of old newspapers in Benson's garage at Mendham one day, I saw headline after headline along the lines of, "Rita Romilly Rages Her Way to Stage Success." It explained everything. But Benson showed tremendous forbearance and extraordinary patience and tolerance. It was a teaching in itself. (So it was a huge surprise when he confided to me one day, "I am so hasty." One might not have known.) And heaven knows, Rita Benson carried on in ways that would have embarrassed the great Beelzebub himself.[4]

Still, we enjoyed the endless retelling of the story Benson told of their wedding in New York in May 1934, during one of Gurdjieff's visits. When Gurdjieff arrived at the church, an usher asked him, "Are you with the bride or with the groom?" Gurdjieff put the usher to rout by responding, "I am father of them both." And even though Rita Benson and I barely exchanged a word for years, she called on me to be the lead pallbearer at his funeral service. He had always said that he wished to be carried into the church (head first) and carried out (feet first) by his friends. It was a prospect that really caught his fancy. The official pallbearers from the funeral home were clearly unhappy at having us amateurs perform this task, but we were being true to his spirit.

What was most striking to me and almost foreign to my own experience in those early years was the genuineness of his feeling. He was not your touchy-feely type. Nothing so cheap or sentimental. He was proud of having had Gurdjieff declare him to be a "compassionate idiot." And he clearly was someone who had suffered. As Roger Lipsey pointed out,

> He was vulnerable, and you could sense that.
> He wasn't cased in anger
> And of course no one touched him:
> Such vulnerability is great power.

Indeed, it was experiences in World War I that had led him to Gurdjieff. Looking at some notes that I had made in my very first weeks at Franklin Farms, I see that he told me of an experience in the trenches in World War I that left its scars. During one battle, he had rescued a wounded comrade, slung him over his shoulder and carried him from the front. They came under attack, and his friend was killed by machine-gun fire. "The court-marshal proved to me that I had killed him," Benson told me. In the moments of my own greatest suffering and remorse at what had happened between Madame Ouspensky's grandson and me—described elsewhere in these pages—he told me, "You are one of my people." He understood my suffering. But we never, ever— and I repeat: *never*—spoke about it afterwards. It was something never to be cheapened in that way.

One fine day, it turned out that Madame de Salzmann had asked him to respond to questions at the Sunday-afternoon meeting at Mendham. When we had all sat down, she looked to her right and to her left, and asked, "Where is Martin?" Benson was nowhere to be found. Later we learned that he had fabricated an "emergency" on the property that required his attention. The following week, he again failed to show at question time. This time, he just stayed away and drank. On the third Sunday, Benson dutifully showed up at the appointed time and in evident anguish made his first halting public response to a questioner. Soon after, Benson himself told some of us that Madame de Salzmann had said to him after his first two failures to show, "Do I have to accept you this way?" And that shamed him into meeting her demand.

Of course, once Benson got the taste of talking on these public occasions, he could scarcely be stopped! Those of us who had lived with him and listened to him and shared adventures with him understood what he was driving at in his awkward expositions. Others, including one prominent member of the medical community in particular, openly scoffed at him. Yet Cynthia Pearce, who herself appeared to have no mean intellect, said that Benson was one of the few people who actually could think. One always had the impression that he thought for himself. Among statements of his that I found in my old notebooks:

> "Civilizations have committed suicide many times."
> "People who 'know' are defeated because they think they are leaving something behind."
> "You can live in contradiction only for so long."
> "No one knows."

I can't remember the context of these thoughts. But one thought that slowly took on a special relevance was, "First you have to be a good animal." In fact, he showed me the transcript of a talk given by Gurdjieff to some young men at the Prieuré, in which he said he would give them money to go to Paris and satisfy their sexual needs. They could then come back and work undistracted. Decades later, when speaking to a group of men, Dr. de Salzmann confirmed that this was indeed Gurdjieff's sane approach to the question of sex.

Benson was indeed a son of the soil, with a special sensitivity towards nature, plants, animals, the weather. Many a night at Franklin Farms when the rains came down and it thundered and the lightning flashed and the winds blew mightily, Benson would roam the grounds, singing some kind of wordless paean to the heavens. He was an elemental man. I would find him in his cottage of an evening listening to Gregorian chants and mouthing shapeless words. "I have to listen to this music to get some of the vibrations of life's force," he said. And pointing towards the source of the music on the turntable, "That is life's force, Christ!"

Benson told a number of stories about being the gatekeeper at the Prieuré at the time of a serious automobile accident involving Gurdjieff. This almost certainly was not the mysterious accident of 1924, when Gurdjieff was the sole occupant of the car. Some questions were raised about the date, which Benson evidently did not indicate, when a private transcript was read in New York at the January 13, 2001, celebration of Gurdjieff's birth. This transcript was based on tape recordings made by one of his young friends[5] in 1969, some 40-odd years after the actual events. In this transcript, Benson told of injuries received by Dr. Stjernval and other passengers. The classic and generally accepted accounts of the 1924 accident, such as those of Madame de Hartmann, have it that Gurdjieff had been alone, so this event was clearly not the 1924 accident. What's more, Benson attributed "his" accident to Gurdjieff's having tried to dodge a chicken that ran out on the road.

The accident to which Benson refers must therefore have been around 1933, by which time Gurdjieff had scaled down activities at the Prieuré, was devoting his time to writing *Beelzebub*, and there were many fewer people living on the estate. In any event, Benson told me a number of times of watching Gurdjieff, recuperating after the accident, lying semiconscious, and "feeding off the efforts of the people working in the garden." There is now some healthy scepticism about the authenticity of Gurdjieff's earlier accident in 1924 and the nature of Gurdjieff's injuries, but if they were contrived, then Gurdjieff must have been a consummate and extraordinary actor. But there was evidently no question that, in the accident to which Benson refers, Gurdjieff and his passengers suffered many injuries. Benson told me, too, of Gurdjieff's going to cafés frequented by prostitutes to "feed" off their vibrations. Gurdjieff advised him, "Go to church, Benson, and *steal*. Their prayers will not reach God. Steal them."[6]

Benson's transcript repeats the graphic stories he told us at Mendham about using a screwdriver and a pair of pliers to remove a slew of metal clips with which Gurdjieff's injuries had been "plugged up." Then, in the early morning, having slept for little more than an hour after performing this "operation," Benson heard a noise at the main gate. Going out, he saw Gurdjieff hobbling along on a crutch, about to leave the property. When Benson asked him where he was headed, he said he was going to Paris to work on *Beelzebub*.

He told Benson, "Nothing will stop me, not even death." Benson asked him to wait so that he could dress and accompany him. This story, which he repeated often, differed in one key detail from that tape-recorded version that he made later. In the transcripts of the tape, Benson reports that Gurdjieff said, "Not even *this*" would stop him, but in his conversations at Mendham Benson repeatedly stated that Gurdjieff had said "not even *death*" would stop him.

While Gurdjieff was recuperating, Benson told me, he called people together and asked them what they thought he should do now. Everyone made some suggestion: that he should retire, take his ease, go on vacation, and so on. Benson, however, said that he could not advise Gurdjieff. Gurdjieff listened to them all, and then he said the "sonofabitch bastard" Benson was the only one to make any sense. (I think "sonofabitch" was Benson's loose but perfectly apt translation of the Russian *svolitch*.)

He told, too, of the extraordinary challenges that Gurdjieff presented. One day Gurdjieff asked him to cash a check for $8,000 in American money. (I heard Benson say $8,000, but the editors of the transcript say it was $7,800.) It was a Saturday, and all the banks were closed. Gurdjieff insisted that Benson go out and cash it. Benson was put "on the spot" (another of his favorite expressions). Gurdjieff would brook no excuses. Not knowing what to do, Benson wandered forlornly through Fontainebleau village. After a while, he chanced upon a man working in his garden. He told him his problem. He turned out to be the local bank manager, who obligingly opened the bank and cashed the check.

Benson was acknowledged to have been one of the last three American residents at the Prieuré, and he told us many a story of one—"my friend [Caesar] Zwaska"—who was evidently as wild as Benson himself must have been. They reportedly moved out in the winter of 1933-34.

Meeting up with a man like Benson was the last thing I had expected when I came to Franklin Farms. There I was, a would-be intellectual, teamed up with a man of little formal schooling and no sophistication to speak of. But being with him opened up a whole new world for me. In reading over my notes from that first month at the farm, I discovered that Pentland had presciently said to me that Benson "might be your chief hope." With his essential compassion and earthiness, Benson helped heal some deep psychic wounds, and through him I came to the basic sanity and rationality that had eluded me in all the years until then. But he never allowed me to indulge some pleasant dream about my "growth" or "development." Once, when I remarked with some surprise that the ladies of the house appeared to consider me a rather good man, he almost spat at me as if I ought already to have known: "You are neither good nor bad. You are nothing. You are shit."

Never an idler, and like an old-time peasant and man of the soil, he was quite contemptuous of Madame Ouspensky's grandson. Their exchanges at the table were always testy. Benson mocked him privately with references to the "sly old bastard"—a favorite Bensonian epithet—who, he alleged, was Savitsky's father.

Benson's unabashed loyalty to Gurdjieff burst fully to the fore when we learned one day that John Bennett would be visiting Franklin Farms with the Indonesian mystic Pak Subuh in tow. The scuttlebutt—and this was all new to me, a mere newcomer, a real green and callow youth—was that Bennett had fallen from grace with Ouspensky over the alleged theft of material from his as-yet-unpublished *In Search of the Miraculous*, but Madame Ouspensky kept the lines to Bennett open. This time—it must have been some time in late 1959 or early 1960—Bennett was bringing Subuh to see if he could help with Madame's condition.

Benson pointedly stayed away when we all came to lunch. "He is the enemy," he muttered to me. Furthermore, Benson said, "He wants everything to happen in his own lifetime." This was evidently a reference, as I later learned, to Bennett's periodic "discovery" of yet another "successor" to Gurdjieff. Not to speak of a number of other actions relating to Gurdjieff's family and the forced publication of the Third Series, which did not exactly help the cause.

There were perhaps no more than a dozen of us at the lunch table that day. I had actually changed my shirt for the occasion, and found myself sitting directly opposite Subuh. Bennett made a big show of translating questions for Subuh and then translating Subuh's responses. But as I sat watching this display, I had the dawning realization there was something familiar about Subuh's features. Subuh was from Indonesia, which had long been a Dutch colony, and of course in the colonial days of the Dutch in South Africa they had brought over many East Indians as slaves, the beginnings of the Cape Malay community. He looked like one of my own countrymen. Overcoming my reserve, I ventured to ask Subuh in Afrikaans whether he understood Dutch. Subuh beamed as if I had thrown him a lifebelt. He began speaking in Dutch, which I barely understood, and I countered in Afrikaans. After a few minutes, I noticed that Bennett was becoming increasingly agitated: he had lost control of his prized exhibit. So I stopped speaking and ceded Bennett his place at the helm.

A great deal of scandal and perhaps misinformation has sprung up around Subuh. I suppose much of this was deserved. To me, however, he seemed a quiet, contained man. But one thing that Subuh said that day has stuck with me all these years. When asked if there were one piece of advice that he might impart, he said, "Look at everything as if for the very first time."

Evidently, Subuh was unable to do anything to alleviate Madame Ouspensky's condition. The visit was supposedly kept a secret from all but the permanent residents at the farm, although I have no doubt Benson muttered dark thoughts to the people in New York.

I have no idea what Benson was doing while we were at lunch. My guess is that he took a hefty swig or two of gin to ease his hurt. At that time, he had a huge capacity for liquor, mainly gin, which he could drink neat. But eventually Madame de Salzmann weaned him from that.

During the last years of Franklin Farms, Benson gathered three or four young men around him. One of them was Donald Victor (Don) Petacchi, who had come to Pentland in New York after having lived alone on Kodiak Island, Alaska, where he had prospected for nine years. He had been terribly affected by his experiences in World War II. When he came to Franklin Farms, he looked like a wild man. But he was a master carpenter, a skilled woodsman, and very strong, and Benson drew on his skills to start building a sled of oak. They built a special contraption to steam and bend the runners, and in time they produced a superb sled. As I write, Petacchi probably is still living on a small mountaintop in the Catskills, without the benefit of most modern conveniences, and perhaps even trying to beam thought waves to Mars. A true "original," Petacchi developed his own rather eccentric version of the Gurdjieff teaching. It was always fascinating to hear him speak about the great ideas of Gurdjieff: everything sounded quite plausible and yet faintly improbable, as I dare say they should.

When the farm was closed, a new place of work was bought at Armonk, New York. Typically, Benson revolted against the sophisticated skills of the young group entrusted with the direction of the practical activities. These representatives of the New Breed were quite outspoken in their contempt for the hardscrabble life at Mendham: they were going to bring a new direction to the Work, they said. But while they went their ways, Benson staked out an old icehouse as his domain, a place that no one else wanted. He had assembled a team of maverick if not entirely rogue characters to work in his free-form way. Rogue or street-smart, they knew how to do things.

The icehouse, which was in disrepair when he arrived, had once served as a bakery, with an old brick oven in one corner. Benson disdained the use of levels and plumb lines, and used some rather primitive and unorthodox methods to shore up the building and repair the roof. Since the "management" team (the council) evidently resisted making a formal allocation of funds or supplies, Benson's team became expert foragers. They roamed the property and quietly appropriated anything that wasn't tied down. They did, and made, all kinds of things, including bronze casting using the lost wax process.

One of the mainstays of the icehouse crew was a professional drummer, Jack Moscrop, who had played for several years in the band on the ocean liner *Queen Elizabeth*. He had served as a Spitfire aircraft mechanic during World War II, and was a wizard at repairing motors and machinery. He had often noticed Madame de Salzmann on these transatlantic voyages and wondered who she might be. He had shown up unannounced one night at Mendham, demanding to see Madame Ouspensky. And here he was now, a key member of Benson's crew.

About six or seven years into the Armonk period, Benson died. But not before he had realized one of his personal dreams. He was fascinated by the idea of the aeolian harp, and the icehouse gang eventually produced a beautiful and sonorous harp.

The making of this harp is commemorated in a poem by Mary Kennedy, an old friend of his. I met her coming from his funeral. She mentioned that she wished to publish a book of poetry, and I subsequently helped her to have it printed under my imprint of The Sinclair Press. She spoke of him with real affection. This is what she published:

Out of Winter [7]

He is making a wind harp
For he longs to hear the voice of the wind,
Its song, its own secret note.

He is deep in snow.
A mountain rises above his house
Tall and unbroken to the sky,
A barrier of white.
If it spoke, it would only say
"I am here."

The wind harp will have two strings.
Does the wind blow high or low,
It will sing with a voice from space
And tell him secret things.

He is making a wind harp.
He struggles to rouse
From the waking sleep of the snow.
In the morning he takes courage
In the lion-colored light.
Snow birds, austere and silent
In monastic dress, feed from his hands.

At night, his nearest neighbors
Are the planets. The wind
Brushes by the house, rushing
And filling the valley of the garden;
But it is only the sound of a passing,
A movement of air, the shiver and thrust of winter.

He has made a harp
That sings with a voice from space.

Perhaps it took someone with a more intellectual bent to compress all these impressions into one cohesive image, and that is what Roger Lipsey was able to do in his poem titled, "Martin Benson at Armonk. In Memoriam."[8] I quote it in its entirety.

I. The Wind Harp

A motionless box, not threatening but immensely
    tranquil
Stood on a hillside exposed to the wind.
The air was filled with vibrations,
Waxing and waning slowly,
A mix of sounds as intimately linked
As they must have been at Creation.
And I stopped like a creature caught in a beam of light
(It was a beam of sound),
Wondering how such music could come to be,
And what its significance was for me,
So brute and dense.

II. Martin Benson

Martin Benson sometimes reeled,
He was a man with sea-legs.
You didn't know
Where his voyage was taking him that day,
But you felt inclined to make your own.
His face was open
With blue eyes that never focused on faults
But somehow counted you into a vision of things
That embraced both you and various kinds of organic
    knowledge
Such as farming, carpentry, wood-warping,
Sled manufacture, glass-blowing, wind harp design,
And occult fields like the languages of animals.
Given his breadth, there was no reason to suffer in
    his presence,
Only a need to reel a little, to stand on his ocean
    with him.

He spoke in waves—
You couldn't parse his sentences
Any more than you can parse waves,
Advancing and receding, bringing all sorts of things,
Often stuff that only the sea knows the origin of.
He was wise but never set things in order:
You caught what you could and put it in your bag,
Knowing that it didn't add up to a whole
But represented the whole directly.
He was vulnerable, and you could sense that.
He wasn't cased in anger,
And of course no one touched him:
Such vulnerability is great power.
His workshop was off the beaten path
Not far from where the wind harp stood on that
      memorable day.
It was an antique shop, a laboratory, a bird house,
A historical restoration, a cottage industry,
An asylum for left-over materials,
The last outpost before the woods.
And it was a club for heavier men
Who lumber up the path of consciousness together
With fair doubts about lighter men elsewhere on the
      grounds.
They worked with a sense of ritual, it seems:
Given his openness, there was no routine
But something more like the discovery of sensible
      gestures.
A rhythm in an atmosphere—that describes it.

In one of his last talks he had in mind
Some Eskimo tools made from meteorites,
Metal originating in other worlds.
He wanted to get one for us to see,
Although he acknowledged their rarity.

There is no laying to rest,
Only the unrest and warmth
That he and others of his friends now gone
Have sown.

What law is there other than forgetting?
Is the chain of friendships in some way
More enduring than monuments and books?

*   *   *

Those others of us who lived close to the man have as much difficulty as he himself had in trying to articulate the scope of his warmth and the depth of his insight. But we felt it through some secret influence, and we were never really the same for it.

It even permits me to modify the impression that Lipsey gives, so that Benson might be seen even more in the round. Benson did have one glaring and awkward weakness—a surprising negativity that seeped through at times during his last years. When that mood took hold of him, he would come seek me out at Armonk on the Saturdays when I worked with the newer people, and bend my ear with dire complaints about some of his (uncomprehending) peers. It was part of my own payment, perhaps, that I had to hear him out. I could appreciate his difficulties. I saw a parallel in the description given by Laurens van der Post in his book *The Dark Eye in Africa* [9] of the difficulty of communicating across cultures and, perhaps even more precisely, across differing centers of gravity—and never the twain could meet. Perhaps Benson's flaw reflected the vast dichotomy existing between a man preponderantly in his essence and others, his peers, with their consuming culture and sophistication.

I had only infrequent contacts with Benson in his last years, largely because I was taken up with earning a living.

A little while before he died, he telephoned me. In the course of a long rambling earful, he reminded me of the first day I had arrived at Franklin Farms about 12 years earlier. Certainly that day was etched in my memory, because I had found him with a team of men melting pitch up on the chicken-house roof. He said that he had been dismayed to see me take my hat off when I was introduced to Christopher Fremantle. "I thought I was seeing a pure soul—and for this I wasn't prepared!" As we soon got to know, I was far from being a pure soul. And he helped me to recognize that. He had his feet on the ground, like "a good animal."

There had been a little wooden panel on the kitchen wall in Benson's cottage at Mendham that carried an American Indian inscription. It read: "Every press of my foot upon the earth springs a thousand affections." Martin Benson loved life, as surely and affectionately as he walked the earth.

He died on December 13, 1971. He was 72.

NOTES

1. Ravi Ravindra, *Whispers from the Other Shore*, Quest, Wheaton, Illinois, 1984, p. 90.
2. From my personal notes, February 19, 1968.
3. Paul Beekman Taylor, *Shadows of Heaven*, Samuel Weiser, Inc., York Beach, Maine, 1998, p. 137.
4. It was some time after I had written this that I came across Paul Beekman Taylor's own further assessment of Rita Benson: "Rita was a serious actor in her day, and later a noted teacher in Actor's Studio, but I felt, in the late 1930s and 1940s when I saw her often, that she was wont to perform roles of self-importance. She carried herself with an air of dignity, and always had a better story to tell than anyone else on any topic. I would not say that anything she said was not true . . . but my gut reaction to her stories was negative." *Gurdjieff and Orage: Brothers in Elysium*, Weiser Books, 2001, footnote, p. 161. As I have said, she was always on stage.

5. Stanley Isaacs.
6. This injunction to "steal their prayers" evidently predated the dramatic Christmas Day, 1948 meeting at the Hotel Wellington, in New York, when Gurdjieff gave as an exercise the work to "steal" the energies being poured out towards Christ. See chapter 12.
7. Mary Kennedy, *Behind the Day*, The Sinclair Press, New York, 1972.
8. Originally published in *A Journal of Our Time*, No. 1, Traditional Studies Press, Toronto, 1977.
9. Laurens van der Post, *The Dark Eye in Africa*, William Morrow & Co., New York, 1935.

Out in the cold: Martin Benson, left, and Rene Zubert, author of *Who Are You, Mr. Gurdjieff?*, walking up from Benson's cottage to the main house at Franklin Farms. Winter 1958.

Iron man Donald Victor Petacchi at the manure pile, Franklin Farms, 1959.

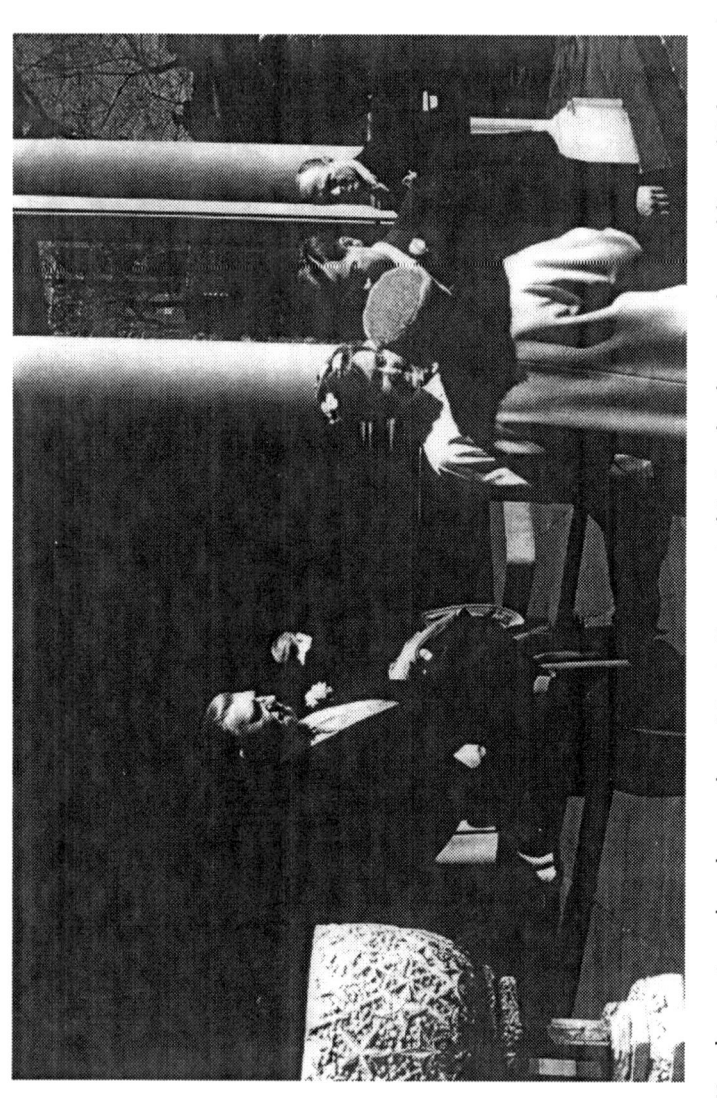

Handsome is as handsome does: Martin Benson in his Sunday best at the wedding of Adam and Rosemary Nott at St. Mark's-in-the-Bowery, March 1962.

No agriculturist, this: Rita and Martin Benson at
Adam and Rosemary Nott's wedding, 1962.

What strange pursuit: Martin Benson, right, on the Franklin Farms chicken house roof, August, 1958. This was the author's first sight of Benson.

Mrs. Margaret Flinsch, right, in the potato field at Mendham. Martin Benson is second from right in his railroad cap.

Thomas Forman and Molly D'Arcy Thompson,
with Pete and Duffy, at Franklin Farms,
about 1959.

CHAPTER 8

Thomas Vivian Forman:
Harrow; Trinity College, Cambridge;
Franklin Farms, New Jersey

"Here people are neither clever nor stupid, neither English nor Russian, neither good nor bad. There are only spoiled automobiles, the same as you. It is only thanks to these spoiled automobiles that you can attain what you wished for when you came here."
—G.I. Gurdjieff, *Views from the Real World*

"The priest is subject to the same weaknesses and sins as anyone else."
—From the *Divine Liturgy of the Armenian Church*

"To the living, we owe respect; to the dead, we owe only the truth."
—Voltaire

*   *   *

I CAN RECALL the exact day that I first met Tom Forman. It was in the autumn of 1958 when I first stepped on the grounds of Franklin Farms after flying in from South Africa.

In the succeeding four decades, he and I were participants in some of the variously dramatic, humdrum, extraordinary, enlightening, strange and trite events that inevitably—it seems—arise in the circumstances of the Gurdjieff Work. After all, the tone had been set for us all by Mr. Gurdjieff himself. (Gurdjieff was still *Mister* Gurdjieff for decades after his death, even to those of us who had never met him.)

As I launch into this account, largely a reprise of my eulogy at his funeral service, I recognize that I shall be accused of performing the ultimate character assassination, perhaps even a "sin against the Holy Ghost." I have no illusions about the contumely that will be heaped on my head by his loyal pupils. But here in this chapter, I also, perhaps quite gratuitously, may be performing something approximating an ancient ritual of which Gurdjieff speaks in the Third Series. He tells of his revulsion at the expression of the customary "senseless words" of sympathy upon the death of someone. Instead, he tells of a ritual dating back "many thousands of years" in which the mourners participate in "washing the bone of the dead down to the white of the ivory."[1] In this so-called "Remembering Feast," the mourners recalled to mind and expressed "only the bad and evil deeds of the deceased during his life." Gurdjieff does not elaborate, but clearly this ritual is intended, I think, to "loosen the ties that bind" and to hasten the deceased's departure. It is also very explicitly to remind us that the egoism is "the cause of all evil in our common life."[2] Still, what I am about to write is not all dire and black. Rather, it is a commentary on how mercilessly the Work works, and in ways that are not predictable or foreseeable.

As I have said, I arrived at Mendham as a consummate neophyte in the Work, originally intending to stay only two months. Contrary to the original plans, I remained "in residence" for about 15 or 16 months, and continued to take an active, if only minor, part in the life at Franklin Farms after Madame Ouspensky's death on December 30, 1961.

Forman, meanwhile, was already considered an "older" member of the Work, having been with the Ouspenskys at Lyne, England, and having met Gurdjieff in New York during Gurdjieff's last visit. At Madame Ouspensky's death he, along with other Mendhamites like Miss Dorothy Darlington and Miss Nancy Pearson, was placed in Group One in the New York Foundation. Attaining that kind of "eminence" was the farthest thing from my own thoughts: I was consumed with a need to know, not to speak of making my way in life ("paying for my arising," in Gurdjieff's language). Yet I ended up some 20 years later as a member of this group, taken in by them, in the continuing dance of the generations, to work alongside Lord Pentland, Dr. William J. (Bill) Welch, William C. (Bill) Segal—and Tom Forman.

Forman and I more or less went our separate ways after the closing of Madame Ouspensky's estate in 1964, but in July 1998 it was proposed that I visit Cleveland to work with him and to prepare to step in as the New York representative "at his passing." Forman was then 88 and in fragile health. It was not a role that I had sought, and I expressed my misgivings to the trustees of the New York Foundation at every opportunity. On the occasion of my second visit two months later, Forman must have felt comfortable with my being there, and quite unexpectedly expressed the wish that I would deliver the eulogy at his funeral. His health had always been precarious, and the thought of dying could never have been far away. I assured him that I would, and I took the opportunity to ask him to clarify a few minor "historical" details to round out what I already knew about him. He agreed, and spoke quite freely for a while. Again, I felt he could do so because I had spent some time in close proximity to him in those final years at Franklin Farms.

He was very proud of the fact that, while at Mendham, he was "the only Englishman on the Eastern seaboard to have received the [U.S. Department of Agriculture] soil conservation award." The truth was that not until his late 40s or early 50s (by my calculation) did he actually work for a living. During the years of World War II he had served as the head of security in the New York offices of British Military Intelligence (MI5 and MI6), along with another Mendhamite, Baron Bissing, and other British expatriates. But that was the war effort. He said that it was Lord Pentland who had urged him to find a job after the closing of Franklin Farms, and I half suspect it may even have been through Pentland's connections that he landed a fascinating job as one of half a dozen general editors of the new *American Heritage Dictionary*. That job lasted five years.

Forman was especially well prepared for that kind of undertaking. As a privileged British youth, he went to Harrow School and later to Trinity College, Cambridge. Only much later did I learn that a number of others, including my own first group leader, B. Fairfax Hall, had been at both Harrow and Trinity College. Pentland, too, had been at Trinity. Moreover, Molly D'Arcy Thompson, a member of Fairfax Hall's Cape Town group who visited Franklin Farms while I was there, was the daughter of yet another Trinity College man, D'Arcy Wentworth Thompson, a Scottish embryologist, who had been professor of natural history there and was renowned as the author of a work titled *On Growth and Form* (1917).

Forman seemed rather proud of having been sent down from Trinity—that is, expelled—for an escapade with Malcolm Lowry, the author. He and Lowry had been out on the town and returned somewhat under the weather. They were pursued by a policeman, and according to Forman he "ran interference" for Lowry. Lowry was able to escape, but Forman was arrested and subsequently sent down. Forman said that Lowry later dedicated a book to him, and also used him as a character in Lowry's best-known book, *Under the Volcano*.

I must say that when he first told me about being drummed out of Cambridge, I laughed. After all, generations of luckless (and underprivileged) young men in the old British colonies shamelessly (and hopefully) flaunted business cards announcing that they had "Failed B.A."

Largely, I suppose, to try to prove that he had been a daredevil, a young man of the world, and no stranger to sex, Forman occasionally referred, quite publicly, to having had a youthful bout of gonorrhea. In any event, this led to his meeting Dr. Kenneth Walker, a Harley Street physician who specialized in such problems, and through him, Ouspensky. (I did point out in my remarks at his funeral that this was "certainly not a course to be emulated" in one's introduction to the Work.)

When I first met Forman back in 1958, he had graduated to playing the role of the "squire" of Franklin Farms. He had accompanied Madame Ouspensky from England, and he was responsible for the management of the 300-acre estate that the Collin-Smiths had deeded to Madame Ouspensky. Besides Ouspensky's grandson, Lonya Savitsky, there was a small band of women in residence at the time. Among them (as I have noted) were Miss Dorothy Darlington, who had been Ouspensky's secretary; she was an accomplished violinist who had renounced that gift, and she was reputed to have appeared in vaudeville with Sir Harry Lauder of "Roamin' in the Gloamin'" fame. Another was Miss Nancy Pearson, a true egghead who briefly had been secretary to John Steinbeck ("briefly," because Steinbeck soon discovered that she had the common failing of many women in the Work: she tried once too often to tell him what to do). Also resident on the estate, but not in the main house, were Dr. and Mrs. Ralph Phillips, staunch devotees of the Ouspenskys who had their own cottage, and Martin Benson, who, as noted, lived in a cottage at the main entrance on Route 22.

Also living there was Bill Forman, Tom Forman's brother. Bill's responsibility was to milk the cows and drive the tractor. Bill often had difficulty milking Starlight, who tended to be a bit rambunctious and somewhat uneasy at Bill's rather rough-and-ready methods. I can recall Bill's exasperated shouts of "Starlight!" resounding through the barn when she became especially obstinate and uncooperative, sometimes stepping into the pail of milk and knocking Bill off his stool. Starlight figured in a nice story that some of the expatriate Britons felt epitomized "the American way." One spring Starlight was in heat, and Tom Forman called the local veterinarian to come over and artificially inseminate her. However, the vet. was fully booked. So Forman went to Pitney's farm across the highway (Route 22) and arranged for a real live bull to perform the rite. Forman met up with the veterinarian in the village a few days later and explained what he had arranged. The veterinarian nodded thoughtfully and said, "Ah yes, that's a good way, too."

Forman had his own little den at one end of the barn, where he would practice the accordion. I remember learning there the song "The Er-i-ee was arisin'/And the gin was a'gettin' low," as well as the trick of drinking wine from a gallon jug hoisted over the shoulder. He was responsible for sowing and reaping the annual wheat crop. But by the time I arrived on the scene he was already suffering from the ear ailments that plagued him for the rest of his life, and many a day he did not stir from his room. I do recall my complete astonishment the first time I was asked to take something to him in his room in the main house—it was on the "red corridor," down from Madame Ouspensky's room. (I was a mere outsider, and therefore assigned to the end room on the third floor, the "green corridor"). Forman's room was rather awesome in its look of total abandon and disorder. Back in the Old Country, he would have had a valet or a manservant from the "lower classes" to keep things in order. One tiptoed over and around wine and whisky bottles, piles of books, fishing and hunting gear, and heaven knows what else, to reach him.

Forman was on especially good terms with the local firemen, and periodically arranged for them to hold their fire drills around the barn. Their fire trucks would be parked in the barnyard with lights flashing, long lengths of hose were run from the pond down by the Phillips's cottage, and the drills were rounded off with lots of beer and whisky provided by Forman in his role as the "squire." Of course, Benson, who could scarcely disguise his distaste for Forman's pronounced Englishness, was openly derisive. Looking at the little dribbles coming from the fire hoses, he muttered, "I could pee better than that."

Like others who had been around Ouspensky, Forman had sat through many a night drinking flavored vodkas and listening to Ouspensky expound on a vast range of subjects. Ouspensky had a huge and evidently well-deserved reputation for drinking. Indeed, his grandson often said, "My grandfather was never sober." From all accounts, that was no exaggeration. I remember the large, tall glasses in the pantry at Franklin Farms, and being told they were not flower vases but actually Ouspensky's cocktail glasses.[3]

It was not only in his huge capacity for alcohol—mainly Armagnac, cognac, Scotch whiskey and vodka—that Forman reflected Ouspensky's influence. The truth is that he had an excellent mind. He could recall exactly the things he had heard, he could organize his thought, and he could make orderly presentations that we all might envy. But there was a serious down side to this gift. Once Forman got started, and especially when—out of town, away from the chastening influence of his peers—he was deferred to as the oldest, he tended to surf rather effortlessly from one association to another. I once endured a two-hour monologue of his at a dinner in Cleveland, and I vowed that I would never again expose myself to such an endless chain of association. When he went on like that, it was a cause of great consternation and discomfort to many of those who were compelled to listen. There was the story of one young man who irreverently brought a remote control (TV channel changer) and pointed and clicked it at Forman during one of his long monologues, but nothing happened! To my mind, these long ramblings gave a misleading impression of the role of the leader, and many a budding "group leader" sedulously aped him. It seemed that Forman often instilled qualities of forbearance and long suffering more by default than by intent. In his last year, in my presence—and perhaps because of my presence—he openly owned to this weakness, and he occasionally tried hard to forego the impulse to expound. But those efforts did not last long. I suspect that the admission was more a well-meaning public relations gesture than an expression of an achievable intent. I felt that he was indeed a font of familiar orthodoxies, gleaned by a retentive mind from the old leaders. But I have always felt that what the Work calls for is the *present* understanding, freshly mined and newly met, here and now.

I suspect that this rather common predilection for the "declarative statement," or "the ultimate pronouncement" based on seemingly incontestable orthodoxies, probably was the most noticeable unintended legacy of the Ouspensky "method." At his best, Forman was a supraliteral exponent of Ouspensky's declarative method, a method which Ouspensky himself had renounced at the end of his life. Ouspensky appears to have had a remarkable mind: consider his extraordinary reconstruction of the teaching of the early years in *In Search of the Miraculous*, in which he reported with profound objectivity on the great psychological and cosmological teaching that Gurdjieff had brought to the West. Consider, too, how many spurious leaders not connected with the mainstream have built their little empires purely on the basis of Ouspensky's extraordinary recollections—at secondhand.

In the end, Ouspensky's saving grace was that some kind of revelation was evidently bestowed on him. In his final days, Ouspensky "was a different man," Rodney Collin-Smith observed. I myself had some inkling of this purely from seeing a beautiful silent film taken of Ouspensky at Mendham. It was shown to us one evening, and it totally demolished my old image of him as a stiff, rigid, humorless, and remote intellectual. It was evidently taken surreptitiously by his grandson, filming through the crack in the sliding doors leading to the parlor off the dining room. Ouspensky sat at the same end of the dining room table where Savitsky installed himself in subsequent years. He looked like a blond Buddha, gentle and calm, as he expounded on some idea, turning to each of his listeners in turn. When his gaze fell on the camera, he smiled in recognition. I was bowled over by this impression. This was not the harsh, cold, and tough-minded Ouspensky whom most people seemed to recall. This was a warm and generous human being who manifested real feeling and obvious compassion.

So it was no surprise, then, to read Collin-Smith's report that, "In the bitter early spring of 1947 he called several large meetings in London of all the people who had previously listened to him, and of others who never had. He spoke to them in a new way. He said that he abandoned the system." The truth is that he had actually said in response to a question by Dr. Kenneth Walker, "There is no system."[3A] Be that as it may, Collin-Smith (writing as Rodney Collin in his *The Theory of Celestial Influence*) observed, "It is difficult to convey the impression created. For twenty years in England before the war, O[uspensky] had almost daily explained the system. He had said that everything must be referred to it, that things could only be understood in relation to it." To those who had listened to him, the words and the language of the system "had become more familiar to them than their mother tongue." Several months later, Ouspensky said to a few friends, "You must start again. You must make a new beginning. You must reconstruct everything for yourselves—from the very beginning."[4] Collin-Smith drew this telling conclusion: "Every system of truth must be abandoned, in order that it may grow again." (Of course, around Mendham, Collin-Smith had been dismissed as a dilletante, and his death in South America—where he fell from the bell tower of Lima Cathedral—was attributed to his alleged messianic ambitions: the story around Mendham was that his death was not an accident but that he had deliberately walked out into space, believing himself superhuman.)

In any event, Pentland himself was able to acknowledge some decades later that he had gained little, if anything, from his years with Ouspensky and from Ouspensky's rigid exposition of the "method." "It was after Ouspensky died and I went out to India and on the way back, actually, it became clear to me that even all those years with Ouspensky, I hadn't arrived at anything. I came to nothing."[5] The moral to be drawn is perhaps that "ideas are not enough," to use Madame de Salzmann's compelling admonition. Ouspensky evidently came to that realization too at the end of his life.

Forman also echoed many of Madame Ouspensky's singular habits in dealing with members of his groups. Madame Ouspensky was well known, if not notorious and feared, for her practice of embarrassing people without mercy, of pointing out what *she* considered to be their weaknesses and failings. She also liked pointing out people's animal counterparts, I understand: so-and-so is a wolf, a sheep, a snake, and so on. I was fascinated to find in Pentland's book a subtle criticism of this approach. I suppose it passed by many people, but it could not be more obvious: "[S]elf-observation becomes something far beyond the psychological sort of stories that can be related to nature by the head, as in the idea of a menagerie or something. All of that is old hat, so to speak, compared with what's at stake."[6] I recall being told by the women at Mendham that with Madame Ouspensky one could say one thing, or another, or yet a third thing, but whatever one said, it would be wrong. Forman was a shameless practitioner of this putdown. Of course, there were people who had no other experience of the Work, so they considered this standard operating procedure. Or, if you wish, the "method."

I have harped on this issue because—and of course, it will no doubt be seen as a failing on my part—I have never liked bullies, in any guise, whether they were from Petersburg,

Poona, Paris, Pittsburgh, or Pretoria. And least of all, in the pursuit of the sacred.

In any event, back in those last days at Mendham, Forman sported a natty blue blazer with a Royal Air Force Volunteer Reserve badge on the breast pocket. Almost invariably accompanied by his two collies, Pete and Duffy, he would tool around the estate and Mendham village in a sporty little Austin pickup that was rather the worse for wear. There were rumors down at Joe's Bar and the Black Horse Inn that he was a World War II air ace, one of those gallant few who had saved the Western world for democracy, and Tom neither affirmed nor denied them. But he was, by his own admission to me, just an amateur airman who had not seen aerial combat. Forman was also a keen fly fisherman, and would tie his own flies. He spent his free days fishing at Lake Hopatcong, occasionally bringing back a bagful of pan-fry fish for our supper. He was, like most people in the Gurdjieff work, adept at many crafts, particularly leatherwork.

But those were not easy times for Forman. His marriage to Madame Ouspensky's granddaughter Tatiana (Tanya) had unraveled, and the so-called "Ouspensky people" were considered somewhat beyond the pale by many in the New York Foundation, partly (I suppose) because of Gurdjieff's contemptuous treatment of Forman. Indeed, Forman was considered something of a pariah by a few true-blue (or is it died-in-the-wool?) Gurdjieffians who for decades could barely hide their disdain. But Forman stuck it out, and Madame de Salzmann especially treated Forman with great consideration. At 88 years of age in Cleveland, and at my prompting, Forman told me a little more about his encounters with Gurdjieff back in 1948, and they were enough to daunt anyone less resilient or stubborn.

According to Forman, Gurdjieff was all sweetness and charm when Forman was first introduced to him by Madame de Salzmann. But on their second meeting, when Madame de Salzmann mentioned that he was married to Madame

Ouspenky's granddaughter, who was many years younger than he, Gurdjieff blew his lid. He raved that Forman was a *svolitch*—the Russian equivalent, it seems, of a sonofabitch. The story goes—and I did not get this from Forman—that Gurdjieff said, among other things, that he could have married her to a prince. And he made a point of lambasting Forman at every subsequent meeting. Forman told me that he had married Madame Ouspensky's granddaughter "to save her," and I did not try to probe into that. Certainly, those were hard times, and there was very little money, as those of us who lived at Mendham even as briefly as I did can testify. The food was especially poor. I should point out that Forman was in no way to blame for the quality of the food at Mendham. There was just no money.

Still, I should tell this rather shameless story. I had been working out in the fields one hot Sunday with the Englishman Jack Moscrop. When the lunch bell echoed around the grounds, he looked at me and said, "There's no way I'm going to lunch. I need real food." I think that by that time I was no longer living on the estate, and must have resumed a "normal diet," so I was as desperate for "real food" as he was. We drove a couple of miles to Joe's Bar at the edge of the town. As we sat at the bar, I had the eerie feeling that there was "someone else" down at one end of the bar. I slowly stole a look that way, and lo and behold, there was one of our senior people—a group leader—sitting there. Evidently his need was as great as ours! We all pretended not to notice one another. Moscrop and I ate our hamburgers and drank our beer, and returned to the estate just as the others were going back to work out on the grounds. I have no moral to draw from this. We worked like horses and we were just hungry.

Forman frequently mentioned the contempt with which Gurdjieff referred to Ouspensky. Gurdjieff dismissed Ouspensky as a hasnamuss—a hassnamuss being, by Gurdjieff's definition, a person without conscience. However, when he was presented with Ouspensky's *In Search of the*

Miraculous, Gurdjieff declared that he could hear his own authentic voice in Ouspensky's account. Gurdjieff said, "It was the way I spoke then [to the Russian intelligentsia]." Others have reported that Gurdjieff also said, "I love that man [Ouspensky]."

Forman said Gurdjieff laid into Ouspensky's followers in order to make them "think for themselves." In Forman's opinion, Ouspensky was biased towards the intellect, an opinion, I should add, generously shared by some of the Europeans, who nevertheless make liberal use of Ouspensky's extraordinary exposition of the ideas.

At Mendham, Forman told me this classic story about Ouspensky. One night Ouspensky admitted to him that if he (Ouspensky) heard Gurdjieff was coming in at one door, he (Ouspensky) would slip out of the other door. Because Ouspensky, Forman felt, was afraid of Gurdjieff. I kept this story to myself for many years, but others have given similar accounts, so it has the ring of truth. Then, too, Jessmin Howarth told an equally fascinating story in a letter written in November 1948 as the people around Madame Ouspensky were preparing for Gurdjieff's visit. She recalled that Madame Ouspensky had asked her what would be her reaction if ever Mr. Gurdjieff came to America. Mrs. Howarth said she would probably hide under her bed. To which Madame Ouspensky laughed and said, "No, I think Mr. Ouspensky already there!"

It would seem that Ouspensky had for years waited in vain for Gurdjieff to call him back to the fold, but the call never came. That—and his tearful regret that he had never had any ecstatic experiences[7]—was perhaps the grave disappointment of Ouspensky's life until his evident "breakthrough" at the end.

Forman believed that Gurdjieff had begun to relent in his treatment of him towards the end of his New York visit. On one occasion, when Gurdjieff was railing against Ouspensky, who by then had died, Forman dared to say, "If it were not for Ouspensky, these people would not be here." Forman said that Donald Whitcomb (of Providence, Rhode Island, and a Prieuré "alumnus") reached to him in a silent gesture of support. Thereupon, Gurdjieff made a remark about God's needing to have a strong devil with whom to struggle, which Forman took to be a compliment for standing up for Ouspensky. Forman regretted that Gurdjieff was interrupted, apparently as he was about to say something further. He seemed to feel that Gurdjieff had come round to conceding that he was not such a bad egg after all. He told me Gurdjieff had invited him to go to Paris, but Forman declined because of his obligations to Madame Ouspensky at Franklin Farms, where he was the "only man" at that time.

Whatever the truth may have been, Forman was totally committed to the Work. He regularly visited Madame de Salzmann in Paris, and one had the impression from the way she treated him that she understood his great need of the Work and his great isolation from his peers. As others have borne witness, he labored long and hard over the old tapes of Thomas de Hartmann playing Gurdjieff's music, for which the Work must be indebted to him. It is said that Michel de Salzmann, who characteristically turned a deaf ear to the grumbling about Forman's Ouspenskian teaching "methods," once declared that all of those who, like Forman, had worked so selflessly to preserve the Gurdjieff music were "candidates for immediate beatification." Even this claim needs qualification in fairness to the roles both of Madame de Salzmann and de Hartmann himself. It was de Hartmann who "saved" the music. Madame de Salzmann several times told the story of being sent by Gurdjieff to see de Hartmann at the time of his parting from Gurdjieff to ensure that she take possession of the music on Gurdjieff's behalf. She recalled her trepidation at having to demand the music from de Hartmann. But when she arrived at his residence, she was astonished to find that in his total devotion and loyalty to Gurdjieff he had already gathered all the music so that it could be handed over intact and in proper order.

I think Forman's role—certainly a formidable one—was in the salvaging of the tapes of de Hartmann's actual playing. This he accomplished through long hours of editing on some truly antediluvian equipment, most of which was reverently preserved by the faithful. It was Madame, an accomplished musician in her own right, who made the final choices among the pieces to be preserved. De Hartmann's performances are seldom played anymore: for some, the music would appear to have taken a subtler turn, it would seem, and Madame herself exerted a huge influence on the direction that the playing took. Of course, I speak subject to correction. But "from where I was sitting," that is how it has sounded to me.[8]

* * *

In any event, Forman was devoted to the Ouspenskys, devoted to Gurdjieff's teaching, and devoted especially to Madame de Salzmann. He gave all his energies and all he owned—as well as a great deal of money that he squeezed from others in the spirit of Gurdjieff's own fund raising—to the support of the Work. In his last years, Forman had virtually no other life apart from the Work.

I was profoundly relieved then, for my own conscience's sake, to learn that in his very last months some breakthrough evidently did take place. I do not believe that I saw him after that, but I shall quote the words of a physician who had known him since the middle 1960s.[9] They had been on their last visit to France to be with Michel de Salzmann in Beau Préau. "Towards the last few days we had with Michel at his home, Tom [Forman] said to Michel (only a few people heard this), 'You have turned my understanding of the Work upside down in the last few days.' I had a chance to ask [him] about this because I was concerned as to what [he] was so shaken up about . . . and also because he had been the 'plenary member from New York' for over 30 years.[10]

"When I asked [him] specifically about what he meant, he indicated to me that he always had been under the impression that attention (consciousness) came from the mind . . . but that Michel had provided a new way of seeing and experiencing consciousness from 'another source' . . . a higher, unknown, much greater source. Tom wouldn't speak much more about his 'new understanding' except to say that he always thought of attention [as] related to the mind much like a muscle . . . and that if you exercised it like a muscle that it would grow stronger. But after our visit and work with Michel de Salzmann, he said, 'I now see that consciousness is everywhere in the universe and is contacted in the here and now . . . as in the "I Am" presence.' With that he ended the conversation. He did appear genuinely physically and psychologically shaken at the time . . . and since he also seemed in a frail condition, I didn't pursue it any further."

My correspondent, who, as a longtime member of the medical profession might legitimately be considered a trained observer, added: "As you know, Tom usually didn't like to be seen in the light of 'not knowing' but at Beau Préau he had a childlike appearance when he was 'turned upside down' for a couple of days . . . and his personality wasn't so dominating."

In a subsequent note, the good doctor wrote: "On a couple of occasions, Michel said to us (and especially to Tom) [that] this physical body is nothing, it was given to us temporarily and will perish. We need to assist the creation within us of a finer[,] second body . . . and we prepare for this by coming to this deeper, more central space within us, in the deeper silence . . . ." Michel de Salzmann added that "the attention (consciousness) that we need comes from a higher source . . . and not from us. We need to become empty and without pretense."[11]

*   *   *

In accordance with Forman's wishes, I delivered a brief eulogy at his funeral service. I did not offer the seemingly harsh pronouncements that I have made here. Speaking "in the beaten way of friendship," as Hamlet would say, I noted that he had given his all in support of the Work. I said that he had indeed become what Dr. de Salzmann termed "a living treasure"—"with his blemishes and warts and all." And in acknowledgement of the extraordinary struggles with what Gurdjieff would call the weaknesses of his nature, I said, "Tom Forman truly bore witness to the search for being."

It was unfortunate that the graveside service was not pure Church of England, as befitted an old Trinity man and someone whose personality was so thoroughly and determinedly English. But it was no longer important. Surely he had finally crossed to

> . . . where was ended the talk and the great
> Understanding began . . . . [12]

NOTES

1. G.I. Gurdjieff, *Life is Real, Only Then, When "I Am,"* p. 158.
2. Ibid., p. 159.
3. Colin Wilson elaborated on this feature—or weakness—of Ouspensky's character in his book *The Strange Life of P.D. Ouspensky.*
3A. J.M. Cohen, "In the Work," an unpublished radio script first broadcast January 5, 1966, quoted in James Webb, *The Harmonious Circle,* G.P. Putnam's Sons, New York, 1980, p.449.
4. Rodney Collin, *The Theory of Celestial Influence,* Vincent Stuart, London, 1954, pp. xx-xxi.
5. John Pentland, *Exchanges Within,* p. xxi.
6. Ibid., p. 224.
7. James Webb, op. cit., p. 406.
8. My own image of de Hartmann as a resolutely dour and perhaps unimaginative pianist was shaken when the Dutch music researcher, Gert-Jan Blom, made new recordings of the orchestrated music that de Hartmann had prepared for Gurdjieff's first visit to America in 1924. These orchestrations certainly

undermined the dogmatic assertions by some that the true Gurdjieffian oeuvre can be represented only by the piano music.

9. Dr. Edward Tupta, in private correspondence to the author, September 5, 2002.

10. For some 40 years, the so-called "plenary member" was the ultimate authority on matters both spiritual and secular, and whose word was law. Needless to say, this arrangement has been changed.

11. Dr. Edward Tupta, in private correspondence to the author, September 8, 2002

12. John Howland Beaumont, "Poet's Epitaph," *Poems*, A.A. Balkema, Cape Town, 1957.

Tom Forman, on his old tractor, ploughing the potato field at Franklin Farms, 1959.

PRONUNCIATION GUIDE

for words invented by

GURDJIEFF

in

ALL AND EVERYTHING

Beelzebub's Tales to His Grandson

The Society for Experimental Studies
Armonk, New York
1984

The title page of the *Pronunciation Guide for Words
Invented by Gurdjieff*, showing the elegant colophon.
Originally printed in an edition of 120 copies in 1984,
it was reprinted in 1986. This little guide was
subsequently superseded, if not overwhelmed, by the
impressive work of the Traditional Studies Press in
Toronto.

CHAPTER 9

Annals of the Antic Press

I T IS PERHAPS not out of place to offer this postscript to my faint recollections of Fairfax Hall's timely appearance in my life.

Sometime in the late 1970s, the opportunity to start up a real printing project presented itself at the work place in Armonk. The obvious place to set up the press was the old icehouse, an unheated building that had served for a few years as a forge (and, before our acquisition of the property, as a bakery). After their mentor, Martin Benson, died, the forge team lost interest in coming, so it was decided to convert the forge into a print shop. I led a team in laying a concrete floor, installing as much insulation as possible, and adding windows, doors, and a little vestibule to ward off the icy winter cold. A potbelly stove and some electric heaters provided the heat.

We already had acquired an old Vandercook proofing press, which had been housed in the basement of the main house, where some early efforts at printing had been made. We maneuvered the press out of the basement and over to the icehouse, along with some old letterpress type and equipment that we had obtained from commercial printers who were fast abandoning letterpress.

Soon after, another Vandercook press was added. Its acquisition was somewhat serendipitous. One morning, a printing salesman with whom I dealt in my business affairs and who knew of my interest in printing called me from a telephone on the corner of 45th Street and Madison Avenue, in New York City, a block away from my office. He told me there was a printing press on the sidewalk. I went out to look at it. There on the sidewalk was a late-model Vandercook proof press similar to the older version at Armonk. What to do? Reluctantly I decided that it was just too heavy and bulky to move. I told my friend that only if the press were still there at the end of the day would I try to get some help. By the end of the day it had disappeared, and I thought no more of it.

A few days later, I got another telephone call. "Do you believe that lightning strikes twice in the same place?" my friend asked. The press had reappeared on the sidewalk. By then I had thought better of losing such a gift, and I told him to stand by it and I would come right out and join him. Once out on the street, we borrowed a dolly from the superintendent of a building nearby, manhandled the press onto it, and pushed it up the street where the superintendent allowed us to park it in a side entrance to his building. All the while I hoped that none of my business colleagues would pass by while I was out on the sidewalk pushing this heavy piece of equipment. Back at the office, I called a few men in my group to bring a van. Once back on the street, I actually accosted a strapping passer-by to help us load it into the van, and he jumped at the opportunity to display his strength. By the end of the day, our new press was on its way to the print shop at Armonk.

A purely subjective decision determined the type chosen as our "house" type. As a young man, I had been infatuated with Lawrence of Arabia, who had dreamed of setting up his own press and printing with Caslon type. So Caslon it was, and over the next few years we produced several small, limited editions with this typeface. All were quickly snapped up by our membership, and as far as I know only one of our pieces ever found its way into the "larger world." I should mention here too the good young people who contributed their time and energies to the work in the print shop. Almost all of them "moved on" over the years and went their ways. It was a labor-intensive craft, requiring efforts that are rarely made anymore in this age of digital typesetting and printing.

Our first production was an elegant booklet using linoleum cuts in several colors of a text of dubious origin and merit titled *Desiderata*, which we printed (in 1980) primarily as an exercise.

The first original production was a softcover book titled *To Live in Emptiness*, by Genevieve Lanfranchi. This was a translation from the French by Nancy Pearson and Irving Friedman. We published it in 1981 under the imprint of The Antic Press. The name Antic came about because I had chosen a stylized letter "A" (for Armonk) as the colophon. But then I had concerns that the name "Armonk Press" might present a conflict with some existing business establishment in the town. And "antic" seemed to reflect rather accurately some of the character of the print shop.

The next year we published 50 copies of an oversize book titled *A Book of Traditions*. This had begun as an exercise in the use of linoleum cuts in the style of Fairfax Hall's Rupert Shephard book. We added short texts from four traditions. The book was our first attempt at formal bookbinding.

Next came a reprint from *Parabola* (Vol. 5, No. 3) of Dr. Michel de Salzmann's essay, "Footnotes to the Gurdjieff Literature." Dr. de Salzmann visited the press while the work was in progress, and he himself selected gold as the second color. This softcover book was printed in 1983 in an edition of 100 copies under the imprint of The Society for Experimental Studies.

In 1984, the group printed *A Pronunciation Guide to Words Invented by Gurdjieff*. The text was prepared by Mrs. Margaret Flinsch and Emil Hana. The softcover book was printed in an edition of 120 copies, also under the imprint of The Society for Experimental Studies. It was later reprinted commercially in offset to meet an unexpected demand from members of the groups. And 16 years later, I was more than gratified to see a lone copy of the reprint listed in the catalog of By the Way Books for the sumptuous price of $150. The *Guide* has now been superseded by the scholarly second edition of *A Guide and Index to G.I. Gurdjieff's Beelzebub Tales to His Grandson*, published by Traditional Studies Press, Toronto (2003), but I can assure whoever has acquired that lone 1984 edition that it is worth every penny.

For a few years, there was a sense of experiment and accomplishment in the print shop. The printing group was especially taken by the fact that Madame de Salzmann would visit the shop whenever she came to Armonk. In winter, she would be specially chauffeured through the heavy snow and ice to spend time there. Often, too, she would visit the press and simply stand to one side while we went through the various procedures involved in letterpress—setting and distributing type, proofing galleys, inking the presses, getting the right impressions, making the minute adjustments in the make ready, checking the registration. In fact, simply getting 100-odd acceptable pages was always an achievement, and the little core group thrived on this exacting work.

One of the particular difficulties we encountered was the big swing in temperature during the winter months. Since the icehouse was unheated during the week, the first order of business on Sunday mornings was to light the potbelly stove and turn on the electric heaters. It generally took until the 11:00 a.m. coffee break for the room to be adequately heated and for the steel presses to "thaw out." The print run was generally timed to take place between the coffee break and lunch. It was difficult to control the consistency of the inking if the print runs were undertaken earlier or later: either the materials were not warm enough, or they were too warm.

One day I sent Pentland a copy of *Footnotes*. I learned then that he had himself worked at printing under Ouspensky, and he sent me a gracious reply that acknowledged the "lineage" stemming from The Stourton Press. Since it is perhaps the only letter I ever received from him, I quote it in full:

Dear Frank:

Thank you for the very handsomely bound and printed booklet. It follows, after much too long, as the first authentic footnote to [T]he Stourton Press. I am particularly happy to see it because I did a little work with Fairfax Hall at the press in Colet Gardens and this led in the later fifties and early sixties to some reasonably nicely done hand set productions in San Francisco, although they never reached a Stourton quality.

Where will you go from here? We decided through the years to go on to linotype, then to photo-offset and now computer word-processing which we hoped would also be a work for attention. What a question!

All the best.
John Pentland.

I also sent a copy of *Footnotes* to Pamela Travers, who had retired to London, and she too sent me a charming "thank you" letter.

She wrote: "It was so good of you to send me through Jessmin Howarth the beautifully printed *Footnotes*—the format is a lovely one and the whole thing is so well set out. Best of all you have sent me No. 36 which is of course 9. What could be luckier? I am glad, though what I have done is so minimal, to be mentioned in it."

The Armonk team's experience with the Vandercooks prompted the later use of similar presses by the Work in Los Angeles and New Hampshire. When Armonk closed in the mid-1980s, the presses were put in storage before being given to another New York group on "permanent loan." Subsequently, one of the presses found its way to the New York Foundation's Lake property near Monticello, New York, in March 2000, and the other to another work place, the old Firehouse at Sparkill.

I have hesitated to point any morals or draw any inferences from the work around the presses, but perhaps it is enough to say that the demands of this particular craft enabled a few of us to explore unknown and unexpected reaches of ourselves. For myself, it was never any question that Fairfax Hall had given the initial impulse, and I think he would have appreciated—and perhaps even have been surprised at—the sincerity of our efforts.

*   *   *

The icehouse at Armonk being readied for its last season as the print shop in 1988.

The print shop at Armonk being spruced up for its last season of use, in 1988.

CONSONANTS

g is hard, except in Akhaldangez-poodjnisovors (p. 300).

All *h*'s pronounced *kh* except in the words Heropass (p. 35), Hasnamuss (p. 203), Hanbledzoin (p. 871) where it is pronounced *gh* like a stronger *kh* (voiced).

The *h* is omitted in Heptaparaparshinokh (p. 84) which is pronounced *Eptaparaparshinokh*, and in Hadji (p. 568) which is pronounced *Adji*.

r is slightly rolled.

s is usually *s*, but more like *ss* in Ors (p. 52) [Orss], and Kesdjan (p. 764) [Kessdjan].

z is pronounced *ts* except in the following words:

Khaizarian (p. 13)
Beelzebub (p. 31*)
Triamazikamno (p. 137*)
Aliamizoornakalu (p. 175, 176)
Zadik (p. 210)
Akhaldangezpoodjnisovors (p. 300)
Zalnakatar (p. 308)
Alstoozori (p. 312)
Dzedzatzshoon (p. 542)
Zoostat (p. 559, 564)

4

This is a typical page in the *Pronunciation Guide* showing the consonants.

TRULY spiritual life is characterized
by the experience of emptiness. In itself this emptiness is presented as absolute freedom, in a consciousness linked
on all sides; as an ultimate experience,
which however many experiences con-
ceal; and having the taste of eternity:
however, it is initially so fleeting that
it is not clear whether it can be compared with one whole second of our
earthly clocks. And the subtle joy that
it uncovers, such that all other joys
seem coarse in comparison, will not
save us from the sorrow of discouragement—if not despair, from which it
seems the certainty that it gives should
preserve one—sorrow, discouragement,

To Live in Emptiness: The first page of text, all hand
set in 14-point Caslon type, the "house" font of the
print shop at Armonk. Printed in an edition of 100
copies in 1981.

The icehouse at Armonk, in summer.

The icehouse at Armonk, in winter.

CHAPTER 10

John Pentland:
The Lordly Line of High Sinclair

HENRY JOHN SINCLAIR, Lord Pentland, has been accorded such a central place in the history of Gurdjieff's work in the West that, aside from my own sober respect for him, anything I might I add to the rich lore of glowing paeans, baseless scuttlebutt, fawning adulation, endless gossip, cult-like worship, gratuitous slander, and outright ignorance of the man could be considered superfluous.

Like many others who were around the Gurdjieff Foundation in New York in the '60s, '70s and '80s, I have my own personal remembrances of my encounters with him. Each of them was *sui generis*, unique, one of a kind: he rarely seemed to repeat himself. As so many have made evident, he seemed a subtle and ubiquitous presence, whether you were in his groups (as I was not) or merely "knew him" by dint of passing him on the stairs.

I first heard of him while I was in the Cape Town group, preparing to go to Franklin Farms. Fairfax Hall ran down a brief list of people I was likely to meet, and Pentland was among them. I immediately imagined a pompous and plump and self-important Colonel Blimp, of the kind who hung out

Lord Pentland at Armonk, 1965.
Photo: Library archive, Gurdjieff Foundation, New York.

in stuffy oak-lined clubs and spent much of the day smoking cigars and reading the London *Times*. Having grown up in the colonial—and anti-colonial—setting of South Africa, I was used to, although not inured to, the type. I had done my own reading on the circumstances surrounding the Boer War, and had taken an instant dislike to people like the imperious Alfred Milner, who had rather presumptuously (as victors do) chosen the title of Lord of Cape Town and St. James when he was elevated to the peerage. And out there in the former colonies, those who put on British airs put them on to the nth degree, imitation being the ultimate form of ingratiation. I remember a headmaster of a leading school—he had been a well-known South African cricketer—who was so stiff and formal and put on such airs that one would think he had the handle of a cricket bat irretrievably stuck up his rear. So I already had half a notion about this British aristocrat whom I might meet at Mendham.

Of course, looking back at *my* own inconsequential self, I realize now what a half-conscious fog I lived in, and I could hardly be representative of anything but the somnambulistic "machine" that Gurdjieff so tellingly described. Indeed, as Madame de Hartmann put it when I first arrived at the farm, I was just "a piece of the furniture." Taking the kitchen swill to the pigs each day was probably the occupation for which I was best, if not eminently, qualified.

My first meetings with Pentland were minimal. Three minor incidents stayed in my mind. One was an occasion when I actually asked a question at the Sunday-afternoon question period at Mendham. He gave me a response that went way over my head, and I countered by saying that he had not heard my question! Another was at Christmas, when he came through the woods below Madame Ouspensky's garden. I was doing something or other at the top of the so-called kitchen gardens. He stopped, said a few words, and then pulled a folding hair brush from his pocket and offered it to me as a Christmas present. I wasn't sure "where he was coming from," but I accepted it and thanked him. Intuitively I knew that he was sizing me up. In any event, I have kept the brush to this day, along with the safety razor given me by Miss Dickson, who assured me that it had belonged to Mr. Ouspensky; I could never be sure! And the third was once when I had helped to make up a list of the men's teams and he asked me on what I had based my assignments. It was a question that put me to wondering how I did indeed approach that work.

I saw very little of him in the next few years, as Mendham was closed about a year after Madame Ouspensky's death and the practical work shifted first to the Foundation and then to Armonk. At Armonk, which formally opened for work in January 1965, I was automatically labeled an "Ouspenskian" because of having lived at Mendham, and the new Young Turks of that time rode rather roughshod over one and all as they ushered in what they hoped would be the total antithesis of the Mendham experience. It did not turn out quite the way they had imagined it would, and after a year or two of rather healthy ferment there were quite a few casualties and defections.

I had been quietly if not dutifully taking part in the activities while at the same time watching some of these antics when Pentland came to me one day and said Madame de Salzmann wanted me to be on the Armonk council. By then I was in Group Two, which met regularly with Madame de Salzmann, so she had some knowledge of me. After having borne the gratuitous slights of those early Armonk years, I took some satisfaction in announcing to the council—at my very first meeting with them—that I was there "because you are failures." The worm had turned! I have no doubt that this instantly endeared me to them. Meanwhile, Madame de Salzmann had asked me to meet with Henri Tracol, her chief aide, who, to my astonishment, laid out for me some of the immense problems that the New Yorkers faced. There were many divergent undercurrents at the time, since the leadership was comprised of Gurdjieffians, Ouspenskians, and Orageans, each camp steadfastly loyal to their origins and claiming their own tangents on the truth. In any event, I sensed that what was needed from the council was some independent thinking, and not, "What would they [the leadership] like us to say?"

My early "elevation" to the council was really the beginning of my long acquaintance with Pentland. Our dealings were still more or less at arm's length, since I was not in any of his groups. But he made a practice of lunching once a week with the council, while we were always drawn into meetings with Group One (and Madame de Salzmann when she was in town). Additionally, there was always some interchange with Pentland about Foundation and Armonk matters.

I got my first real taste of the sharpness of his mind—or wits, perhaps—one morning before the day was to begin at Armonk. I was walking towards the house when he passed me by the fountain, pondering (I imagined) the material he was about to bring to the gathering. He asked me something. I responded with an idiomatic expression that I don't now remember. I was only halfway through the idiom when, quick as a flash, he had already responded as if he had already heard the whole thought.

Pentland held me—as I am sure he did others—in thrall with the rapier-like incisiveness of his thought. When he spoke about Mr. Gurdjieff's ideas, I would find myself raptly following his reasoning step by step, and then feeling a sense of satisfaction at having been able to do that. And in the very moment of silently conceding how absolutely right he was in his argument, I would wake to the new fact that he was in the process of establishing what appeared to be a totally contradictory position. (Indeed, I recall that I once subtly contradicted one of my older fellow speakers at lunch. She waited for me as we left the dining room, and in icy tones declared, "Frank, you did a Pentland on me," and stalked off.)

I suppose it took me many years of turning mental somersaults before I began to step back, as it were, allowing him to make his assertions without being intellectually seduced, and accepting this demonstration of a way of thinking that could embrace the contradictions and the opposites. It was a challenge to my ordinary way of thinking. At the same time, it demanded an awareness of my lack of suppleness, my automatic judgment, and the limitations of my own rigidity of thought.

Of course, I came to learn that he had been president of the Cambridge Union, the university's debating society, which was a traditional stepping-stone to high positions in politics and public life. Although he did not go into public life to the same extent that many eminent members of his family had—they ranked high in the annals of the British raj in India, among other places—Pentland was a natural-born politician. If he had not found his true vocation in serving the Work, I have no doubt that he could certainly have made his mark in politics. It was said that he considered politics an art of a high order. When I once muttered ever so delicately to Madame de Salzmann about some alleged "stunt" that he had pulled, Madame quietly assured me that "the Work would not be what it is today without the things he has done."

In later years I came to appreciate Pentland as indeed a "remarkable man," fit perhaps to be numbered among the pantheon of eminent Gurdjieffians. Pentland certainly met one of Gurdjieff's criteria—that "he can be called a remarkable man who stands out from those around him by the resourcefulness of his mind." I think he made exceptional efforts to live up to the second of Gurdjieff's criteria: "to be restrained in the manifestations which proceed[ed] from his nature." And especially in his last years he surely was an exemplar of the third: "conducting himself justly and tolerantly towards the weaknesses of others."

He was able to move with seeming ease in many worlds, and was indefatigable in his attention to and care for the integrity of the Work. Several people occasionally recalled that Gurdjieff had "appointed" a number among his followers to be his representative in the New World, but no one apparently took it as seriously as Pentland, or was better qualified. As he expressed it in his own obtuse style, the way Gurdjieff left things at his death "made it perfectly easy for me to have to really enter in a position of responsibility as such."[1] He had found his true calling.

Pentland had spent roughly 10 years under the Ouspenskys' wing before meeting Gurdjieff. Like so many others of the post-World War II era, he spent only a short time—a mere nine months—with Gurdjieff before Gurdjieff's death. I believe he had been irrevocably touched by these encounters. Yet I am sure it was the enormous influence of Madame de Salzmann that enabled people like him to find their true bearings in their understanding of the Work, and I felt that he had conscientiously accepted to work under her extraordinary guidance until his death in 1984.

Pentland was an engineer by training, and the methodical and sober application of his thought was clearly demonstrated in the unpublished writings and talks, some of which I had been privileged to read when Lady Pentland occasionally would show me his drafts on different subjects. I received the impression of a man who would consider a subject from one "angle" of approach; then there would be another paper that might include much of the same material but in a different order of progression, and often yet a third paper. I imagine that these were more often than not his drafts in preparation for the Tuesday-evening theme meetings at the Foundation. In the end, however, he appeared to have moved beyond the language of those eminently rational and masterfully constructed expositions to a subtler understanding. In any event, I had always thought of those meetings when he was "up front" as being perhaps in the tradition of those great fiery debates in the old Tibet that one reads about. I, for one, rarely missed the opportunity to be present when he spoke.

Of course, he was not always (as many of his pupils would have one believe) absolutely infallible or immaculate in his perception. For example, I was once given the responsibility to finish some project associated with the new house at Armonk. I made all the preparations, and then to my chagrin someone came in during my absence one weekend and took over the job. I met Pentland in the basement of the Foundation and I told him rather sourly that I felt he had undercut the responsibility with which I had been entrusted. It was a question of principle, I said. He responded, as quick as a flash, "There is no principle. There is only the man on the spot." I believe that I countered that it was wrong to have "taken *my* work from me." The next day, we saw each other again in the basement, and he said, "I have thought about what you said. You are right." That was perhaps the only time he ever conceded to me that he might have been wrong or actually expressed his regret.

Of course, one had always to have one's wits about one. I often suspected that "commands" that supposedly came down from Pentland were probably often of the same order as those that came down from Madame Ouspensky's room, where she was bedridden and mute. So I must confess that I did not always automatically jump to attention when certain "orders" were conveyed. One day, on walking into the Foundation, someone unceremoniously greeted me with the words, "Lord Pentland wants you to do such and such." True or not, I felt there would be no feudal throwback for me! My "Gurdjieffian calm" was instantly shattered by their presumption that I would simply come to heel, but I said slowly, cuttingly, and quite audibly for all within earshot, "I am not Lord Pentland's dog." It was a more or less formal declaration of independence that was true to the spirit of our ancestry, should one need to give a reason! I half suspected that *my* remark would be reported back to him. But I was quite relieved that I heard no more.

Towards the end of his life, Pentland revealed something to me that cast further light on his own mode, or style, of thinking. One day we were the first to arrive in the room known as the Apartment, waiting for the Group Two members to arrive. I had been thinking about the nature of thinking. I said I was interested in the different kinds of thought; that I thought that Ouspensky's recollection of Gurdjieff's ideas was an extraordinary feat; and that this was something beyond my own capacity. Pentland responded quite matter-of-factly that neither could he ever do what Ouspensky had done: "I could never do that." Elsewhere, Pentland had written with total generosity: "Probably his [Ouspensky's] achievement will never be equaled."[2]

My greatest impression of Pentland was that he was invariably prepared. Often, what appeared to be brilliant improvisation also had the feel of calculated intent. He would deftly introduce a seemingly unrelated idea and establish the connection as if it were totally natural and spontaneous, or he would steer an exchange as if extemporaneously to a premeditated idea that he considered more central. Whether it was premeditated or a sudden inspiration, his ideas invariably carried provocative weight and conviction.

But I also saw him as a true man of action. He himself drew the extraordinary image of such a being in a talk titled "On Economy of Energy."[3] "The image of economy we are speaking of is not of the engineer who dams up the river but the man of knowledge who is able to leap from rock to rock across the crest of the waterfall, that is, who is aware of the apparently superabundant energy that is flowing out in all directions outside him and inside him, but even while this is going on is able to preserve intact his own sense of will and movement." He added: "What is this inner movement, this inner sense of economy, which makes it possible to feel the [flow] of energy with wonder, without losing perspective and at the same time to move up against the stream—and so escape altogether from the idea of potential energy and entropy, an energy that is running down?" And in a subtle delineation of the forces at play, he concluded that we indulge our desire for energy "when in fact it is only the feeling of lacking energy that brings me back to awareness."

Lord Pentland, Madame de Salzmann, and William Segal at lunch, Armonk, 1965.

Understandably, Pentland's subtlety and finesse were more than many could fathom. Quite a few senior people, both in the Americas and abroad, confessed that they could not understand him, and one senior Briton once admitted to me that Pentland's was a language with which he was not familiar. Naturally, he had many imitators among his students, tortuously attempting to play with contradictions and often tying themselves in mental and verbal knots, while muddying the waters with their shallow obfuscations.

Of course, there were inevitable and often pathetic misunderstandings, just as there obviously were with Gurdjieff. Complaints by some with overly delicate sensibilities, and who soon passed from the scene, that he did not "succor" them enough. Gratuitous assessments by total outsiders and strangers of his comparative worth as a leader of the Work. And heaven knows what else. But like Gurdjieff, he appeared to understand this as an inevitable part of the price to be paid in the service of the Work.

As with one or two others of my elders, I could never bring myself around to calling him by his first name. He was always *Lord* Pentland to me. And although we were namesakes and members, as it were, of the same clan, I doubt that we were even remotely related. Still, Madame de Salzmann said to me in private one day that it was a "big thing to be a child of the Work," apparently thinking, I suppose, that I must be Pentland's offspring. Indeed, on one of the first occasions on which I went to Los Angeles, a woman waylaid me after a group meeting, demanding to know if I was related to Lord Pentland or to Lady Pentland. I said to her, "I am related to both—by blood!" I placed an intentionally cryptic emphasis on the *blood*. She hurried away appropriately mystified.

As I learned only much later when I began to delve into these things, Pentland's lineage was—at least in the British world, where these things appeared to count—quite impressive. He was the son of the first Baron Pentland, who was Secretary of State for Scotland and Governor of Madras,

India. It seemed his father had been "kicked upstairs," booted into the peerage, as it were, to get him out of the way, as is the custom in politics. When I first met John Pentland, in 1958, he was about 51. He had come into his title at 18. He was the grandson of the seventh Earl and first Marquess of Aberdeen, who was Governor-General of Canada, and of the ninth Earl of Elgin, who served as Viceroy of India. Elgin, of course, was a name not unknown in South Africa or, for that matter, in Greece, which to this day claims that the so-called Elgin Marbles were stolen.

The Sinclair clan has a rich and honored lore. The current chief, the Earl of Caithness, quotes an unnamed source in saying, "No family in Europe beneath the rank of Royalty boasts a higher antiquity, a nobler illustration, or a more romantic interest than that of St. Clair." The senior branch of the clan, "the lordly line of high Sinclair," as Sir Walter Scott phrased it, is descended from the Norse Jarls, or princes, of the ninth century. Beyond that, I have difficulty unravelling the lineages, since cousins contended with cousins in the intricate intrigues of medieval times. For example, while one "branch" of the clan arrived in the British Isles with William the Conqueror, one of whose principal knights, Sir William Sinclair, was a Norman, another branch was fighting against the Conqueror.

In any event, the Sinclairs were firmly established in Scotland in 1162, when Henry de St. Clair of Roslin was granted lands in Lothian. A descendant, Sir William, gained the Barony of Rosslyn in 1280. His son, Sir Henry, fought with Robert the Bruce when the English were routed at Bannockburn, and was one of the Scottish barons who signed a letter to the Pope asserting Scottish independence.

The Sinclairs (St. Clairs) of Rosslyn, which is situated in the Pentland Hills, near Edinburgh, have long been linked with the Knights Templar, for example. It has been argued that the Knights Templar, an order of warrior-monks dissolved by King Philip of France in 1307, underwrote the struggle by the Bruce and Sinclair clans to gain independence from England. The castle and chapel complex at Roslin is "considered one of the wonders of the medieval world."[4]

In recent years, a number of books have even alluded to romantic assertions, seemingly deriving from the French branch, that the "bloodlines of Christ run through the Sinclair family."[5] But this "rank nonsense," as one reviewer described these claims, has now been totally discredited as a patent hoax, and any claim that Pentland was, as some of his more starry-eyed "devotees" might have wished him to be, a descendent of Jesus Christ and Mary Magdalene, must be considered to be totally groundless, thank heaven!

Pentland made quite a few casual references to our ancestry. One day he said to me, "Frank, did you know that one of our ancestors is a white god?" I said I did not know that, but that I did not doubt it! He told me there was a tradition among the Micmac Indians of Nova Scotia that a white god had come to them over the ocean. This "god," it turned out, was [Prince] Henry Sinclair, a Scottish navigator who landed there in 1398, almost a century before Columbus "discovered" the New World. I was intrigued by this, because one of my own forbears, as I have noted, was a Scottish sea captain who was shipwrecked in the 1800s off the rather forbidding southwestern coast of South Africa.

Then there was one occasion when a subtle reference to his nobility helped us both out of a tricky impasse. He had just returned from Paris, and he said to me that he had a message from Madame de Salzmann that he would like to bring to Group Two. In those days, there was a distinct coolness between certain members of Group Two and Group One. Most of Group Two were older people who had met Gurdjieff. However, in one of those odd injustices that characterizes the Work, they were consigned to Group Two, often considered by the supercilious in those early days as a kind of spiritual limbo. Many of the early members of Group Two had no particular regard for their supposedly "more qualified" counterparts in Group One. I myself was in neither camp since I had never met Gurdjieff and owed my presence in Group Two—apart from my objective merits!—to having married someone who had herself met Gurdjieff. (Indeed, for many years I was simply referred to as Miss Rego's husband, hardly the mark of spiritual eminence.)

In any case, I took an active part in the many activities, so it seemed only natural that Pentland should ask me to be the go-between. But I funked the mission, leaving the ticklish confrontation literally to the very last minute. As we gathered for our meeting, and with no escape in view, I hurriedly told them that Pentland wished to join us, and before they had time to respond, why, there he was at the door. "Here he is," I said. He took a seat, and a painful silence followed. I was quietly writhing in discomfort. Suddenly I remembered that, in parliamentary circles—and, I imagine, in the British House of Lords—when the sergeant-at-arms saw someone who did not belong in the chamber, he would call to the Speaker, "There is a stranger in the House." I spoke up, saying how difficult I found the moment, especially since "there is a stranger in the House." That broke the ice, and Pentland was able to bring his message.

I was rather pleased at having got us all out of a difficult situation. But the next day, as I stood at the urinal in the men's room, I was aware that a tall person had arrived at the adjoining space. Inclining his head ever so slightly my way, he said, with a slight touch of feigned sadness, "Frank, how could you call me a stranger?" He was right, of course. But I was still rather pleased at the way I got us out of that predicament.

It was always evident, from the things he said and did, that he himself was keenly aware of the unhealthy adulation and its inevitable opposite that surrounded him as a "leader." He was aware, as he once wrote of New Age leaders, that "the higher energy released under the leader's direction has to go somewhere and will inevitably be associated by the members [of the group] with the leader's person and organization, causing an emotional cycle: first affection, then loyalty, and finally disappointment at the lack of 'progress.'"[6]

There was little danger that I would have fallen into that adulatory trap. For many years there had been a deep streak of cynicism in me, stemming from events in my childhood, and I found I could not resist a compelling urge to provoke him at every turn. I was fascinated by the quickness and sharpness of his mind, and I figuratively jumped through hoops to joust with him. It was a lopsided match. Only years later did I find out that there were times when I had crossed the line of decency and decorum, and that he had been dismayed by my antics. Only then did it dawn on me that in his measured responses to my not-so-subtle goads he was resisting mere automatic reaction: instead, he gave me "his work." I believe I came to this realization while he was still alive. By that time he too had mellowed. I even heard it said that he had regretted having hurt some people in his lifetime (with his cleverness and quickness of mind). He showed himself to me to be a man of compassion and feeling.

I am probably not mistaken when I say that the only time he did not play quite so dazzlingly with his sharp wit and intellect was in the company of Madame de Salzmann. In meetings with her he was clearly more muted, less indulgent of his lightning-quick wit. He acknowledged her profound understanding. I had an unexpected confirmation of this when I made my first visit to Los Angeles with him, probably in the late 1970s or early '80s. (Lady Pentland had just begun to go there, and I surmise that she had recommended to him that I accompany her. He had therefore invited me to dinner to size me up, saying, "I know nothing about you," which gratified me immensely to hear. I had no particular interest in "togetherness" as such: I too valued my own privacy.)

On my first morning at the work house in Los Angeles, as I sat at breakfast with him, he unexpectedly announced that I should bring the task for the day. I countered that people had come to hear *him* speak, not me. He looked at his wristwatch, and said quietly, "You have ten minutes." I raced back to my room to gather my thoughts, and then returned to face the music. After I had delivered my rather lame opening remarks, he and I walked out of the room together. I found myself moved to confess to him, "In moments like this, we who are younger can grant that you who are older know more than we do." With unexpected candor, he shot right back, "And Madame [de Salzmann] runs rings around *us*."

And Madame runs rings around us. What a telling corrective to all the benighted talk down the years of his infallible pre-eminence. I felt that in the true feudal spirit he had pledged his fealty to Madame de Salzmann, and he never appeared to betray that. Yes, he was the president, but anyone who overheard or participated in meetings of his own peer group in those decades would know that no single person set the tone for them or gave the orders, and no quarter was given. How he was perceived "out there" on the street or in the provinces was quite another matter.

Certainly the most "delicate" moment in our acquaintance occurred once when we had one of our periodic "men's lunches" with Madame de Salzmann. There were perhaps a dozen of us. The conversation had stalled for a moment. Searching for something to contribute, I spoke about the conflict that arose in me when working with leaders who had "feet of clay." I suppose my allusions were quite blatant. One might even say that the behavior I alluded to was simply his exercising of some old feudal prerogatives that shall be nameless. Pentland, who was sitting beside Madame, turned to me with a studied deliberation that barely concealed his icy anger. The image sprang to mind of a fox turning on its pursuers. He curled a lip and said, "I am not a role model." There was the proverbial deathly silence. After what seemed a long time, and no one having dared to speak, I mumbled something that appeared to ease the tension, and the conversation resumed as if nothing had happened. Later I connected this incident with Ouspensky's report of Gurdjieff's having said, "We do not teach morality. We teach how to come to conscience." Pentland's dramatic response was another pointed lesson for me about being in the real world.

I must state very clearly that I did not have—and still do not have, and certainly never will have—even the remotest understanding or knowledge of his vast and seemingly ubiquitous labors in helping to organize and maintain the Work in the United States. He played a major role in bringing Gurdjieff's and Ouspensky's books to publication in English. It is a matter of record that he advised many authors and wrote a number of forewords to books published by Far West Editions. He was, it was said, a "pivotal force" behind the biennial program of public lectures in San Francisco between 1974 and 1984 that saw a variety of prominent speakers explore some of the timeless concerns for meaning in a materialistic world. He was also, I suspect, the major fundraiser for Madame de Salzmann's film projects. And it was he, I gather, who set up Triangle Editions, Inc. in New York to guard the copyrights, ensure the authenticity of the Gurdjieff books and films, and achieve an uneasy peace with Gurdjieff's heirs who under French law were entitled to profit from Gurdjieff's books and music.

And like so many charismatic leaders, he drew around himself—just as Gurdjieff himself had—not only a range of sober citizenry and people of responsibility in all walks of life, but also a strange spectrum of the odd, the unstable, the borderline, and the definitely abnormal. Of the latter, I recall at least one man who believed himself to be Jesus Christ; fortunately, he went off, I assume, to pursue his messianic dreams on his own. Pentland was indeed a man of the world, "organizing and reorganizing and reorganizing," as he once pointed out,[7] to achieve the conditions required to bring the necessary pressures to bear. There are others who were close to those events and undertakings, and they can better bear witness to those endeavors than I can.

Given my seemingly peripheral relationship to Pentland, who was old enough to be my father, I was truly surprised when, at his death in February 1984, his family called me after midnight to ask that I read a passage from the New Testament at his funeral service later that day. Although Pentland was nominally Presbyterian, the service was held in (the Catholic) St. Vincent Ferrer's at Lexington Avenue and 66th Street, a church with which I was familiar because I would often go there to sit quietly before my meetings. The priest who had arranged the service and who "directed" the proceedings had actually attended meetings and movements classes at the Foundation, although I never saw him again after Pentland's death.

The text I was given to read was from Corinthians II. I read it again and again that night, and again in my office, to be sure I could read it without falling into a priestly drone. It was an extraordinary moment for me—a nonentity of the first order—to mount the pulpit and to read this profound material in front of that large and attentive congregation. There were several hundred people, most of whom probably had far more direct and intimate contact with him than I ever had. I was especially alert because his daughter, Mary, had preceded me in the pulpit, and her voice broke momentarily as she read a moving description of the death of a Sinclair chieftain.

Purely for the record, I should correct two statements in a later book about my role in that service.[8] I was never, as the author declared, "a long-time pupil of Lord Pentland's," nor did I end the reading by saying, "Lord Pentland believed in the mystery of the Resurrection." The truth is that I read only the text from the Gospel, and added nothing to it. I also had no idea whether Pentland "believed in the mystery of the Resurrection."

I suppose there was some awesome irony in the fact that, about 16 years after his death and about four decades after I was booted out of Mendham, I was elected (in April 2000) to the role of co-president[9] of the Gurdjieff Foundation. As I explained it to anyone who asked, someone had to sign the checks. I never considered the presidency in itself to be a sign of spiritual advancement. In any event, no one could conceivably regard me as even remotely Pentland's equal.

Is there one thing that, for me, encapsulates Pentland's significance in the Work? Perhaps he expressed it best in one of his last interviews: "The growth of being and the balancing of deficiencies takes place through the interaction between people, of whom the leader is a principal but with whom the leader is sharing his life, subjecting himself to all the forces and pressures and difficulties."[10] In this he was indeed a role model.

It was an extraordinary privilege and a rare gift to be engaged, however peripherally, in the search for understanding with this unusual and remarkable man.

NOTES

1. John Pentland, introduction, *Exchanges Within*, Continuum, New York, 1997, p. xxii.
2. John Pentland, foreword to Jean Vaysse's *Toward Awakening*, Harper & Row, New York, 1979, p.xi.
3. John Pentland, unpublished paper, courtesy of Lady Pentland.
4. Steven Sora, *The Lost Treasure of the Knights Templar*, Destiny Books, Rochester, Vermont, 1999, p. 116.
5. See Michael Bageant, Richard Leigh, Henry Lincoln, *Holy Blood, Holy Grail*, Dell Publishing, New York, 1983.
6. Lord Pentland, "On Growth Centers," *Material for Thought*, No.12, Far West Publications, San Francisco, 1990, p. 1.
7. Lord Pentland, interview, *Gurdjieff, Essays and Reflections*, Needleman and Baker, Continuum, 1996, p. 389.
8. Wm. James Patterson, *Eating the "I"*, Arete Communications, San Anselmo, CA, p. 350.
9. A position shared with Paul Reynard.
10. *Gurdjieff, Essays and Reflections*, p. 389.

Bill Segal working on the roof of the new dining
room at Armonk, 1965. *Photo: Library archive,*
Gurdjieff Foundation.

CHAPTER 11

Bill Segal: The Radical Reorientation

WILLIAM C. SEGAL was the "quiet American" among the older men at the Gurdjieff Foundation. Soft-spoken and courteous, he had a big influence on many in and around the New York Foundation in my time. But behind this gentle self-composure one could discern a man with all the street smarts of a boy who had been expected to provide for himself from an early age. He had a steely grasp of the ways of the world. A successful businessman, he knew how to run a tight and profitable ship.

I knew Bill Segal from my earliest days at Franklin Farms. For years I would recall with some embarrassment that when Beatrice asked that I meet him and his first wife, Cora, at his home in Chester, a few miles from the Ouspensky estate, I regaled him with my ideas of what the Work was all about. He listened with a gracious bemusement, but made no comment.

I had few direct dealings with him for several years, since my ties were primarily with Martin Benson when I was at Franklin Farms and later at Armonk, and increasingly with Lord Pentland. Still, there was one interesting occasion that cast a revealing perspective on the man.

In the last year or so of Franklin Farms, Madame de Hartmann told us she would be visiting India, and Beatrice asked her to try to "find" her sister there. Her sister had taken her vows as Swami Lalitananda after following the well-known Swami Sivananda to his ashram in Rishikesh. Madame de Hartmann, who could be relentless and dogged in any pursuit, eventually tracked her down. She was living off the premises in rather squalid conditions. When Madame de Hartmann returned to the U.S., she reported that Beatrice's sister had an extraordinary companion, Swami Jyotirmayananda, a brilliant young Hindu monk. When her sister eventually returned to the States, she brought Swami Jyotirmayananda with her. At Madame de Hartmann's invitation, they both appeared at Mendham one Sunday in their orange robes and sat at one end of the "head table" during the afternoon question-and-response period. I am sure the swami would have loved to respond to a question or two, but of course he was not given the opportunity. He truly was—and is—a brilliant man, a classic yogi. He was fluent in English, had earned a degree in biology, and made a deep impression on me with his command of Sanskrit and his chanting of the Bhagavad-Gita and other sacred texts.

Soon after visiting Mendham, Madame de Hartmann arranged that Swami Jyotirmayananda meet Group One for tea at the Foundation. All went swimmingly until Segal spoke rather condescendingly of the swami's "withdrawal" from life. The swami asserted his own vision, and Segal countered with his, saying that those in the Fourth Way were more advanced in their understanding. I don't know exactly what transpired then, but I could see that Segal was just a bit ruffled by the encounter. The swami, on the other hand, reveled in the exchange and in the rectitude of his own tradition.

Segal, of course, was well known around Madison Avenue for his interest in Zen. In fact, once when I dropped his name at a business lunch, my guest said, "Oh yes, Bill Segal the yogi." Indeed, members of Segal's groups habitually meditated quite openly, sitting cross-legged around the property at Franklin Farms, much to the consternation of the old Ouspenkians.

It was perhaps only in the last decade of his life that I had a more direct involvement with Segal, and I think the common ground between us was the understanding that the Work is in and for life (both in terms of the sacred and the profane). I believe we both understood that it is meaningless to "make a career" in the Work, as some appeared to do, while being an unregenerate misfit in "the world out there."

I came to see more of Segal after his automobile accident. The fact that his car was a massive old Chrysler New Yorker, a pre-OPEC gas-guzzling monster that resembled a truck, must have contributed to his extensive injuries. It was a shock to see him walk into the building on his return. For one moment I did not believe it could be the same handsome athlete I had seen around Mendham. I had not been prepared for the change. Here was a man humbled both in his pride and in his prime. The man whom I used to see jogging to work in the woods, where he would swing a mean axe, was now mangled and bent.

Having lived somewhat in the ubiquitous shadow of Pentland, he slowly came into his own at the Foundation. Although he did not speak much, he brought a certain sense of presence that communicated what was timeless. I append the following little review of Segal's collected writings (under the title of *Openings*) because I believe I caught in it something of the essence of his vision. He managed to meld a special insight into the way of Zen with the teaching of Gurdjieff in such a way that neither appeared to be compromised. This was not a "synthesis" of the paths, but rather a special understanding of the "transcendent unity" of all the ways. As Gurdjieff would say, all roads lead to Philadelphia.

Of course, such a vision is barely comprehensible to most people. After I had plied an obituarist from *The New York Times* with endless source material, quotations, and explanatory e-mails following Segal's death in 2000, at the age of 96, the reporter confessed that he really did not understand what it was that Segal "did." I think Segal would have been pleased both at the writer's mystification and his honesty.

In any event, this is the review that I wrote for *Parabola*:

This small compendium of writings by William Segal is disarmingly modest in scope. Yet it provides a timeless authentication that the mystery at the core of the great traditions can be approached only through a radical reorientation. Now in his nineties, Segal is clearly a man who, in his own words, has learned to love the Silence.

A careful reading of these pieces, many of them quite short, reveals that his spiritual linkage can be traced to several profound—and direct—influences. Among them are P. D. Ouspensky, the Russian mathematician/philosopher, G.I. Gurdjieff (Ouspensky's own mentor), both of whom he met in the 1940's, and Dr. Daisetz Suzuki, the Japanese Zen master. Through the latter, Segal was able to spend a great deal of time at the main Rinzai and Soto monasteries in Japan. Moreover, as a successful businessman, he has in his own individual way combined a life devoted to the wisdom of the East with the practical and secular opportunities available to people of the West.

In this collection, he echoes Gurdjieff's special vision when he declares that "The role of a conscious human being is to provide the phenomenal earth world with energies which otherwise would not be effectively transmitted to the creations and units which make up our world." And following Gurdjieff, he calls attention to the largely neglected need to study "the relationship of oneself to the interplay of energies that make up the body/mind structure." Change, he adds, begins with "seeing the state of one's body, tension-filled or tension-free; with seeing one's vagrant associations and reactions; and with the hard-won capacity to maintain the priority of that which sees."

Similarly, he echoes his monastic friends in Zen in typically brief meditative passages: "Quietly watching, anticipating nothing, I am open to what is here, now . . . . I am the witness and the witnessing, passively watching and actively being watched."

Certainly, one senses that Segal approaches his writing—as he does his painting—with the same mindfulness or "all-embracing attention." The disarming simplicity and directness of his writing might belie the profundity of the experience that clearly informs it. Yet what he conveys through these authentic insights is a call to a deeper understanding. This understanding, he reminds us, can be found only through a "deep alteration," a "radical shift" in our being. Clearly, certain inner conditions need to be met in order that this occur. "Change, movement, liberation are possible. But until conscience, deeply buried in the subconscious, is aroused, one may never unveil the feeling needed to create and sustain the human link to another order of energy."

As those who know and respect him can attest, Segal's insight and simplicity enable him to convey with conviction that "The sole reality is consciousness, and consciousness only." Both in word and in deed, he bears sober witness to the presence and the force of "an unchanging inner stillness." *Openings* is a book which speaks to those who share an interest in opening to this "hidden reality" while remaining firmly planted on the earth. [1]

Segal left his benign mark on many people, both in the Work and outside—and especially on people who themselves were very much men (and women) of the world. As for my own special memories of the man? I will mention one more— the occasion when we attended a performance of Peter Brook's "The Man who Mistook his Wife for a Hat" at the Brooklyn

Academy of Music. At the reception afterwards, we were offered some wine. I asked Segal if he would like some. Segal, who was close to 90 then, declined. He said to me, "At my age, I only drink the best." He was always, as they say, a class act.

NOTES

1.   *Parabola*, Vol. XXIII, No. 3, August 1998, p. 88.

Madame Jeanne de Salzmann.
Photo: Institut Gurdjieff, Paris.

CHAPTER 12

Jeanne de Salzmann:
A Compelling Call

IT TOOK ME many years, as it did for so many others, to catch the drift of Madame de Salzmann's most compelling call—her invitation to us to follow the movement of an energy coming from "a higher part of the mind."

Although some intrepid souls like Ravi Ravindra have written openly about this special work—risking, as he said, both misunderstanding and misappropriation[1]—trying to describe it to the unprepared probably leads to wild imaginings, like the wishful attempts by pious Western devotees to rouse the Kundalini and other fanciful projections of the sort. [2]

Now that Gurdjieff's ideas have reached academia—a destination often fatal to the transmission of essential meaning—there is good reason for the lowly "troops in the trenches" to be reminded that a special work whose avowed end is transformation lies at the core of the teaching. All else is truly secondary.

Certainly, there are timely warnings coming from both within and without the pale that serious seekers of the post-Gurdjieffian era need to have their wits about them. One sympathizes completely with those who would wish to help "the Gurdjieff tradition avoid the trap of becoming an institutionalized religion,"[3] if it is indeed a "new" tradition. One also appreciates the ever timely scholarly reminder of the "paradox that while all religious institutions seek to protect and preserve the teachings [of the founder], they do tend to kill them."[4] As well we all ought to be warned. Nevertheless, one should question in these warnings the further inferences about the alleged passivity of the "establishments," and the ostensible movement towards the establishment of "the Gurdjieff Church."[5] The point is that these assertions, as well as others made on the esoteric lecture circuit, raise some fundamental questions: Can the teaching be sustained and preserved through vacating the true center, that is, by "being mixed in with other traditions,"[5] or in searching for the "teachers of Gurdjieff" a la Rafael Lefort and others, and—if I may say it—thereby abandoning its very specificity?

It might seem hugely paradoxical to some that when Gurdjieff and his fellow Seekers of Truth sought a hidden teaching, it must have been shielded, sometimes even for many generations . . . and sustained . . . and once again rediscovered, alive and intact—*in an institutional setting*. How else but as institutions does one describe those hidden monasteries, world brotherhoods, anonymous schools, and other repositories of an ancient knowledge to which Gurdjieff alludes? This does not discount the insight that the real preservation is accomplished through an exchange that takes place between the institutional establishments and the individual seekers. There are levels within these institutions, circles within circles, all ensuring the invisibility of the understanding at the center.

For all the "critical appreciation of Gurdjieff's texts"[6] that some academicians might provide, I think one must be cautious, wary of their often all-too-literal "mathematik." If there are those who would see the value of Gurdjieff's teaching primarily in the help it might give to those interested in (say) "the Turkic Oral tradition or in occultism in Russia in the 19th Century, in astrology, Gnosticism, Theosophy," etc., etc.,[7] what then of the teaching's real and deeper significance as an actual *work* for transformation? The teaching loses all its true relevance if it is not seen as Gurdjieff clearly intended—a means to arrive at awakened conscience and the experience of "an unnamable emptiness and silence" while at the same time meeting "the demand to attend to the ordinary life of ourselves as we are," if I may invoke the perceptive insights of Jacob Needleman, an academic well-versed in Gurdjieff's ideas.[8]

Of course, there are those within the "institutions" who understand very well that speaking about the teaching even in its most worldly aspects is so fraught with danger that they wisely choose to remain silent, unseen, unheard, and steadfast to their understanding. One respects that. And it is an example, perhaps, that I myself ought to heed. So, what I am launching into, in what follows, is purely my own personal indulgence. It is not in any way an "institutional" position, not a "party line." My "justification" is that I have attempted simply to point to the central and (to use Rene Daumal's cogent term) "non-Euclidian dimensions" of Madame de Salzmann's message (and consequently of Gurdjieff's). I have done so without benefit of clergy, well knowing that in spite of my seeming "disclosures" it will still remain an essential secret and a mystery. The Unknown does not yield itself through abundant description.

Madame de Salzmann did not appear to speak of some psychic movement of energy, as in healing, but rather of something profoundly subtler. She would indicate the flow of this subtle energy with a gesture almost (dare I say it?) of papal authority—a gesture whose wide adoption by some of her pupils flags the unmistakable provenance of their work. I found for years that this movement or flow was virtually impossible to "achieve." I always felt that the work she indicated derived from deep experience, virtually unfathomable to the rest of us. She spoke with such conviction, with such force, that for several years I sat in thrall in front of her, confounded by my inability to experience what she so clearly called us to experience. When working in front of her, this was the most desirable action to which one could open: to allow this energy to enter and to circulate.

Yet we all—including some vaunted "leaders of the Work"—sat there, it seemed, like dumb oxen, secretly puzzled, mystified, totally inept. I recall that she once said to us assembled "elders" working in front of her, "There is only one among you who understands this effort." And secretly I accepted that it was someone else who understood, and not I. Then, too, "There must be absolutely no tension," she said. We discovered we were full of the most unexpected tension, sometimes barely perceptible. Once while working with her she even pointed to the area of my navel, and said, "You are tense there." And that was exactly where the tension was.

In her last years, she spoke so often, so insistently, so relentlessly, so single-mindedly about this movement of energy that I occasionally thought to myself that she must perhaps be in her dotage, and that her mind was slipping. I discovered only years later that one of her more outspoken critics appeared to contrast Madame unfavorably with his own teacher by saying that she—also a woman—did not "retreat into a single grand verity, wearing it threadbare by endless iteration."[9] I will not dwell too much on this charge, since I did not find that verity to be worn threadbare, rather that one was repeatedly called to turn yet again to the elusive central effort.

Certainly, in her last years, approaching 101, Madame de Salzmann could no longer remember names, even of family members who were close to her. Yet she never sank into the selfish fog of some old icon in decline. But slowly it had become clear to me that this opening to a new inner circulation of energy to which she was so resolutely pointing us, to the very end, was the "next step," the real "inner work" to which all other efforts led.

I recall her saying, in that "endless iteration" at the last January 13 celebration she attended in New York in 1985, that the body needed to be open to a force that comes from a higher part of the mind. This force, she said, was really a second body. Furthermore, this force needed the body, yet the body itself was secondary in importance. One had to let this energy fill oneself entirely, so that one could feel there was in oneself a body which had its own life. Needless to say, this new movement in oneself could not merely be imagined. It required a very exacting engagement of all one's parts.

To some of the Work's old-line practitioners, this kind of language seemed not only difficult to accept but also impossible to understand. It also required a new category of effort not readily comprehensible to the literal mind. Better, they appeared to mumble, to continue making their customary strenuous efforts, punishing the body, taming the mind, obeying the edicts of a "leader." It was quite instructive to see a few of the once loquacious reveal through their body language their unease and discomfort. And yet—Madame de Salzmann had spelled out the enormity (and the subtlety, and the near impossibility) of this work when she had compiled Gurdjieff's early talks. When these talks were published in 1973, she had indicated the implacable conditions that needed to be met: "The transformation of the human being . . . can only be achieved if there is *a real meeting between the conscious force which descends and the total commitment that answers it*. This brings about a fusion" [emphasis added].[10] But *a fusion* is not so easily attained, even though any number of new Young Turks both within and without the "institutional" ranks, ever eager to claim the prize, readily profess their almost proprietary insights into this way of working.

Undeservedly maligned as she was by those "outside the pale," at least Madame de Salzmann had one overarching advantage in conveying this mysterious inner movement of the Work. Her intimate involvement with Gurdjieff and his methods over several decades empowered Madame de

Salzmann to express her understanding with the quiet assurance and conviction that we came to know.

She had no need to apologize for having been able "to study very thoroughly a fundamental characteristic of [Gurdjieff's] teaching, namely, that while the truth sought for was always the same, the forms through which he helped his pupils approach it served only for a limited time. *As soon as a new understanding had been reached, the form would change* [emphasis added]."[11] Many peripheral groups who hold tenaciously, and often even fastidiously, to the "strict" formulations of the teaching as received through Ouspensky and others, appear to find it impossible to bear, or to understand the need, to relinquish old forms and old habits. It was often equally impossible for certain of the mainstream "leaders," several of them of my own acquaintance.

One of the apparent modulations in the undulating landscape of the Work is even considered by the unforgiving to be a paradigm shift of such magnitude away from Gurdjieff's presumed intent—"a doctrinal corollary of seismic implications"[12]—that it might possibly warrant a charge of heresy, as it were, or something of that order. These insistent critics, including some perhaps reluctant to give up their conscious labors in the last ditch (or even their infatuation with those tortuous and misleading redundancies and unwitting structural somersaults in the 1950 *Beelzebub*), have roundly impugned Madame de Salzmann's motives, and continue to do so. Several of them were people who actually worked for a while with her, but most would appear to be people who never met her, or who had only the remotest contact. Many no doubt have only the purest of motives. Yet there are those who argue that Madame de Salzmann and her cadre of "elderly apologists of the new quietism"[13]—noble souls, nonetheless!—have imposed a "New Work," a supposedly passive approach to the work for consciousness and conscience.

I am not familiar with that formal passivity or its promulgation as an institutionalized procedure.

In any event, the general outline of the work that Madame de Salzmann brought so forcefully in her last years is—at least in a rudimentary and external form—no longer entirely a secret, no longer known only to the groups immediately around her. Much of its outer form is, to all appearances, more or less in the public domain now. And she herself contributed to that by speaking freely and openly, to young and old alike, of what had become her central directive, that single grand verity.

Already in the year after my own neophytic arrival at Mendham, Madame de Salzmann was revealing to those budding elders, including John Pentland, William Welch, Christopher Fremantle, William Segal, and their compatriots, a deeper level of the Work. Ethel Merston, visiting New York around that time, was moved to describe it as being the Ramana Maharshi's teaching "word for word." She added, "Gurdjieff must have gone on to it with his more advanced pupils during the Paris years; what he had meant, perhaps, by his 'mesoteric' work."[14]

The truth is precisely in that recognition: that Gurdjieff appears to have been measured and exacting in his unfolding of the essential secrets of his teaching—nothing before its time and nothing without a corresponding preparation. But as he demonstrated in his so-called Fifth Talk to the New York Group on December 19, 1930, and in his challenging "gift" to the people who gathered in the Hotel Wellington, New York, in the early hours of Christmas Day 1948, he could also be almost quixotic in dispensing his spiritual largesse. Several people of my acquaintance, including Louise March and my then-future wife Beatrice, were there that Christmas, and like Martin Benson and others they would recall his extraordinary injunction to go out and "draw in," "steal," or "suck in" the energies being poured out "by millions" of people in prayer, as on that Christmas. (My old notes reveal that within days of my first arrival at Mendham, Benson was drumming into me his account of how Gurdjieff had told him,

"*STEAL* those energies, Benson, *STEAL*. Their prayers cannot reach God." And in the way he spoke, I felt that those injunctions must have dated back to his time at the Prieuré, and not just to that Christmas Day.)

Inevitably, there were only partial recollections of that occasion. For instance, Louise March, German translator of *All and Everything*, displaying uncharacteristic sensitivity, ventured only a skeletal summary of his instruction. Expressed in fewer than 50 words, her recollection has been all but unnoticed in subsequent exegesis:

> "I wish give *real* Christmas present. Imagine Christ. Somewhere in space *is*." Mr. Gurdjieff forms an oval with both his hands. "Make contact, but to outside, periphery. Draw from there, draw in, *I*. Settle in you, *Am*. Do every day. Wish to become Christ. Become. Be."[15]

I dare say that this exercise—in its original formulation and perhaps wrapped up with Gurdjieff's sexist insults, of which the hapless recipient was no doubt fully deserving—will emerge in time on the Internet, reconstructed from the primitive wire recordings made by Donald Whitcomb on that occasion, endlessly fiddled with by Tom Forman over the ensuing years, and now finally in the possession of the Family. Even from this one unadorned account, largely ignored and almost totally overlooked in the literature of the Work, it would appear that Gurdjieff counseled his listeners to turn towards a point "somewhere in space"—someone even said he had referred to a planet, but clearly, then, "above the head," even perhaps "a higher part of the mind"—and consciously draw in a fine energy. One may legitimately say, then, that this was a movement "all of a piece" with the work he had been giving for years and which Madame de Salzmann later brought as her "single grand verity." Indeed, the kind of directives given later by Michel de Salzmann in his turn were equally all of a piece with this distinctive Gurdjieffian line of work.

But to return to that Christmas Day. As some were still able to recall, Gurdjieff claimed to speak as "a Christ," commanding his listeners to undertake this exercise because only through it would they "understand reason to live."[16] To those of "new formation" and "the daughters of the Philistines"[17] in our midst, this extraordinary claim must have sounded like the ultimate and most inexcusable heresy—among the many seemingly heretical statements Gurdjieff liberally and mercilessly dispensed over the course of his life.

Those who were there, like Whitcomb (whom I met early on) and Benson, recalled that he warned them that no one should try to explain this exercise. Rather, they should consult with Madame de Salzmann. The rather primitive and almost chaotic recording of that occasion, painstakingly re-examined more than 50 years later on more technologically advanced equipment, appears to bear this out: "She will explain in real English language because my English perhaps not understand everybody," Gurdjieff can be heard to say.[18]

Most people could recall only the barest outlines of his extraordinary directive that day. Yet to "steal" was the defining thought—the common denominator—of the recollections that one heard down the years. For the majority of those who attended that remarkable gathering in the Wellington, the memory of his extraordinary declarations appeared to have vanished entirely from their awareness—from our "apelike consciousness," as Whitehead so keenly characterized it.

It is evident then that Gurdjieff brought methods of awakening that were extraordinarily creative, astonishing, indefinable, often shocking, and seemingly at odds with known spiritual norms. And yet, even so seemingly blasphemous a statement as the one he made that Christmas morning—that he was "a Christ" and therefore could command what his listeners were to do—is completely conforming to the timeless mystic experience, as I have dared to note in Chapter 5. In certain states such as Gurdjieff surely experienced, the notion of "God-as-other" falls away, as the great Meister Eckhart put it. And as the physicist Erwin Schrödinger noted with the awesome insight that I shall repeat once more, the mystics of many centuries have described "the unique experience of his or her life in terms of what can be condensed in the phrase: *Deus factus sum* (I am God)." To claim to be "a Christ" is to declare that equivalence. To be a member of the Trinity, Gurdjieff would appear to be saying, means that I am not only the Son of God, but as such I *am* God also. Indeed, *I AM*.

There are those who would presume to "protect" Gurdjieff from needless misunderstandings (among the infidels? the Gentiles? the unwashed? assorted academics?) by covering up his use of such language—yet even so distant a spiritual figure as the Ramana Maharshi, speaking from a totally different heritage, had been known to borrow this Christian language and to declare, "I and my Father are one." No one presumed to "protect" the Maharshi's image or reputation— the least of a master's concerns—by excising any "dubious" mystical terminology. But we who would delve into Gurdjieff's teaching should also know our traditions—the Great (and Immemorial) Knowledge—in order to recognize the echoes in his teaching of "the powerful ancient stream of knowledge of being"[19] that underlies both his and all the timeless teachings.

To assuage the delicate sensitivities of Gurdjieff's "protectors," wherever and whoever they may be, I shall comment only that, of course, as logical as some traditional doctrine may appear to be to the *rational* mind, its deepest meaning is also beyond one's ordinary comprehension.

Given all of the accounts of Gurdjieff's profound understanding of "the inner world of man" and the directives such as that Christmas Day instruction, the evidence is, to my mind, incontestable that the special work that everyone attributed to Madame de Salzmann—and which some would

even "blame" her for allegedly "adding" to the teaching—
actually derived directly from Gurdjieff himself. Mesoteric or
esoteric, it came from Gurdjieff.

In view of the misunderstandings that appeared to have
grown around the direction that Madame de Salzmann gave,
it is salutary indeed to ponder the extraordinary silence with
which she appears to have met these charges that she had
brought a "New Work" or strayed from Gurdjieff's effort-
driven path. I was never in, or even remotely near, her "inner
circle," although many of the Parisians were almost fanatic
(and perhaps justifiably so) in their pride of possession, so I
can only speak as one of "new formation" who could merely
look on from a distance. But I never heard that she had
launched counter propaganda, or offered any justification.
She occupied some rather high ground, and had no need to
stoop.

So it seems not inappropriate then to attempt to review
the "evidence" that, in hindsight, was available to everyone,
and to venture some thoughts about the clearly seamless
lineage of the special line of work that became the "single
grand verity" of her final years. Some may feel that I am
trying to solicit some questionable legitimacy for my
inferences about that work. Certainly, I have neither the
spiritual nor the institutional standing to speak with any
implied "authority" in such matters. Yet I shall risk these
particular connections since they have not been made
elsewhere, which is understandable, because most of those
who were able to work directly with Madame de Salzmann
seldom indulged in any philosophizing about the meaning or
the purpose of the exercises and directions she gave.

*   *   *

So, for what it is worth, let me re-state my understanding
that the circulation or movement of energy that she called us
to understand was never a departure from what Gurdjieff had

brought, but *was "all of a piece" with indications given down the years by Gurdjieff himself.*

Those indications were there for all to examine, for example, in the so-called Fifth Talk to the New York group on December 19, 1930.[20] Reading that talk after all these years, one is astonished at the generosity of spirit that he displayed, if only as a counter to the seeming misdirection that Orage had provided. Some may consider it a "stretch" to suggest that Gurdjieff was speaking then, on that particular occasion, of the same subject. But it appears to me now that he was describing to his listeners a prototypal form of the descending movement of energy that Madame later brought as that central "grand verity" of her transmission.

In this Fifth Talk, Gurdjieff speaks (I shall use the present tense) of the effort to divide the attention, and then of directing one half of the attention to the head brain "for the purpose of observing and possibly constating any process proceeding in it." Then he adds: "And already I am beginning to feel in it, from the totality of automatically flowing associations, *the arising of something very fine, almost imperceptible to me. I do not know what this is nor do I wish to know,* but I definitely constate, feel and sense that this is some definite 'something' arising from the process automatically proceeding in my head brain of associations of previously consciously perceived impressions" [emphasis added].

After a reference to the role of the breathing in this process, Gurdjieff continues: "I now consciously direct this second half of my attention and, uninterruptedly 'remembering the whole of myself,' *I aid this something arising in my head brain to flow directly into my solar plexus. I feel how it flows*" [emphasis added].[21]

To repeat, this was for me Gurdjieff's prototypal (perhaps even generic) explication of the movement of an energy—an unknown energy—arising above, or in, or at the general level of, the head, and proceeding or flowing "down" into the organism. Gurdjieff emphasized that his audience should not expect "such a definite result" from their intentional repetitions of the exercise, since they had not had the appropriate preparation for this new action in them. This is certainly a warning that applies as much to the casual reader as to those who would profess to be "in the Work." One must be guided by those who have been before.

In any event, a careful study of this revealing material, and serious personal efforts to enter into the meaning of that particular exercise, led me to the inescapable conclusion— that Gurdjieff himself was the source of the work that Madame later brought so single-mindedly.

There was yet further support for this assumption in the accounts of Gurdjieff's meetings in Paris before the War. For example, in a meeting recorded in Solita Solano's copy of the transcripts, now freely accessible on the Internet, Madame de Salzmann responded to a questioner, quite openly and *in Gurdjieff's presence*:

> *Madame de Salzmann:* "For the moment the necessary thing is to feel the path along which something must move and that you grow familiar with the sensation of this path."

> [Gurdjieff himself tells the questioner that he must do the exercise "to the end," and "Gradually as you have need of it, you shall use this path."]

> *Madame de Salzmann:* "It is for training, for exercising in feeling these passages. *You must know how you can flow* [emphasis added]."[22]

While little that is meaningful or relevant has been written specifically about this kind of work, apart from Ravindra's thoughtful attempt—"a necessity laid upon my soul," he feels[23]— I should note at least one random and independent commentary on Gurdjieff's exercises. This too was evidently based on observations made from outside the "institutionalized" framework, that is, without the benefit of a direct contact either with Gurdjieff or Madame de Salzmann. While not addressing the specific work brought by her, it nevertheless appears to throw some light on the actual movement of energy implicit in this "effort." The observer, who is associated with the Work as brought by Bennett and is therefore not part of the "institutional" mainstream of which I have been writing, states "that it is important to observe that concentrating the attention is not really a matter of effort. Nor is it a matter of 'I am doing this.' There is more the sense of an impersonal act proceeding by itself. One intends something such as a flow from the head brain to the solar plexus and then one has to allow it to happen as it will: it is no good 'doing' anything to try and make it happen."[24]

All of these accounts point up not only the scope but also the centrality of Gurdjieff's exercises to open to the movement of energies from another level. As I have noted already, Louise March referred to Gurdjieff's instruction as being to "draw" in that energy. She evidently preferred not to use the word he actually used on that and other occasions—to "suck" in the energy. But elsewhere, as in the transcripts of his talks in Paris in 1938 (that is, about 10 years before), he spoke unreservedly about "sucking" in the energy:

> *Questioner:* Mr. Gurdjieff speaks of ways for flowing. And in order to suck in, how does one do it?
> *Mr. Gurdjieff:* Imagine that you take in air. Consciously, you feel you suck it in. It is the same occasion. Good breathing leads to better sucking in. Good sucking in leads to better breathing.[25]

Given the "generic" character of these descriptions, it should be remembered that Gurdjieff brought the Work to his students in an abundance of creative forms. Furthermore, in some of his exercises the movement of energy sometimes coincided with the breath, and in others it was clearly independent of the breath.

I will forbear from mentioning any of my own efforts to explore this line of work. But Madame de Salzmann always spoke of this work with great exactitude, and with a profound understanding of the forces at work. Once when I asked her a question, she reached into her tote bag, brought out a simple wire-bound exercise book, and referred to something she had written, clearly in the course of her own seemingly unending inquiry and exploration. I dare say that when her own notes are collated and published, there will be surprising indications of the precision with which she followed the movement of the attention and the work for Presence.

So, I believe it is not totally out of place to mention just one extraordinary, independent corroboration of what we of new formation came to know as Madame de Salzmann's indication. It occurred almost two decades after her death. I was visiting a place of work out of town. At the end of an intense day, a young man spoke of his silent, inner struggle to hold his attention in a very difficult surrounding. I had never spoken to him about Madame's specific directions. Nor had I ever mentioned to him, for instance, that Michel de Salzmann had once indicated to me that this movement of energy can be quite swift, sweeping down from above the head. And here was this young man, unexpectedly describing his experience of an energy that *swept down*, "from above." He illustrated the movement with a swift sweep of his arm. "It came down, whoosh," he said.

I could only listen in wonderment and silence. No one could ever allege that this man had been brainwashed, or that he was suggestible, or that he was simply parroting something that had been pumped into him. His unexpected experience confirmed for me yet again that when the centers are mobilized, in a strange new unity, in a new alignment, then a new energy, an energy of an unknown quality, can appear. It can flow. From another level. As if by grace.

*   *   *

As I delved over the years into writings of the great teachers, this indication was there to be found, clearly stated, for example, in Meister Eckhart's sermons: "There is a higher part of the mind which keeps itself above time . . . ."[26]

A *higher part of the mind*. So easily imagined and so easily spoken about by the discursive mind. And so readily dismissed by some who would appear to regard any notion of a new receptivity—an *active* receptivity—as the negation of "the need for incessant struggle against passivity and sleep."

Of course, Madame's own teacher, Gurdjieff, had said it so explicitly in the Third Series—that all man's possibilities "come from On High."[27] One might take that quite figuratively, and at the same time—in working in this special way—it is without any doubt literally true.

So, there was never any question in my mind—and there is none now—that the Work that Madame brought was Gurdjieff's Work. She was clearly Gurdjieff's closest, most faithful, most dedicated, and most comprehending pupil— the only person whom Gurdjieff declared to be "going out of idiocy"[28]—and I never doubted that she was communicating her understanding of his direct, oral teaching. I felt that as she reached out to other traditions and teachers—she openly and unashamedly attended Krishnamurti's talks in Saanen, Switzerland, for example—it was Gurdjieff's teaching that provided the touchstone, rather than that she was looking for help or importing "alien" practices. After all, she had had a master as her teacher.

Having said all of this with all appropriate circumspection, well knowing the scorn that will be heaped on me for daring to "uncover" something of a work which, like Gurdjieff's metaphorical dog, still lies deeply buried, I am confident that when some of the material among Madame de Salzmann's private papers, notebooks, and even some voice recordings are eventually published, her own authentic voice will yet be heard speaking directly to these deeply esoteric matters—and corroborating this rather halting assessment of the work she brought to us.

*   *   *

So, to continue my digression into what I have termed the seamless lineage at the heart of the Work, nothing could be more evident than that Madame de Salzmann was, among other things, totally committed to carrying on Gurdjieff's great legacy, the Movements. She herself deepened their exploration, and she ensured, through the documentation on film of the spirit and the form of the Movements, that an archive for the mainstream groups would be preserved, all of which required intense inner and outer preparation. It is a work that still continues "at the center" and whose intensity is only remotely reflected in the materials that are now a seeming commonplace on the Internet.

I believe she also saw it as her duty to ensure that successive editions and translations of Gurdjieff's source literature were issued. Some of this sense of duty was evidently imparted to the Canadians at Traditional Studies Press through whose endeavors the Russian-language *Beelzebub* was able to appear in the year 2000, several years after her death and 50 years after Gurdjieff's death. All of the publications that she herself saw to press helped to ensure that the voice and intent of Gurdjieff were faithfully conveyed. I should add that there have been some suggestions, which have found their way into print, that she more or less "sanitized" and even bowdlerized Gurdjieff's talks along the way. I dare say some of his talks might indeed have been sanitized in the Nietzschean sense: " . . . I will fence my thoughts round, and my words too: so that swine and hot fanatics shall not break into my garden!"[29] Moreover, as Madame de Salzmann noted in her foreword to *Views*, "The writings of Gurdjieff, as well as certain exercises which he brought to his pupils, were not all meant to be published."[30]

As Gurdjieff's editors have noted down the years, some of his language certainly needed cleaning up—but not always to hide secret meanings. Expletives like "sheet of sheets" (shit of shits) were rather mild, to say the least, but I dare say that most of his choicer expletives and references to (say) the sex organ of the female crocodile could be considered downright demeaning and uncouth to the unpracticed and unfriendly ear. He might profess to be "Oriental gentleman," as he admonished a Lady of the Rope applying her makeup in his presence, but would this language cut any ice in the present day and age? Better, then, to leave out the most scurrilous and the vulgar.

*   *   *

Madame de Salzmann also worked tirelessly to bring together the disparate and contending groups of Gurdjieff's immediate followers, a task of Herculean proportions. Speaking of the early adherents in New York, for example, William Segal could concede 50 years later, "We were really a pretty rough crowd of people."[31] Frankly, I think he put it rather mildly!

It was Madame de Salzmann too who equally tirelessly conveyed to the early leaders the spirit of the Work, the central necessities of the work with others, that is, *the work together*, and the deep understanding that, except when "I AM," there is little that is real about us. (What was it that Gurdjieff had said about our being mere "shit factories"?) Indeed, on reading some of the early notes of those meetings in New York, I could not help saying to a few of the surviving members, as a "young upstart" still only in my seventh decade on the planet, "You really knew nothing in those days!"

For several decades Madame was legally the *only* "member" of the New York Foundation. I had the impression that that legal arrangement had been made to ensure that she alone determined the authenticity of the Work, especially since there were clear factions stemming from Ouspensky, Orage, and later Bennett, Nyland, and others. That raises some questions about the assertion made by an insistent and aggressive lobby that any one particular person had been designated to "lead" the Work in America. There were quite a few designees—and contenders—for this role, it seems. Who appeared to "win out" in the end in Gurdjieff's esoteric rough and tumble was another matter

Indeed, I recall one of the last meetings of the New York trustees at which Dr. Welch was present. He had succeeded to the presidency on John Pentland's death, in 1984, and assiduously downplayed any interest in the seeming aura and the supposed glamor surrounding that position. He told his fellow trustees that the title of president gave the false impression that the Foundation had a "leader," and he actually urged that the presidency not be perpetuated after his passing. One felt his sincere wish to forestall such ambition. While this was agreed to by those present, the position was subsequently filled (with a co-presidency, of which I was one "half"). This was done as much for corporate reasons as for spiritual. In this day and age, someone has to sign the tax returns.

Still, today, at least among the mainstream foundations and their affiliates, the Work in the New World may have a wider, although not necessarily a surer, footing than in those early years. One can only hope that those (again, I can speak only of the New World) who would follow in such sober footsteps should not forget these origins. The aim of the teaching is, after all, to enable us to wake up—and that aim is only "dumbed down" to the basest, or exoteric, levels by indulgences in the "power possession," the trappings, the competitive superficialities, that come with being "group leaders" (like those bishops in the resplendent robes of the Order of the Star who surrounded the young Krishnamurti), or in heavy-handed attempts to enforce imagined dynastic claims, whether at the national or at the provincial levels! If anything is automatically passed on by heredity, I am sure it isn't consciousness. As Gurdjieff himself said, "Heredity is not important for the soul."[32]

*   *   *

In any event, I was always hard pressed to regard Madame de Salzmann's contribution as a "New Work." Indeed, one of the leading proponents of this point of view, in writing about the change to an allegedly "passive" work, asserts, quite correctly, that "Gurdjieff stressed that active man serves evolution and passive man serves involution."[33] True, but as this industrious onlooker does concede, Gurdjieff's meaning is not always to be inferred so categorically.

The key issue regarding a New Work in contrast to a supposed Old Work would more properly be whether one ever "achieves" anything in the spiritual realm through one's own subjective affirmations or whether, in being "acted upon" (which some Westerners appear to find abhorrent and effete), one is experiencing the affirmation of a "higher" (and therefore objective and impersonal) force. This particular observer adds: "Although Gurdjieff may have introduced new teachings at the end of his life about which no records are available, [Madame] de Salzmann's teaching differs from Gurdjieff's demands for unremitting struggle and effort that are echoed in his pupils' writings of their experience with him." However, judging from my experience—and I speak only for myself—I would only say that whether one has found oneself shoveling away on the manure pile at Mendham, or engaging the mind, the body, and the feeling in the comprehensive laboratory of the Movements, or experiencing the intense call "to be" that is evoked in the so-called "new type of sitting," or bearing the unpleasant manifestations of others towards oneself (a seeming specialty of institutional life), "the demands for unremitting struggle and effort" are never absent.

The point, surely, is that it is the nature of *effort* that needs to be more clearly understood as it becomes more refined and purified, as well as the transition (never guaranteed or predictable) from effort to non-effort. For instance, Peter Brook, reflecting on his work with Madame de Salzmann, provides a perceptive insight into this subtle transformation when he observes, "Effort only has a place if it leads to a mystery called noneffort, and then if for a short instant one's perception is transformed, this is an act of grace."[34]

The latter-day traditionalist Rama C. Coomaraswamy, too, throws an interesting light on some of the modernist confusions regarding the inner work. "One frequently hears that prayer" —this might perhaps also be read as meditation, self-remembering, work in the quiet—"(with wires attached to prove the point) induces a 'trance state' which is productive of tranquility. Clearly those who hold such views have no real experience with this form of prayer—where every effort is engaged in avoiding trance states—or putting it more precisely, where alertness and concentration is a *sine qua non*. Closer to the reality is St. John Chrysostom's statement that 'prayer is a torture chamber.'"[35]

This is, moreover, an oral teaching, and not all directives, not all exchanges, are recorded. And the oral teaching includes the non-verbal communication as much as the verbal, the right and timely gesture, a respect for the intangibles, and the work for Presence. Not everything that Madame de Salzmann imparted to several generations of pupils, as with Gurdjieff himself, was written down. Indeed, I recall that more often than not she insisted that no notes be taken: the work was in the active listening, the seeing, the immediacy of the inner, experiential exploration that engaged the whole of one's being.

To repeat myself, the work to be still and to be sensitive to this quiet becomes as intense, in its way, as all those overt efforts to push the body, or to contain and align the disparate energies of the mind, the body, and the feeling in the sittings and in the Movements. The "demands for unremitting struggle and effort" are there—it is just that the form and the shape of the "struggle" become more subtle and interiorized. Gurdjieff himself gives the ultimate guidance, it appears, when he indicates that true interiorization requires that a process proceed "in absolute quiet."[36] And what do our discursive minds, not to speak of our other brains, know of this absolute quiet? It is hardly a matter to be settled by conjecture, that is, by resorting to more thought: "Which of you by taking thought can add one cubit to his stature?" (Matthew 7:27).

So it is, as Henri Tracol observed, that Gurdjieff "reserve[d] an important place for profound meditation, for silence, as the return to the very source of all knowledge."[37] If we are indeed to relate to the source, if we are to penetrate beyond even the here and the now, as Eckhart urged, then we must "become wholly still and detached from all images and all forms."[38] Thus it is an ironic tribute to the force of Madame de Salzmann's overarching sensibility and her alignment to the Higher that some of her so-called "New Work" practices, such as the sittings, are now increasingly adopted (if only in form) in non-mainstream circles.

And then, as I have mentioned, long after these great principals had departed this life, there it was for some, the corroborating evidence, as it were, barely discernible on those antediluvian voice tapes amateurishly recorded in the Hotel Wellington in the early hours of Christmas Day 1948. Those old wire tapes, more or less dating back to the Stone Age of sound recording, had languished in storage and for a long time they were accorded only a certain curiosity value. Primitive and scarcely intelligible, they are nevertheless authentic. And there, those who have attempted to unravel the near chaos of sounds, have heard Gurdjieff, in his own voice, speaking in barely understandable English to his largely uncomprehending audience about an energy to be drawn in—"sucked" in—from a point out in space, above the mind. It was all of a piece with the teaching he had always brought. And it was that teaching that was the source of the directives that Madame de Salzmann faithfully imparted in "endless iteration."

So Gurdjieff had spoken, but he had not been understood out in the wider circles. It was all too esoteric. It was only for those who had "ears to hear"—and until Madame de Salzmann brought this to the groups in the full force of her understanding, it had been quietly alluded to and equally quietly shielded from those who, like myself, were still unprepared. Browsing through my own old notebooks, I found this simple entry dating back to January 26, 1965: "Madame de Salzmann said to us that 'Beyond our contradictions is a life which has no beginning or end.'" The teaching was all in that. And how was one to open to this? It was an understanding—a mystical illuminism—not lightly "achieved": it had to be opened to by unremitting struggle and effort.

Even 50-odd years after Gurdjieff had given his remarkable directives, this opening to a movement of energy from another level appears to be little understood, as well it must. Perhaps there is a handful of people at the very core who do understand. It was nothing that Madame de Salzmann had invented. But it was something to which she, as "a real pupil" of Gurdjieff's, had dedicated her life.

Quite frankly, I have never been able to believe that there was either a New Work or an Old Work. At the heart of the teaching, there is only one Work, and Madame de Salzmann clearly was faithful to that.

NOTES

1. Ravi Ravindra, *Heart Without Measure: Gurdjieff Work with Madame de Salzmann*, preface, revised paperback edition, Morning Light Press, Sandpoint, ID, 2004.

2. I am reminded of a verse quoted in Herbert Whone, *Church, Monastery, Cathedral*, Element Books, 1990:

Once a chela, eager ninny,
Tried to raise his kundalini,
Having heard that it would shower
Every kind of magic power.
So he read and practiced breathing
Till he had his centers seething:
Bubbling until overloaded
Cell & nerves & brain exploded.
Fifty volts for a five-watt mind
Nature surely had never designed.

3. Seymour Ginsburg, quoted in *Gurdjieff International Guide*, interview with Sophia Wellbeloved, October, 2002.

4. Sophia Wellbeloved, interview, *Gurdjieff International Guide*, October, 2002.

5. Ibid.

6. Ibid.

7. Ibid.

8. Jacob Needleman, "G.I.Gurdjieff and His School," *www.berkeley.edu/people/misc/School.html*, 1982/1996.

9. James Moore, article on Henriette H. Lannes, *Gurdjieff International Review*, *www.gurdjieff.org./moore3.htm*

10. G.I. Gurdjieff, *Views From the Real World*, E.P. Dutton & Co., Inc., New York, 1973, p. vi.

11. Ibid, p.v.

12. James Moore, interview in Telos/Gurdjieff-legacy.org.

13. James Moore, "Moveable Feasts: the Gurdjieff Work," *Religion Today*, Vol. 9, No. 2, 1994, pp. 11-15.

14. Ethel Merston, quoted in "Miss Merston in India, part VI: Miss Merston at Mendham," *The Gurdjieff Journal*, vol. 9, issue 3, p.20.

15. Beth McCorkle, *The Gurdjieff Years, 1929-1949: Recollections of Louise March*, The Work Study Association, Inc., Walworth, New York, 1990, p. 80.

16. Miscellaneous recollections of a dinner talk by G.I. Gurdjieff at the Hotel Wellington, New York, Christmas Day, 1948.

17. Ezekiel 16: 27. One of Martin Benson's favorite anathemas.

18. The Dutch music researcher Gert-Jan Blom has devoted considerable energies and skill to the preservation of the old voice tapes made on Gurdjieff's last visit to North America. With the exception of the chaotic Hotel Wellington Christmas Day 1948 tape, these have been published in his *Gurdjieff: Harmonic Development: The Complete Harmonium Recordings 1948-49*, Basta Music, 2005.

19. Gurdjieff, *Views*, p. 57.

20. Gurdjieff, *Life Is Real, Only Then, When "I Am"* (commonly called The Third Series), E.P. Dutton & Co., Inc., New York, 1975, p. 131.

21. Ibid., p. 140-1.

22. Gurdjieff: Meetings at 6 rue des Colonels Renard, 1938. Meeting # 32. Probably from Solita Solano's copy in the Library of Congress. Taken off the Internet, 2004.

23. Ravindra, op. cit.

24. A.G.E. Blake, "Possible Foundations of Inner Exercises," *gurdjieff-internet.com*, 2003, p. 3.

25. Gurdjieff: Meetings at 6 rue des Colonels Renard, 1938, #32.

26. Meister Eckhart, sermon titled "Woman, the hour is coming." Quoted in Reiner Schurmann, *Wandering Joy: Meister Eckhart's Mystical Philosophy*, Lindisfarne Books, Great Barrington, MA, 2001, p. 53.

27. Gurdjieff, *Life Is Real*, p. 173.

28. McCorkle, op. cit., p.76.

29. Friedrich Nietzche, *Thus Spake Zarathustra*, translated by R.J. Hollingdale, Penguin Books, Baltimore, MD, 1961, p. 207.

30. Gurdjieff, *Views*, p. vii.

31. William C. Segal with Marielle Bancou-Segal, *A Voice at the Borders of Silence*, The Woodstock Press, Woodstock and New York, 2003, p. 200.

32. Gurdjieff, *Views*, page 151.

33. Sophia Wellbeloved, *Gurdjieff: The Key Concepts*, Routledge, New York, 2003, p. 154.

34. Peter Brook, *Threads of Time*, Washington, D.C., 1998, p. 110.

35. Rama C. Coomaraswamy, "Introduction to Guenon's *Error of Spiritism or Spiritualism*," *Sophia*, Vol. 9, No. 1.

36. G.I. Gurdjieff, *All and Everything*, Viking Arcana, New York, 1992, p. 691.

37. Henri Tracol, "Let us not Conclude: Some reflections on what is specific to Gurdjieff's teaching," *Further Talks, Essays & Interviews*, The Guild Press, Fifield Road, Bray, Berkshire, England, 2003, p. 69. Originally published in *Gurdjieff: Essays and Reflections on the Man and His Teaching*, Continuum, New York, 1996.

38. Meister Eckhart, Sermon 18, *Selected Writings*, Penguin Books, London, 1994, p. 187.

* * *

CHAPTER 13

Some Random Inferences

I N THE HALF century since Gurdjieff's death, the
landscape of what is loosely called "the Work" has
changed, perhaps beyond recognition, from that experienced
by his early followers.

It probably requires discernment of near-archangelic
acuity for the novice "searcher" to sort out the wheat from
the chaff among the self-proclaimed teachers, leaders,
groups, assorted pretenders (with their improbable claims
to be man number 5 or 6 or 7), and the manifold cosmic
standouts who have followed in Gurdjieff's wake like
Tolkien's Gollum, slouching in the shadows to snatch the
One Ring to Rule Them All. The participants range from
the profoundly committed, virtually invisible, at the core
(the "secure line of succession" whose seeming *absence* has
been noted by Sophia Wellbeloved) . . . to undeniably sincere
and doubtless well-meaning reconstructionists . . . to
unmitigated frauds. Accounts of the Work have come to
include the equivalent, it seems, of the Protocols of the
Elders of Zion, with their malicious fiction—and the
idolatry of starry-eyed sycophants readily mesmerized
(and cowed) by the more vocal of Gurdjieff's imitators in
the local crowd.

I trust that I too am not contributing to the cacophony of a latter-day Babel. The particular disposition that I have displayed in these recollections is rather evident. Call it, if you wish, an intuitive leaning towards the sacred and, by implication, the opening to energies that speak of grace and the overarching work for Presence. Why should I excuse myself or apologize for that?

Still, it was a complete and utter surprise to learn, as I brought this supremely unfinished document to a close, that Dr. Michel Conge, one of Madame de Salzmann's closest pupils, had expressed a similar disposition. "The entire universe is prayer," he wrote in notes entrusted to a few pupils and his family. Fortunately, these insights have now been published for others, too, to make the relevant connections. "Contact with a fine energy in ourselves is already a prayer." "Preparing oneself to receive this unknown force—you can call it *God* or *That* or *That Which Is*—is already a prayer and not a demand; not even a call, because that would still be subjective."[1] And, he asks, What will make the two natures communicate? "Self-remembering and Prayer." Which is a direct endorsement, if you will, of my long-felt conviction that what one is learning through the Work is, indeed, how to pray. But not, of course, to some bearded old Middle Eastern patriarch sitting on a throne high in the sky.

As articulate as Dr. Conge was, one cannot ignore Gurdjieff himself in this regard. His talks were replete with unrepentant references to God, to Christ, the intervention of conscious spirits, and to prayer. And it is all very well documented that Madame de Salzmann, too, expressed herself very clearly and often on the subject of prayer.

Perhaps too-well-documented, since some explicit indications given both by Gurdjieff and Madame de Salzmann have surfaced through Solita Solano's papers in the Library of Congress and in other transcripts. They are now out in the open, as it were, available on the Internet both to serious seekers and to the idly curious alike.

There one can learn that Gurdjieff was quite forthright and open in responding to such questions as, "How should

one pray? To whom does one pray?" Gurdjieff replied that
those who prayed could establish a telepathic line, analogous
to a telephone, he said, to "certain inverted likenesses of the
Absolute." Again, this is for most of those who read such
indications, rather mystifying, and perhaps just the rambling
of a pious old charlatan. If these indications were indeed the
truth, it probably could not be grasped merely through the
written word or the ordinary processes of thought. So, what
he spoke about with such certainty might indeed be, as he
said, "for the future."

Be that as it may, for all of the confusion, mystification, and
absurdity that Gurdjieff appears to have provoked around
himself and his teaching—a psychic smoke screen that offers
rich lodes to be mined both by serious academicians and
dilettantes of every persuasion, but a smoke screen
nonetheless—he clearly spoke from real experience of, and real
communication with, "the Higher." It could not be otherwise.
Every real, authentic teaching derives from profound, overarching
experience, a revelation, an opening to the noumenal, a contact
with the Higher. And every real, authentic teaching calls the
seeker to open to, and endlessly renew, a direct contact with a
life force inaccessible to the importunities of the "little self"—a
life force that "supports, enlightens, and unifies" one's presence,
as Pentland so eloquently expressed it.[2]

Indeed, Gurdjieff's original title for the last chapter of *All
and Everything* was to have been "Ecstasy of Revelation,"
according to Orage.[3] And although there are those
Traditionalists who hold that there will be no more revelations
"in this cycle," there must surely be ongoing revelations,
Gurdjieff's included, because one cannot conceive that His
Endlessness, or God, should simply take a leave of absence.
In the Christian tradition, it is understood that "My Father
works till now" (John 5:17). He has surely not terminated his
creative action.

Gurdjieff himself noted that " . . . 'mystical states' . . . when
they are not deceptions or imitations . . . are flashes of what

we call an objective state of consciousness."[4] Clearly, Gurdjieff's realizations were of a very high order. So it is not a little edifying when one begins to hear words like *prayer* and *sacred* surfacing among the otherwise ploddingly pedestrian in serious moments of work, the speakers—many of whom had once been quick to denigrate anything with echoes of the spiritual or the sacred—seeming to refer to a dawning recognition of standing directly, "one to one," before the Higher, as Pentland put it. As if the discovery is being made, rather late in the day, and after long insistence on their own dour vision, that the real meaning of the Work lies in these inner realizations, acts of communion—and even occasional union—with a nameless Source, and not merely in the relentless pursuit of super-efforts, or in espousing some selfish pretensions.

No one brought the insight more forcefully and consistently than Michel de Salzmann that it is the attention that brings order, and that it is the attention that relates us to the Higher. The attention, he pointed out, derives from a very high source—an unknown source. Madame de Salzmann herself emphasized that "pure attention is the way towards consciousness." It was this ever-present study with which she was so unerringly engaged.

And so the overriding, exacting, and *practical* necessity in Gurdjieff's teaching is the *work* for attention. Moments of attention are, in fact, proof that the Work is a movement between levels. But *talk* as we may about attention (and the practice of remorse, and the growth of consciousness) we do not truly see our extraordinary predicament. If we who profess to be "in the Work" find ourselves living in a state of almost unrelieved—and unperceived—identification, can there be any wonder that there are endless misunderstandings about the nature of Gurdjieff's message itself, not to speak of struggles for turf at the worldly level, and other tasteless presumptions?

But why should we be surprised by this? I recall the occasion in April 2000 when, upon being elected to "high office," I duly received in the mail my own personal copy of an anonymous document that had already been sent to a few of the older members, and titled "What Would Mr. Gurdjieff Do?" The author, who claimed to have entered the Work seven years after Gurdieff's death (and was therefore roughly my contemporary), complained that the Work in New York "is now almost the 'Shachermacher-workshop booth'" mentioned by Gurdjieff. "The Work today is only a pale imitation of something that was once alive," the document declared. "If one wants to study identification and inner considering, as Mr. Gurdjieff defined them, one could not do better than observe the Work's current group leaders . . . . One can clearly see the inner slavery of self-satisfied people. One can see vanity, self-love, inner slavery of every kind. But one rarely sees evidence of a genuine inner effort to wake up."

That is quite an indictment . . . if it were true. But again, why should we be surprised by any of this? Even a great Church Father like St. Augustine could express his own grave disquiet at the realization that, although it was written on the lintel of a church (in Numidia), "This is the door of the Lord the righteous shall enter in," the reality was quite the contrary. "The man who enters is bound to see drunkards, misers, tricksters, gamblers, adulterers, fornicators, people wearing amulets, assiduous clients of sorcerers, astrologers . . ."[5] (and, no doubt, some who tend to write memoirs). After all, we are in the world, "in life."

But my predilections and aversions aside, there is, of course, still and always the question, What is the Work? Countless proprietary visions hold among the great orthodoxies such as Islam, Christianity, Judaism. So why should we expect the Gurdjieff scene to be any different? Something of the latter-day state of the search is echoed by James Moore (a seemingly endless source of incisive perceptions!) when he says, "Perhaps we are more realistic to see the Work as a living organism—healthy in parts, sclerotic in parts; spitefully plagued by colorful little parasites;

vulnerable, breathing, growing; browsing on fresh generations of seekers, sloughing off layers of defectors, ingesting the honored dead . . . . Yes, a very mysterious organism moving forward through time, slowly gathering momentum . . . ." And, as he goes on to say, "excreting a dubious secondary literature"[6] —no doubt exactly like this.

Moore himself, as I have noted, appears to have been quite unsparing in his criticism of the allegedly passive redirection of the Work that he believed to have taken place under Madame de Salzmann's guidance. This ostensibly passive approach was to be seen, one assumes, in the publication of the revised 1992 version of *Beelzebub*, while some would feel it in the very way that *Beelzebub* is actually read.

Having been coached by Madame de Hartmann, among others, I can still recall the way she secretly beat me on the thigh, unseen by the listeners and hidden by the tablecloth (yes, we had tablecloths even in those hardscrabble times), to keep the proper cadences as I read. I, on my part, occasionally wanted to throttle the feisty old aristocrat—a spritely survivor of the trek through the Caucasus and other great adventures with Gurdjieff—while at the same time realizing that she understood rhythm and cadence better than I. This was surely an early, if not begrudging, acknowledgement on my part of the validity of hierarchy, of the need to respect the best in "those who have been before." Reading is as much a work as any other activity, and I had never heard of this supposed passive approach until long after Madame de Salzmann's death.

In the original *Pronunciation Guide* (1984) that we printed at Armonk, Margaret Flinsch, who devoted decades to the study of *Beelzebub*, wrote, "The words invented by G.I. Gurdjieff produce a certain resonance in the listener. If one of the purposes of his book is to interrupt the associative, habitual processes of thinking, to reach a deeper layer of thought, then there is a need for these words to sound as the author intended." In my experience, each reading can be new, *sui generis*, each a new opportunity to be in an active mode, questioning, sensitive to the meaning, the sound, the movement of the attention, the presence of the others. To stand out of the way so that the authentic voice of Gurdjieff, in all its manifold dimensions, should come through without being tainted, interpreted, colored, judged, or circumscribed in the process by the reader's subjective vision. A tall order, indeed. But again, as in so much of the activities, this is not a solitary endeavor. There is a reciprocity of effort, a communal work, in the reading. If one is simply assembling pliant zombies for some spooky and meaningless ritual, one could read them the *Racing Times*, or the local telephone book, for that matter.

*   *   *

Another way in which the landscape has changed is in the growing visibility of non-affiliated groups, centers, and leaders—non-affiliated with the core Foundations, that is. In this environment, the Foundations have become, to many of the non-affiliates and strangers at the gate, the bogeymen of the teaching, the forces of rigidity and reaction, putting the brake on "progress," openness, and freedom.

But Heaven alone knows what boundless fabrications circulate among those whose only references are the books and whose relation to the messenger and his message can only be tenuous and sometimes even deluded at best. And how does one "*preserve* the Work *unchanged*, as it had been given," to quote the anonymous author of "What Would Mr. Gurdjieff Do?"

At least there is a consensus both inside and outside the Foundations that Gurdjieff's putative followers come in many different stripes. They have many different expectations, understandings, and requirements. And, of course, along with that comes a wide assortment of "leaders"—perhaps like myself—who may be said to be of mixed and often questionable provenance. Inevitably, then, Gurdjieff's teaching is open to "appropriation and fragmentation," to use Wellbeloved's terms,[7] although this takes place primarily in the exoteric reaches, when the essential link to the Source is absent.

Yet the Foundations—that is, the four original foundations established at the behest of Gurdjieff—remain at the core. Whatever their alleged institutional departures from the doctrinal stasis and "rock-like 'Gurdjieffian fundamentalism'" that are held to be so desirable by some,[8] they nevertheless contain, in their ranks, a dedicated nucleus, *and not always the obvious ones*. They are the pupils who, working selflessly together, have devoted their lives to finding a "relation to the world Above," as Madame de Salzmann would say,[9] and who have protected the authenticity of the Movements, the music, the core literature—the formal underpinnings of the Work, all of which automatically seem to become fair game for every deconstructionist, every new "visionary," every self-appointed Defender of the Faith.

Of course, even the attempt to protect the transmission of the teaching through the revision of *Beelzebub* (1992) has been assailed as a clear betrayal of Gurdjieff's "deliberate stylistic opacity." That action has been dismissively ranked (again by Moore) as "the grand trophy of revisionism."[10] Perhaps, to use the idiom of modern Baghdad, it might even be called the Mother of All Abominations. Still another critic (one among many) has made some charming if unvalidated references to an alleged "party line" in the Work, not to speak of the supposed "authorities," all centered, one imagines, in the Foundations.[11]

As the most articulate (and rather barbed) of the recent critics, Moore, who is nevertheless also the author of perhaps the best biography of Gurdjieff to date, appears to have been particularly harsh in his condemnation of Madame de Salzmann's sponsorship of the "new" *Beelzebub*. He has alleged in a number of articles that today we "grapple" not only with "the irreparable deformation of Gurdjieff's Legominism" (i.e., *Beelzebub*), but also with the "polarization of the English-speaking Work."[12]

What's more, he charges, the revised version panders to "debased comprehension thresholds," leaving it "exposed and vulnerable to neobarbarian trespass," rather like the King James Version of the Bible, one supposes. Better, it is said, to let *Beelzebub* retain its "quasi-scriptural status" than to clean up what some equally sober and sensible minds consider the antediluvian and obscure construction contrived with the best of intentions by those benighted old Russian émigrés charged with translating the book. Yet, with the literary construction now more precise and accurate, and more faithfully rendering Gurdjieff's writing, "the reader's confrontative effort" is still no less required—and the effort demanded of the reader is hardly *passé*. The dog is still buried very deep.

*　　*　　*

Naturally, the new landscape of the Work also harbors a wide spectrum, a murmuring throng, of the unhappy and the disaffected, with their special requirements. Some have complained that they did not receive the proper attention; they weren't adequately pampered, they weren't understood, and often the revered leaders did not measure up to their pupils' exacting subjective criteria. There are innumerable testaments to that effect. I still recall the man who hung out in the corridors at Armonk to waylay Madame de Salzmann, as if his Armenian roots and origins by themselves should vault him into her circle. His were no less "question-begging credentials" than Kathleen Riordan Speeth's assertion that "I was born into the Gurdjieff work," to borrow Moore's incisive assessment. [13]

When we grasp, as Madame de Salzmann pointed out, that "We begin from very far away from the essential," and that we lose the meaning of our work "and have to return again and again,"[14] obliged always to renegotiate our passage back towards the center, towards the Source, then we recognize that *all of these misconceptions are absolutely understandable.* Nor have I been close enough to the scene to know, but perhaps there is more than a little truth to the charge, for example, that Paris may exert a "tenacious hold over materiel and 'orthodoxy,'" that there is "an extensible dynastic line," and that "a single raised eyebrow in Paris may dictate methodology in Caracas 10 years later."[15] (I would say, however, that that particular eyebrow would have to be of cosmic proportions to exert any undue influence in Caracas.)

Yet these are intriguing thoughts, and many could surely add their own modest tales of "patterns of sanction and privilege,"[16] injustices, slights, and insensitivities, real and imagined, to the personalized manure piles in their own immediate neighborhoods. As I imagine my ubiquitous (and unwashed) Bushman might say again under the starry skies of the Kalahari, "If you wish to feed with the lions, you must learn to love raw meat." One needs a strong stomach! Even to ask if all of this grumbling is important or to the point is perhaps of no particular consequence: there are unfathomable forces at play, and we players are ourselves such stuff as dreams are made on.

Still, like beauty, "deviation and revisionism" are most often in the eye of the beholder. I am hardly equipped, still less inclined, to tilt in the lists over such doctrinal subtleties, still less to be able to read Gurdjieff's mind. Yet it seems this new landscape has been enlivened—better yet, as the French would say, *irrigated*—by this fundamental disagreement over the direction that the Work has allegedly been given by the family de Salzmann. It has resulted, that most articulate of the critics alleges, in "a classical theological dichotomy" that embraces "the dialectical tension between 1) personal endeavor and 2) supernal grace."[17]

Moore adds that "Fronting the new doctrine was an oligarchy-led modulation of idiom from active to passive voice:

the pupil no longer 'remembered himself' but 'was remembered': no longer 'awoke' but 'was awoken.' Pupils did not, need not, could not, work: they were 'worked upon' (even while they literally slept!)."

In short, if one understands this argument, we are expected to take seriously the charge that the Foundations have abandoned "Gurdjieff's canon of effort, striving, and self-reliance," and taken up with "a new quietism" marked by "gratuitous, omni-accessible, and invincible grace."[18]

*   *   *

I am afraid that I have not adequately conveyed these expressions of a rather nostalgic yearning for the restoration of the "heroic" and historical Gurdjieff and of "the Work's effort-saturated cosmological matrix,"[19] that is, the Ray of Creation, the Step Diagram, and other elements of the vast scheme of things that Gurdjieff has mapped out. These are eloquent laments for the perceived passing of the "traditional tenor" of the teaching received through a revered teacher. But the Work is replete with revered teachers. Thank God Madame de Salzmann had no interest in being considered a teacher, her reverence for Gurdjieff being monumental and impartible. Inevitably, one must invoke Dean Borsh yet again, and hold to his seminal "indifference to the saints." This is a hard doctrine. But it does not obviate a sense of loyalty and respect.

And if one's leader did not, for example, "place disproportionate and . . . uncanonical emphasis on long 'sittings' with eyes closed,"[20] does it mean that those who actually did so were necessarily effete, spineless, mere nattering nabobs of esotericism, and without "a unity challenged and proved in the arena of manifestation"? Well, those spritely old samurais in New York ran a few revered leaders out of town in their time. Some of the departed displayed their own brand of "rock-like Gurdjieffian fundamentalism" that did not always find a very receptive audience in the New World. But, as in life, those who would live by the sword die by the sword: who said the Work is for sissies? And who knows, New York's "loss" may have been someone else's gain.

There will be no end to contrarian points of view. There are even forums now at which well-intentioned attempts are being made to bring disparate visions and understandings of Gurdjieff's legacy together. And all the while the silent ones at the core remain just that—silent. But rather than gallop into confrontations for which I am ill-equipped and ill-suited, I can only volunteer some random inferences about the Work as it appears to me now, as I await my turn to move off the scene, and always with the caveat that this is how I have seen it "from where I was sitting."

*   *   *

Accepting the alleged "mystical illuminism" that Madame de Salzmann unveiled and brought to us was (and is) perfectly natural to me, given my own lifelong disposition, even though, as I have admitted, I could acknowledge my own massive weakness of will, my permeating laziness, and my pervasive lack of any ability to "do." But there needs to be a next step. One has to be "available" to be drawn beyond the apparent threshold of the moment—beyond the limits of the known, beyond even the here and the now.

After all, how many ditches can one go on digging? How many confrontations can one enter into? Just how many crafts can one practice? How many interactive exchanges can one undertake? It was perhaps something of this that Pentland had in mind when he said, "If the experience that we are looking for is given, given from above, something that we reach when, you might say, we drink from the waters of remembering, it seems to descend on one . . . . Unfortunately, we tend to think of the work as climbing mountains. We don't think of it enough in terms of the taste, which is relatively absolute, of an overview . . . . Once you have had that taste, it should be enough to be able to give up doing projects that keep you up all night."[21]

I recall how difficult it was for some of the old-timers (some of my mentors included) to accept that there could be an intentional "quiet work"—even a few minutes of silence before leaving the breakfast or lunch table before going to the practical tasks. Even in my time, when some groups visiting Mendham were seen to sit quietly, word would be sent down from the Olympian heights of Madame Ouspensky's room, by way of her guardians, that "Madame says we do not practice meditation." Yet how many other old-timers have told of sitting in silence in Gurdjieff's presence. Michel Conge, for example, has reported for the record that "the most extraordinary part was not [Gurdjieff's] answers, it was his silences . . . . They would last for minutes on end . . . ."[22] Louise March tells of the "silent circle" that surrounded Gurdjieff when he wrote *All and Everything* in the café at Fontainebleau or the Café de la Paix in Paris. "All of Gurdjieff's visitors had to wait until he turned to them, and that could take, one, two, or three hours," she observed. "Whoever came sat in his silent circle."[23]

*   *   *

There is the need, on the one hand, for becoming whole— ever more whole—and entering into what some have even termed the process of "individuation." But may such a concept, with all its Jungian overtones, legitimately be used among those of the traditionalist persuasion? I think not, because Gurdjieff and Jung would make strange bedfellows indeed. The traditionalist perspective hardly supports the popular perceptions of Carl Jung's understanding of man's possible evolution. If one is to trust the arguments with which Titus Burckhardt, writing in the old *Studies in Comparative Religion*, appeared to demolish any claim to spiritual legitimacy in Jung's "approach to the traditional metaphysical doctrines," one should also be careful about introducing the notion of a collective unconscious, let alone a collective consciousness, into discussions about Gurdjieff or the great esoteric tradition, as some would do. Burckhardt dismissed Jung's approach because it "relativize[d] the notion of the self by treating it . . . not as a transcendent principle but as the outcome of a psychological process."[24]

My own experience, which I have touched on in these recollections, would certainly bear out Burckhardt's assertion. Even after decades of being "in the Work," many "Gurdjieffians" of diverse provenance continue to speak as if they can *achieve* transformation, whereas—as one of the latter-day perennialists, a distinguished academician and a professor of mathematics, no less, expresses it—the "'door' cannot be forced from below."[25] In other words, no matter how proficient one is in the Movements or in the music or in speaking about the ideas—or even in tracking the teaching back to its purported constituent parts (the "re-fragmentation" of the teaching that Wellbeloved so tellingly discerns in the world-wide Work today[26])—the inescapable truth is that the birth of the "new" can come only from another level, from "On High."

This has been more or less "scientifically" borne out, for example, by Franklin Merrell-Wolff, also a professor-of-mathematics-turned-esotericist, who discovered for himself that "The Awakened State is not an effect of causes set up by the candidate, for it has nothing to do with conditions. It is as though at some moment in the process of preparation the optimum balance is achieved such that an obscuring curtain simply drops, revealing what has always been there." Through his researches and "efforts," Merrell-Wolff discovered that "the realization comes at its own time, spontaneously. All preparation has the value of purification or destruction of barriers *but is not a magical agent that commands the Realization*" [emphasis added].[27]

Again, there are some extraordinary echoes in Meister Eckhart of the metaphysical ground for this fundamental differentiation between the two natures. Where indeed, he asks, is he that is born? "This birth . . . cannot take place in the faculties, but only in the being and ground of the soul," the great Dominican declares. "No creature, but only the soul is receptive of this birth or act." As Eckhart himself put the inevitable question, "What then is the proper use of those faculties?"[28]

So we are brought before the necessity for a work that needs to be undertaken on one level—the temporal, in the realm of the functions or faculties, that is, of the mind, the body, the feeling—*as a support* for the unpredictable movement of a force that descends from another level, that comes from On High, deriving ultimately from a source "wherein no image ever shone nor any power has ever peered."[29]

On the other hand, the ultimate aim must be, as in the great traditions, to surrender, or in Gurdjieff's terminology, to die to the known. An old Welsh hymn makes the case with total directness: "If you really love Him, why not submit?" The aim is not simply more affirmation, but *self*-realization. St. Seraphim of Sarov, working in the path of Eastern Orthodoxy, declared that the true end (of the Christian life and, by extension, of all the traditional spiritual ways) is "the acquiring of the holy spirit"[30]—or its Gurdjieffian equivalent, expressed in terms of energy and higher centers. On the question of equivalence, I should note that J.G. Bennett, for all his alleged "weathercock messianism,"[31] touched on the delicate correspondence between the God-oriented terminology of religion and the energy-oriented terminology of the Work when he wrote, " . . . [A]ll work begins from grace."[32] The strict fundamentalists probably would say that it begins with "an impulse" that appears in a moment of separation. No acknowledgement of a Creator, or God, is needed, thank you. (Some present-day practitioners "out there" now even delete the pronoun when mentioning "His Endlessness," perhaps to exorcise totally any theological overtones—an example of the sanitization [or the de-anthropomorphisation] of Gurdjieff taken to a strange extreme.[33] As if Gurdjieff is being faulted for failing to clean up his own act.

But whatever the language, the real opening to work is through those subtle moments in which "the good" is seen to "diffuse itself"—moments of Presence which reflect the silence at one's very core. Everything derives from the silence. "A master said: 'In order to achieve his inner work a man must draw in all his energies as it were into a corner of his soul, and hidden there from all images and forms, there he can work. He must achieve a forgetting and an unknowing.' For this to be heard there must be stillness and silence."[34] And how silent is our silence? Only long years of keen observation and a concomitant sincerity reveal the true raggedness, disjointedness, and shallowness of the silence we ordinarily experience. If we are to go deeper, we need a pure attention— an unsullied attention. And this requires a rare intentional inner activity free of all taint, free of images, free of all conditioning.

*   *   *

To those who can see past the seemingly intentional obfuscation in *All and Everything,* and the ambiguities surrounding Gurdjieff's vast expertise in the "muddling and befuddling"[35] of people's conventional mindsets, there can be little doubt that Gurdjieff himself must be numbered among the hierarchy of authentic messengers. Certainly, the "metaphysical essence of his teaching, which is self-realization and the correlative capability for true action,"[36] points to a work of a very high order. Now, does the key to this work lie in the importation of (say) concepts of the collective unconscious to further debase the "comprehension thresholds" required to fathom Gurdjieff's implicit traditionalism? Or does it lie in the adoption of (say) the notion of individuation, with the multi-layered implication that I need to aspire to a kind of certifiable deputy stewardship? But the real "I," or the new man, does not emerge from some such psychological process. As I have said, Gurdjieff and Jung would make strange bedfellows indeed.

Or does the key to this work lie in the elaboration of speculative astrological correspondences? Do we have to delve into "underground, subversive occult teachings"[37] to glean the meaning in the dog Gurdjieff has buried? Is the meaning of the Work to be found in "returning, as it were, to a religious fold which had its origins in the pre-Christian era"? [38] I wonder. The key surely has to be found in a realm beyond that of image and symbol—and beyond the so-called orthodox idiom of the Work, literally understood, which its arch exponent, Ouspensky, himself finally abandoned.

And that, in my opinion, is precisely what the Gurdjieff teaching appears to point us towards. In an injunction that applies equally to the leader and the led, "One has to abandon one's apparent richness, one's self-sufficiency, one's own will," as a recent commentator summarized Meister Eckhart's insight.[39] To my mind, any purported astrological correspondences, no less than symbolism such as that of the horse, the carriage, and the driver (clear echoes of the Katha Upanishad, for example), must refer to levels of the search that still lie on the edge of the known—"this side" of the silence, as it were. The real key, and the mystery, one feels, is surely to be found in the action of the laws themselves, the direct experiential understanding of the "blending" of forces, the action in us of conscience and the opening of the feeling, the appearance of "real I," and (if I may be vaguely encompassing)—and so on.

So, like an ant approaching an elephant—as a virtual nonentity—I would unhesitatingly now endorse, if I may be so presumptuous, the vision of the traditionalist Ananda K. Coomaraswamy when he makes the challenging declaration, "Anonymity is a fundamental condition of return to God."[40] Of course, one invokes the traditionalists at one's peril, since they have their own insistent proscriptions on who may or may not be accepted within the pale. Gurdjieff has never even remotely been considered "one of them." Indeed, Gurdjieff is accused by some traditionalists of "indulging . . . in occultist geographical romanticism of the 'Shangri-La' variety,"[41] among other seemingly unacceptable and unforgivable transgressions.

What's more, the desirability of anonymity—as in having "died to the known"—must arouse a certain distaste among the unregenerate, the "daughters of the Philistines," as it were. Not for them the work to undermine (and ultimately, then, to sacrifice) the egoism, or any suggestion of a surrender, with all of its mystic echoes. Yet this idea is in total accord with Gurdjieff's symbolism of the two rivers, in which Gurdjieff presents a compelling image of the way one river or current of life leads to immersion in the boundless ocean, a return to the source, while the other leads to the nether regions, flowing into "the very depths of the Earth."[42]

Progressively one learns that the Work is, on the one hand, a lifelong attempt to attune oneself to the inner call to "establish" a real I, which has nothing to do with one's subjective image and egoism. I recall that even before I arrived at Mendham, I already had a pleasant image of how I would be after my intended two-months' visit was over. I expected to emerge, as a sheep from a sheep dip, sanitized and purified—and calm, serene, forbearing, compassionate. Needless to say, the truth of what was actually revealed shook me to the marrow, as I have tried to describe. What I discovered of the old Adam was totally the opposite of that rosy-fingered ideal. I realized that I had, on the other hand, a lifetime of "undoing" to undertake.

*　　*　　*

Another recent assertion about the post-Gurdjieffian era is that "pupils now remain in the Work for long periods of time and are not encouraged to leave,"[43] as opposed to Gurdjieff's own practice of actually chasing people away. Those who met him caught glimpses that revealed Gurdjieff, behind his relentless acting, as a man of real being (a Man No. 5, according to Ouspensky) who could play with the forces (as Madame de Salzmann put it to me), and could irretrievably "poison" his pupils before packing them off to embark on a lifetime of self-discovery.

For those of us who have come after, it is evident that a real understanding of his teaching takes much time, persistent effort, and a willingness to work with others, *to work together*. And to repeat myself, there are no overnight sensations. I should add that Gurdjieff clearly did not demand blind obedience or passive conformism of those who took to his path. He clearly despised bootlickers, toadies, those who would fawn, as much as he despised pretension in any form. He did not demand, as in a way of faith, for example, that "The disciple must cling to his shaikh as a blind man on the edge of a river clings to his leader, confiding himself to him entirely, opposing him in no matter whatsoever, and binding himself to follow him absolutely."[44] Not quite "the way of understanding."

I am aware, of course, of the general proscription against reaching to other teachings, traditional or otherwise, for corroborating or amplifying Gurdjieff's tenets. Gurdjieff's teaching is so comprehensive and all encompassing—at least, insofar as one is able to comprehend it—that there would seem no need for that endorsement or clarification. In leaning on the insights of Meister Eckhart and others, I have no doubt compromised that wish for purity in the approach to an understanding of Gurdjieff. However, from all that I have gathered, Madame Ouspensky and others turned to the classic sacred texts of the East to flesh out the teaching they had received rather fragmentarily from Gurdjieff.

Yet, as it is has been argued, Gurdjieff too reached out to what was available to him. He evidently made free use of contemporary forms and language, and perhaps to a greater extent than many would wish to concede.[45] Closer examination of those forms and the language he adapted to his own purposes might confound some who charge that, "With each passing year, the Work is becoming less and less like the original. Soon, if this process continues, it will be unrecognizable."[46]

But while many simply accept Gurdjieff's teaching as a mere psychological doctrine—helping them to "make it through the night," perhaps—there are others, mainly members of the mainstream groups, who can discern in his work the great and unmistakable echoes that sound across current language and contemporary forms. Gurdjieff spoke of a Great Knowledge, and St. Augustine, for one, foreshadowed Gurdjieff's understanding that what we know as Christianity derives from a tradition that predated Christ. "That which today is called the Christian religion," Augustine wrote, "existed among the Ancients and has never ceased to exist from the origin of the human race until the time when Christ Himself came and men began to call Christian the true religion which already existed beforehand."[47] Or as Gurdjieff himself declared, "There were Christians long before the advent of Christianity."[48]

"Gurdjieff made it clear," said Michel Conge, one of the stalwarts of the old wartime Paris group, "that there is a source teaching at the root of what he transmitted: a knowledge having the status of an objective science."[49] No question here of *becoming* a tradition, of being "a new Tradition in the making,"[50] rather that Gurdjieff's work is unquestionably in the great mainstream of tradition. But, to emphasize again, this is just the perspective "from where I was sitting."

*   *   *

To continue these "random inferences," I think it is generally agreed that Gurdjieff astutely couches his teaching in terms meant to challenge the literal minded, and even to disguise his intent. As in the great traditions, Gurdjieff acknowledges in the term "the Absolute" an ultimate reality, a primordial ground of all existence. There is only one Absolute. There are not plural or contending Absolutes. Gurdjieff also finds it useful, if not unavoidably necessary, to invoke anthropomorphic terminology. He speaks of the Creator as "His Endlessness," "Our Endless Endlessness," "the Maker-Creator," just as an orthodox Christian would speak of "Our Father." The sense and aim of existence must derive from that Source—and it is also bound in the great movement of return to this Source. At the same time, this Source—as all the real traditions emphasize—is ultimately unknowable.

It is in this vast "scheme of things" (which constitutes the "great cosmic salmon stream" and its "lawful downward spate," of which Moore speaks so eloquently) that the human drama is played out. As Michel de Salzmann expressed it in the timeless language of tradition in one of his last communications, this is where we are called

> to recognize and serve
> the immanent, immutable, immovable, immeasurable,
> immortal and unique source of being."[51]

Gurdjieff clearly understood both the vast scope of the human potential and, equally, the enormity of the human plight. We are indeed many. Our name is legion. We are not one. And of course, the exposure of ourselves to ourselves—and to the truth about ourselves—is a necessary threshold to cross, if not "all at once and forever," then again and again. It can be a shock to those who believe that in the surroundings of the Work they will encounter only the conscious, the liberated, and the enlightened. Instead, as Gurdjieff pointed out, they "get the impression that we have indeed collected here only people who are stupid, lazy, dense—in a word, all riff-raff."[52]

Still, none of the curious antics and the inevitable misunderstandings that arise in the surroundings of the Work can blind us totally to the high service to which we, "mere humans," are called. One is compellingly drawn to Gurdjieff's own special vision that we exist on Earth to serve "a very great purpose." Unlike the orthodox traditions, the formal religions, Gurdjieff did not require that this vision be taken as an article of faith. Rather, and also in accordance with the essence of the traditions, he calls us to work to be whole, to bring all our parts into this service; to be "perfect," as church-going Christians would say in echoing Christ's words, "even as your Father in Heaven is perfect." One notes too the Christian (or is it pre-Christian?) connotations in his second law of striving: "to have a constant and unflagging instinctive need for self-perfection in the sense of being."[53] One senses that at the heart of Gurdjieff's teaching is this call to be principled. Hence the need for his original Institute for the Harmonious Development of Man and its various successor Foundations.

*　　*　　*

Gurdjieff also brings an even more mysterious injunction. He urges us to work—and again we have this anthropomorphic image—in order to alleviate the suffering, or the sorrow, of His Endlessness. One might argue that the Creator suffers at the imperfection of his Creation, which must conform to the metaphysical necessity that there be increasing entropy in the great outbreath of creation.

Certainly Madame de Salzmann appeared to share this vision. Echoing Gurdjieff, she urged us to work, otherwise "the earth will fall." One surmises that certain energies must be manifested, that there is a compelling necessity in the very scheme of things for the movement of return, that we humans are the conduits for the passage of forces unknown, and that these energies cannot pass without this effort towards wholeness, of being real instruments, real conduits, "servants of the Lord."

Inevitably, it would appear, we come to acknowledge the underlying unity of all the great visions. This does not mean that Gurdjieff simply paved the way for each of us to become what one traditionalist has termed a "facile ecumenist."[54] On the contrary, according to this particular traditionalist vision, "if there is a 'transcendent unity of religions,' there are also differences and even irreconcilable oppositions between them which are quite valid on their proper levels." And indeed, there is a singular specificity to the Gurdjieff teaching that distinguishes it from the traditional "ways." This singular specificity lies in the special role that conscious three-brained beings are considered to play in countering the unrelenting and merciless Heropass. The "consequent nature of God," as Whitehead would phrase it, would appear to be critical to the ability of His Endlessness to remember *Himself*.

All the great traditions speak about a movement of return— a return to the Source. The Prophet Mohammed, for example (and we must not forget that Gurdjieff, for all his allegiance to an esoteric Christianity and his profound respect for the Eastern Orthodoxy of his youth, also wore the Muslim fez like a badge of honor), said, "Verily, we are from God, and to Him we return" (Qur'an XX 156). These words of the Prophet are largely used at burials, I gather, but they must apply equally to the process undergone by the living adherents. Of course, this Source is ultimately unknown and unknowable. The Fathers of the Christian Church, both Western and Eastern, have wrestled with this conundrum down the centuries. It is at the center of the great and continuous dialogue on whether any attribute at all may be assigned to the unseen Source.

This Source may be considered to be very, very distant, beyond the beginning of time, beyond the Big Bang (if there were indeed a Big Bang), and it is also absolutely and immediately at hand as the ever-present reality at the very core of our being.

Of course, there are some who would shy away from speaking about these concerns and possibilities, imposing their "psychological knitting" as the only acceptable norm. In the realm of the anti-intellectual, the unthinking will reign supreme, elevating their own limitations and weaknesses into principles of the Work. Yet one must grant some role to the mind, one of our three brains, as Gurdjieff himself clearly did, and be grateful too for corroborative insights such as those of Hubert Benoit: "If the words employed in this [metaphysical] domain do not designate anything that we can represent to ourselves, we can, however, conceive their meaning."[55] A good (and time-honored) use of the mind, indeed!

So it is that the Fourth Way, of which Gurdjieff in his life was the great exemplar, may be understood as an enabler of this return—just as the ways of the fakir, the yogi, and the monk are the classic enabling ways. No one, surely, can truthfully discern the presence of the Fourth Way, but we know it by its action. "By their fruits ye shall know them" would apply equally to this way. And the most discernible and distinguishing feature—perhaps the practical specificity—of Gurdjieff's teaching is that it provides the wherewithal (the means and the methods, if you wish) for this movement of return, a movement between levels, in the midst of life's discordant activities.

My own humbling efforts to open to the overriding reality, the life without beginning or end (in the company of the abundant and diversified "subjectivities" encountered in and around the Work, whether mainstream or not), bear witness to the fact that we are called to fathom a very great mystery. It was that call that echoed and re-echoed in the lives of those special people about whom I have written. They were indeed, each unto his or her own, "seekers of truth." As are so many others who, at so many levels, have been touched—and are being touched—by Gurdjieff's call.

NOTES

1. Michel Conge, *Sur le chemin de l'octave de l'homme; témoignage d'un élève de G.I. Gurdjieff*, [Paris] Set, 2004. Informal translation provided by Jack Cain and Dan George.

2. John Pentland, foreword to Jean Vaysse, *Toward Awakening: An approach to the teaching left by Gurdjieff*, Harper & Row, San Francisco, 1979, p. xi.

3. Unpublished *History of the Work in New York*, Gurdjieff Foundation, New York, Inc., p. 90.

4. P.D. Ouspensky, *In Search of the Miraculous*, Routledge & Kegan Paul Ltd, London, 1955, p. 145.

5. Quoted in Peter Brown, *Augustine of Hippo*, University of California Press, Berkeley, 1967. *de cat.rud.* xxv, 48.

6. James Moore, "Moveable Feasts: the Gurdjieff Work," *Religion Today*, Vol. 9, No. 2, 1994, pp. 11-15.

7. James Moore, interview in Telos/www.gurdjieff-legacy.org/40 articles/moore.htm; *Gurdjieff International Review*, tribute to Henriette H. Lannes.

8. Sophia Wellbeloved, "Changes in G.I.Gurdjieff's Teaching 'The Work,'" a paper presented at the 2001 CESNUR (Center for Studies of New Religions) conference, London.

9. Jeanne de Salzmann, "The Awakening of Thought," *Gurdjieff: Reflections on the Man and His Teaching*, ed. Needleman and Baker, Continuum, New York, 1996, p. 3.

10. Moore, "Moveable Feasts," p. 13.

11. Joseph Azize, "John Lester: An Australian at Gurdjieff's Table," *The Gurdjieff Journal*, Vol. 8. Issue 4, No. 32.

12. Moore, *Telos*, op. cit.

13. James Moore, "New Lamps for Old: The Enneagram Debacle," *Religion Today*, Vol. 8, No. 1, 1992, p. 8.14

14. Talk given by Jeanne de Salzmann, Mendham, N.J., March 4, 1962.

15. Moore, "Moveable Feasts," op.cit.

16. Moore, ibid.

17. Moore, ibid.

18. Moore, ibid.
19. Moore, ibid.
20. Moore, Telos.
21. John Pentland, *Exchanges Within*, p. 204.
22. Michel Conge, "Facing Mr. Gurdjieff," *Essays and Reflections on the Man and His Teaching*, p. 361.
23. Beth McCorkle, *The Gurdjieff Years, 1929-49: Recollections of Louis March*, The Work Study Association, Inc., Walworth, New York, 1990, p.29.
24. Titus Burckardt, "Cosmology in Modern Science," *The Sword of Gnosis*, Arkana, London, Boston and Henley, 1986, p.176.
25. Wolfgang Smith, "Neurons and the Mind," *Sophia: The Journal of Traditional Studies*, Vol. 10, No. 2, Winter 2004, p. 37.
26. Wellbeloved, op. cit.
27. Franklin Merrell-Wolff, *Transformations in Consciousness*, State University of New York Press, Albany, NY, 1995, p. 251.
28. Meister Eckhart, "Where Is He That Is Born?" *Sermons and Discourses*, Pembridge Design Studios Press, London, 1990.
29. Meister Eckhart, op. cit.
30. Vladimir Llosky, *The Mystical Theology of the Eastern Church*, St. Vladimir's Seminary Press, New York, 2002, p. 196.
31. Moore, Telos, op. cit.
32. J.G. Bennett, *Deeper Man*, Tombstone Books, London, 1978, p. 159. This statement appears to have been omitted from the later edition published by Bennett Books, Santa Fe, New Mexico, 1994.
33. This usage appears to have been adopted at the annual International Humanities Conference, also known as the All & Everything Conference.
34. Meister Eckhart, op cit.
35. G.I. Gurdjieff, *All and Everything*, 1992, p. 26.
36. Michel de Salzmann, "Footnotes to the Gurdjieff Literature," *Parabola*, Vol. 5, No. 3, p. 92.
37. Sophia Wellbeloved, "Gurdjieff, 'Old' or 'New Age': Aristotle or Astrology?" Talk given at Alternative Spiritualities and New Age Studies Conference, Milton Keynes, May 31, 2003. Wellbeloved argues that "The multivalence of [Gurdjieff's] texts

reveal[s] a teaching that is more 'New Age' than 'Old.'" My experiences in the Work, as I have tried to recount in these pages, have brought me to a conclusion that is mightily skewed towards the "Old." This is not to discount the challenging perspectives that Wellbeloved brings, but *they*, in turn, need to be challenged.

38. Wellbeloved, op cit.
39. Reza Shah-Kazemi, "Eckhart's Image of the Eye and the Wood," *Sacred Web*, Vol. 10, p.14.
40. Ananda K. Coomaraswamy, "The Indian Doctrine of Man's Last End," *Sophia*, Vol. 4, No. 1, p. 55. This idea was echoed in private correspondence from David Appelbaum, March 14, 2004, in which he wrote that the work for consciousness "would seem to involve cultivating a tolerance for having no identity."
41. Charles Upton, *The System of Antichrist: Truth and Falsehood in Postmodernism and the New Age*, Sophia Perennis, Ghent, New York, 2001, p. 495.
42. G.I. Gurdjieff, *All and Everything*, p. 1126.
43. Wellbeloved, *Gurdjieff: The Key Concepts*, p. 154.
44. Al-Ghazali, quoted by H.A.R. Gibb in *Mohammedanism*, New York, 1955, p. 117.
45. Wellbeloved, *Gurdjieff, Astrology and Beelzebub's Tales*, in passim.
46. Anonymous, "What Would Mr. Gurdjieff Do?" A paper delivered to some senior members of the Gurdjieff Foundation, New York, in 2000. There have been some enlightened guesses as to its authorship. The internal evidence is unmistakable.
47. St. Augustine, *Retract* 1, 13, 3. Quoted by Lynn C. Baumann, *Sacred Web*, # 4, p.104.
48. G.I. Gurdjieff, *Views from the Real World*, p. 153.
49. M. Conge, op. cit., p.354.
50. Wellbeloved, *Key Concepts*, p. 155.
51. Michel de Salzmann, message to the international conference at the Lake Conference Center, Tusten, N.Y., April 2001.
52. G.I. Gurdjieff, *Views from the Real World*, p. 109.

53. G.I. Gurdjieff, *All and Everything*, p. 386.

54. Alvin Moore, Jr., *Sophia* Vol. 8, No. 1, review of Charles Upton: *The System of Antichrist: Truth and Falsehood in Postmodernism and the New Age*.

55. Hubert Benoit, *The Inner Realization*, translated by John Fitzsimmons Mahoney, Samuel Weiser, Inc., York Beach, Maine, 1987, p.3.

Printed in the United States
104242LV00001B/189/A